11-22-77

Meeting the Third World Challenge

The third volume in the World Economics Issues
series, published by St. Martin's Press for the Trade
Policy Research Centre, London, and edited by
Hugh Corbet, Director of the Centre. The first
two volumes were

World Agriculture in Disarray
by D. Gale Johnson

Technology and Economic Interdependence
by Harry G. Johnson

Also published for the Trade Policy Research Centre by
St. Martin's Press

Towards an Open World Economy
by Frank McFadzean *et al.*

World Agriculture in Disarray
by D. Gale Johnson

The Essentials of Economic Integration
by Victoria Curzon

Negotiating on Non-tariff Distortions of Trade
by Robert Middleton

Technology and Economic Interdependence
by Harry G. Johnson

Meeting the Third World Challenge

ALASDAIR I. MacBEAN
Professor of Economics
and
V. N. BALASUBRAMANYAM
Senior Lecturer in Economics
University of Lancaster

ST. MARTIN'S PRESS   NEW YORK

for the
TRADE POLICY RESEARCH CENTRE
London

Trade Policy Research Centre

1986937

The Trade Policy Research Centre in London was established in 1968 to promote independent analysis and public discussion of commercial and other international economic policy issues. It is a privately sponsored non-profit organisation and is essentially an entrepreneurial centre under the auspices of which a variety of activities are conducted. As such, the Centre provides a focal point for those in business, the universities and public affairs who are interested in international economic questions.

The Centre is managed by a Council which is headed by Sir Frank McFadzean. The members of the Council, set out below,

represent a wide range of experience and expertise. Registered in the United Kingdom as an educational trust under the Charities Act 1960, the Centre and its research programmes are financed by foundation grants, corporate donations and membership subscriptions.

Having general terms of reference, the Centre does not represent any consensus of opinion. Intense international competition, technological advances in industry and agriculture and new and expanding markets, together with large-scale capital flows, are having profound and continuing effects on international production and trading patterns. With the increasing integration and interdependence of the world economy there is thus a growing necessity to increase public understanding of the problems now being posed and of the kind of solutions that will be required to overcome them.

The principal function of the Centre is the sponsorship of research programmes on policy problems of national and international importance. Specialists in universities and private firms are commissioned to carry out the research and the results are published and circulated in academic, business and government circles throughout the European Community and in other countries. Meetings and seminars are also organised from time to time.

Publications are presented as professionally competent studies worthy of public consideration. The interpretations and conclusions in them are those of their authors and do not purport to represent the views of the Council and others associated with the Centre.

Contents

To Marion and Holly

Biographical Notes

ALASDAIR I. MACBEAN has been Professor of Economics at the University of Lancaster since 1967, having been an Economic Adviser at the British Ministry of Overseas Development and, earlier, an adviser with the Harvard Economic Advisory Service in Pakistan. Professor MacBean has been a consultant to the Food and Agriculture Organisation, an agency of the United Nations, as well as to the division of the United Nations concerned with public finance and financial institutions. In addition, he has been a consultant to the Organisation for Economic Cooperation and Development, in Paris, and in the United States to the Agency for International Development. In 1973–4 he was a Visiting Professor at the University of Michigan, Ann Arbor. Professor MacBean is the author of a number of publications in the field of trade, investment and economic development, including *Export Instability and Economic Development*.

V. N. BALASUBRAMANYAM is a Senior Lecturer in Economics at the University of Lancaster, which he joined in 1969. Before going to the United States for graduate studies in 1964 he worked as an economist with the Indian Statistical Institute, attached to the Indian Planning Commission. Dr Balasubramanyam has been a consultant to the United Nations, in the division of public finance and financial institutions, and to a shipping company in the United Kingdom. His published work is in the field of foreign private investment and technology transfers, notably *International Transfer of Technology to India*.

List of Tables

Preface

This book is being sent to press as preparations proceed for the fourth session of the United Nations Conference on Trade and Development, to be held in May 1976, and as the Tokyo Round of multilateral trade negotiations settles down in Geneva. Indeed, it has been written during a period of great uncertainty, characterised by the collapse of the Bretton Woods system of monetary arrangements, by world-wide inflation, by the effects of the quintupling of oil prices and by recessions in the major industrial countries.

We have tried to examine some of the effects of these various crises on the Third World, but our general assumption has been that the world economy will survive these shocks without a decline into a major depression. Our expectation is that trade will recover and economic growth be resumed. On its own, the resumption of growth in the industrial countries will have a major effect in stimulating demand for the exports of developing countries, but it should also improve the atmosphere for the removal of barriers to their exports of manufactures.

Most of our efforts have been directed to what seemed to us to be the major factors which, over the longer term, affect the prospects of improving living standards of the two-thirds of mankind who live in the Third World, rather than to the current situation.

We are indebted to Professors Wolfgang Stolper, Robert Stern, Elliot Berg and Richard Porter, and to the members of graduate seminars at the University of Michigan, Ann Arbor, for comments on earlier drafts of some chapters of this book; and to colleagues Nicholas Snowden, Tin Nguyen and Rodney Whittaker for discussions at the University of Lancaster. Hugh Corbet and Cedric Watts of the Trade Policy Research Centre were kind enough to read and comment on almost the whole of our first draft. We are most grateful to all of these individuals, none of whom need feel any responsibility for the errors and opinions of the authors.

We should also like to thank Joyce Bissett, Stephanie Arkwright, Linda Mogford and Denise Chisholme, who kindly typed sections of the manuscript in various stages of illegibility.

ALASDAIR I. MACBEAN

V. N. BALASUBRAMANYAM

Lancaster
November 1975

Abbreviations

c.i.f	prices including cost, insurance and freight
DAC	Development Assistance Committee of the OECD (see below)
DC	developed country
ECAFE	Economic Commission for Asia and the Far East (an agency of the United Nations)
EEC	European [Economic] Community
FAO	Food and Agriculture Organisation (an agency of the United Nations)
f.o.b.	free-on-board prices
FPI	foreign private investment
GATT	General Agreement on Tariffs and Trade
GDP	gross domestic product
GNP	gross national product
GSP	Generalised System of [Tariff] Preferences in favour of developing countries
IBRD	International Bank for Reconstruction and Development (World Bank)
ICA	international commodity agreement
IDA	International Development Association (a part of the World Bank group)
ILO	International Labour Organisation (an agency of the United Nations)
IMF	International Monetary Fund
LDC	less developed country
MFN	most-favoured-nation (non-discriminatory) tariff
OECD	Organisation for Economic Cooperation and Development
OPEC	Organisation of Petroleum Exporting Countries
STABEX	Stabilisation scheme for exports from developing countries associated, through the Lomé Convention, with the European Community

UNCTAD	United Nations Conference on Trade and Development
UN	United Nations
USAID	United States Agency for International Development
WHO	World Health Organisation (an agency of the United Nations)

NAMES OF COUNTRIES

Where the name of a country has changed, we have normally adopted the one in use in the period of which we are writing, for example, Sri Lanka [Ceylon], Bangladesh [East Pakistan].

CHAPTER ONE

What Challenge?

The United Nations has proclaimed the need for a New International Economic Order and a programme of action to achieve it. Neither the objections to the old order nor the proposals for establishing the new order contain much that is different from earlier demands from developing nations. What was new about the Sixth Special Session of the General Assembly of the United Nations, held in April 1974, at which these demands were ventilated, was a change of atmosphere. The oil crisis and the commodity boom of 1973/4 had produced some real change in the balance of power between the developed and the developing nations and a great deal of misconception, too, about the degree of the shift and the likely long-run outcome. The programme of action consists largely of measures which entail sacrifices or concessions – by those countries which are classed as industrially developed – in order to assist the countries of the so-called Third World.

Most of the measures proposed are considered in the chapters on trade, aid and foreign investment which follow. On the face of it, these demands represent the challenge of the Third World. They present the rich industrial nations with an ultimatum to cooperate or to risk political and economic confrontation. As with all previous such attempts to force concessions from them, the reaction of the developed nations is likely to be to compromise and to turn aside, with carefully hedged promises, any too precise demands which they see as running counter to their interests.

The position taken in this book is that the real challenges to the leadership of rich and poor nations alike are much more fundamental than those which emerge from the political rhetoric of United Nations debates. There is also a need to go back to first principles in considering the precise nature of the challenges, to examine where the real interests of nations lie and to seek out, in the end, the areas in which real progress can be made towards making this world a place in which all mankind can live without fear of hunger, crushing poverty and degradation. It is the object of this first chapter to explore the basic questions of the general nature of the challenge and to whom the challenge is properly addressed.

International Inequality

It seems to be widely accepted that the coexistence of extremes of poverty and affluence in any society is a cause for concern to that society. Evidence for this can be found in the universal adoption of progressive taxation and social security schemes in the capitalist democracies of North America, Western Europe, Australasia and Japan. Most versions of socialism call for reductions in the differences in wealth and income common in most societies. Even though earned incomes and special privileges do differ markedly in the Soviet Union, Hungary, Poland and other centrally-planned economies, the relative insignificance of unearned income means that they have fewer examples of extravagant consumption in the midst of relative poverty than occurs in South America or some parts of Europe. China appears to demand a high degree of equality among her citizens.

Practically all societies at least pay lip service to the idea that enormous differences in standards of living between the citizens of their society should not be permitted. Most governments enact legislation to reduce inequality of income within their nations. The reasons behind these attitudes, and why governments behave in this way, are questions of great interest to the moral or political philosopher, as well as to the student of political economy. It is not at all clear that the philosophical foundations of progressive taxation are particularly firm,[1] but this is not the main focus of interest here. The main question is whether the challenge to reduce inequality, apparently accepted within nations, can be extended to the international community.

If the citizens of the various nations looked upon themselves as citizens of a world community, recognised the common element of humanity and ignored differences of race, religion and nationality there would be no problem. But the world seems far from that position as yet. Nationalism, racialism and religious bigotry remain extremely powerful forces dividing the nations of the world. Given that political reality is characterised by nations which put national self-interest first in their dealings with other nations, is it anything more than mere sentimentality to suggest that the relative poverty of the mass of mankind represents a challenge to the rich nations to reduce the gap?

One thing, however, is clear: whether the rich countries accept it as a challenge or not, it must be a challenge to the leadership of the poor countries. However much the religions of Asia may preach the virtues of asceticism, all recent experience suggests that when people become aware of the possibility of raising their standard of living they want it raised. In many cases the political leaders of the independence movements in colonial Asia and Africa promised great material gains when the shackles of colonial rule were thrown off. Those of them who still rule and their successors have invariably promised to make the growth of their economies a paramount objective. Given the explosive developments in communications, through mass media and foreign travel, it is hardly surprising that many of the citizens of the Third World have some notion, perhaps an exaggerated one, of the affluence of the citizens of the rich industrialised nations. Many are aware that the absolute gap in living standards between the majority who live in the poor countries and the citizens of the better-off nations is growing. This must be a challenge to their leaders. Put at its lowest, political survival depends on their demonstrating some measure of success in raising living standards.

This represents a general challenge. But how can the governments of the developing countries show that they accept the challenge? What are they challenged to do? If they are to speed up the improvement in living standards of the Third World there are a number of things which they could do individually and collectively.

Internally they must set aside resources to create physical and human capital so as to raise the productivity of labour and land. These resources must come from sacrificing current consumption or reducing government expenditure on other purposes – of which perhaps the most conspicuous is military. They must also ensure that these resources are invested in those activities which hold out the greatest promise for increasing the output of goods and services desired by the mass of their citizens or which can be most profitably exchanged through international trade for items needed to raise consumption standards now or in the future.

Externally, they must judge all their relationships through trade and foreign investment with foreigners in terms of achieving the maximum contribution to raising present and future consumption standards of their own citizens – not in terms of political ideology.

These are all very real, very tough, challenges to leaders in the less developed countries (LDCs). In most cases they will not be pre-pared to make the sacrifices involved. If an all-out pursuit of econo-mic improvement for the mass of their citizens were their real goal, governments would not build up defence forces to strengths well beyond those necessary to meet any likely threat to their territorial integrity or other major economic interests.[2] They would not invest large sums of money in prestigious national airlines and international airports which involve them in a constant drain on resources to subsidise their loss-making operations. They would not set up heavy industries destined to run at low capacity for lack of customers and requiring endless hefty subsidies. They would not permit the continuation of the income differentials set by the colonial regimes which place the higher civil service and professional classes on a completely different income plane from the rural and urban masses. They would not allow their national resources to be squandered on the importation of expensive foreign wine, cars and processed foods for the sole benefit of the favoured social groups: the politicians, civil servants, military officers and upper business class.[3] They would seek to break down social and religious taboos which conflict with material progress and they would not discriminate against or drive out the most enterprising and skilled sections of their populations on racial grounds.

To confront and eventually overcome most of these challenges represents a most formidable task. No one could expect human beings to effect the necessary changes quickly and to make rapid and sustained progress towards equality with the present-day advanced countries. The time scale implied is not one or two decades; for some, it may even be centuries.

Conscience of the Rich

While the very existence of a Third World, inferior in income and status to the richer nations, is a challenge to Third World leaders, it is not self-evident that the citizens or leaders of the rich nations need feel challenged to do anything about this situation. The utility of enjoying a high standard of living may even be partly a function of having someone poorer to look down on. The feelings of satisfaction enjoyed by the rich may be a matter of relative as well as absolute standards of living. Where there is no feeling of social obligation, such as may exist in a single society, there may be no tendency to make concessions to raise the standards of the poor. Is there in practice any likelihood that the rich nations will feel a moral obligation to assist the poor nations to raise their living standards? This depends on whether a convincing moral case can be made out and, also, on whether morality does or can govern the actions of sovereign nations in their dealings with one another.

It is not even clear that the policies for reducing income differences between citizens within a country stem from morality. They could simply be the result of the enhanced political power of the working classes, which itself stems from a complex of economic and social forces unleashed by the industrial revolution. The existence of external threat, illustrated by the great wars of the twentieth century, has also emphasised the need for social cohesion. Nations at war cannot afford to have disaffected citizens. Times of war have seen sharp leaps forward in economic and social progress for the working classes. Most of the developed nations seem to have recognised that survival and prosperity for their societies require that observed differences in standards of living between various social groups should not become too great.

It is at least a plausible case which argues that, even within nations, such concessions as have been won by the poor from the rich have resulted *either* from a shift in the balance of bargaining power resulting from full employment and the growth of trade unions *or* from the recognition by the better-off that it was in their own self-interest to make these concessions. The existence throughout the ages of private charity may be taken to qualify this argument somewhat, but the magnitude involved has always been small and the motives of many of the 'charitable' frequently suspect. In the same way the conscience of the rich can be jogged by the reports on television of disasters and famine in poor countries. Nations often respond with help. But the amounts are small. These spontaneous outbursts of sympathy for fellow-humans do not appear sufficient to sustain a longer-term desire to aid development of the poor nations.

It is true that human beings are capable of what certainly appear to be completely unselfish acts because humans, like many creatures, are social animals. A lioness may die in defence of her cubs. A mother bird may act as a decoy to draw predators away from her young. Cow elephants may give their lives in defence of the herd. But these actions are normally regarded as instinctive, bred into the animals by the Darwinian process which has led to the survival of animals with these cooperative characteristics. With human beings these instincts have been reinforced by social conditioning, religious and moral teaching, and further strengthened by legal sanctions. But they are basically family – or tribal-oriented patterns of behaviour which have only gradually been to some degree extended to the national consciousness of the developed countries.

In many of the emergent nations of Africa and Asia the transfer of such attitudes from the family or ethnic group to the nation is only beginning. The recent history of tribal wars, linguistic riots and racial persecution bears testimony to this situation. It has taken centuries to develop within Europe the loyalty to the nation required to generate social behaviour consistent with some concern for the

weaker and poorer members of these societies. The current movement to make people feel members of an international community
may be achieved more quickly because of the spread of education
and the awareness of the immense risks of nuclear or bacteriologi-
cal warfare. But will it be extended quickly to include a concern to
reduce the differences in standards of living between the rich and
the poor countries? It is arguable that it will only do so if the leaders
in the industrially developed countries see it as in their own national
self-interest to promote the development of the poor countries.

Self-interest

In the recent past it is probable that the main reason for economic
aid, not necessarily identified with a desire to promote economic
development, has been the existence of the Cold War. Both the
Americans and the Russians saw aid as a means of bolstering up
the economies of nations which were either friendly to their ideology
or at least not friendly to the other side.[4] Sometimes it was a more
straightforward matter of a concealed payment for the provision of
military bases and other facilities. For various reasons this motive
has lost much of its strength. New weapons systems have reduced
the need for overseas bases and the Cold War has thawed somewhat.
Mankind appears, for the present at least, to have pulled back from
the abyss of open war in an era of mass destruction. In addition,
the naïve faith in the ability of the dollar to win friends and influence people has taken severe knocks. Americans have grown tired
of the stream of insults heaped upon them by nations in their debt.
As a result the American administration's aid programmes have
been drastically cut in real terms by Congress. Public opinion polls
in most of the rich countries show dissatisfaction and waning support for international economic aid. As the United Nations' targets
for official aid have risen to 0·7 per cent of gross national product
(GNP), the actual aid flows have declined to less than half of that
proportion. In the halcyon days of Marshall Aid to war-torn
Western Europe the United States disbursed over 2 per cent of
national income as aid; now its foreign aid is just over 0·2 per cent.

If strategic considerations have lost their force, what other arguments of self-interest remain? No doubt there are other foreign
policy objectives which can motivate particular nations. The desire
of France to sustain the French language and culture and to retain
influence in francophone Africa underpins the French aid programme and is clearly revealed in its heavy regional concentrations
in that area. Similar points can be made about the concentration of
British aid in the Commonwealth. On their own they have a senti-

mental ring about them and one doubts the real interest of the electorate in such matters. They reinforce, however, the undoubted commercial motive which attaches to all bilateral aid programmes. Preservation of the language and culture introduced by the colonial power helps to sustain commercial links in many evident ways, such as helping to retain markets for exports and sources for strategic imports.

Commercial Interest

The commercial element in aid programmes is partly promotional and partly defensive. Since each country knows or assumes that other rich nations will use aid-tying to promote exports to new markets, traditional supplying countries will tie their aid to goods purchased from their farms and factories to help preserve their old markets. If aid-tying is reduced, or if aid is channelled through international agencies such as the World Bank, the direct commercial motive will be significantly reduced. One should, of course, be aware what this commercial motive amounts to. The aid burden on a donor country is simply the cost of the resources used in providing the goods or the cash wanted by the receiving country and is not directly reduced by aid-tying. Exports still have to be increased (or imports replaced) by the donor country in order to provide the goods directly or release the foreign exchange to pay for the required goods from a third country. Because of some associated factors, aid-tying may reduce the burden (the price of tied goods is often higher than goods obtained through free international tender),[5] but it does not produce any net benefit to the donor country. Whether tied or untied, aid remains a real burden save in conditions of under-utilisation of capacity in the specific industries which manufacture the aid goods. Even then, difficulties in the phasing and directing of aid make it hard to arrange that production for orders made under the aid programme will occur at a time of slack in a particular industry.

Commercial benefits only occur if the provision of the aid leads subsequently to sales of exports on normal commercial terms. For example, the provision of a certain type of tractor under aid may lead the recipient country to place orders for more. Receipt of a particular firm's computers or business machines under aid may lead a government to standardise its equipment on these on grounds of compatibility and economy in stocks of spares.

It would appear that commercial benefits to the donor from the provision of capital aid for development are at best problematical and often negligible. Of course this assumes that the aid has been in the form of grants with no repayment or interest required. In loose descriptions of the flow of financial resources from rich to poor countries the term aid is often used to cover a range of transactions of which many cannot truly be termed aid. If a firm goes to its bankers and obtains a loan for which it pays the going market rate of interest, this is a normal commercial transaction from which both parties expect to profit directly. There is no question of aid involved. Equally if a rich country makes a loan to a poor country at a commercial interest rate this can hardly be called aid. If the loan is made for a longer term than normal in commerce, if repayments are not required until after some years of grace and the interest charged is below what would be expected by commercial lenders, then the transaction involves a subsidy element which is true aid. Most of the official flow of financial resources is in fact a mixture of grants and loans at relatively low interest rates and generous repayment terms which do involve a grant element. True aid does mean an economic sacrifice on the part of the donor and is seldom likely to have directly associated commercial benefits to the donor which could be regarded as motivating it. But the flow of financial resources as a whole will often have strong links with commerce.

Long-run Self-interest

It is, however, also argued that the economic development of the Third World will, in the long run, confer economic benefits upon the developed countries which will compensate them for the short-term costs of programmes of aid and cooperation in development. There are several possible lines of reasoning in support of this view. One is an extension of the Marxist-Leninist view of the motives for imperialism. Capitalist nations must eventually arrive at a stage where they cannot absorb all the outputs of their industries. They then require, in order to stave off a crisis, to extend their markets through the development of colonies which will absorb the surplus manufactures.[6] This line of reasoning can hardly stand up nowadays when the domestic governments of the rich countries accept responsibility for the maintenance of full employment and have the means at their disposal to do so through fiscal and monetary policies or even more direct intervention in their national economies, and when the rates of return on manufacturing investment seem to be higher in rich than in poor countries.[7] Up to 1974, the problem for the rich nations has been to find workers rather than to find jobs; they have been large importers of labour from developing countries. The 1975 recession was due to a special combination of measures to counter inflation and the deflationary effects of oil deficits caused

by the quintupling, since late 1973, of the price of crude oil. It bears
no resemblance to the crisis of capitalism caused by under-consump-
tion as predicted by Hobson and Lenin.

Associated with the Marxist argument is another which, in these
days of conservation and concern over depletion of natural resources, may seem more plausible. This maintains that the rich
countries have a clear interest in the procurement of non-renewable
natural resources such as basic fuels, scarce metals and other minerals, rubber and natural fibres, all of which are major products and
exports of the less developed countries. Investment in production
and transportation in the developing countries by the rich countries
can bring returns in lower prices, through increased productivity, and
in reduced risks. It is argued that the latter is achieved by making the
poor countries indebted to the rich and by achieving control through
investment in key resource industries. Most of this type of investment in the twentieth century has been by private firms.

The recent history of the oil industry suggests that a combination
of increased political risks and the successes of the oil-producing
countries in raising oil prices and their share of the profits of oil
production have greatly reduced that motive for overseas investment. The rich nations are searching for alternative sources for their
vast energy requirements, for example in Canada, in the North Sea,
in American shale oil deposits and in nuclear power. Alternatives
for certain natural resources, however, are not always easy to come
by. Governments may see a case for backing up the private overseas
investments of the big companies with some official aid in that it at
least affords some leverage over the domestic policies of the less
developed countries. If they become sufficiently dependent upon a
flow of official and private funds, the threat to cut off or suspend it
may deter the developing countries from policies of nationalisation
or of discrimination against foreign enterprises. Legislation in the
United States forbids the Government to provide aid to countries
which nationalise property of American citizens without prompt
and proper compensation.[8] This then may be a genuine self-interested reason for providing aid to certain developing countries. It
should be noted, however, that it does not represent any interest in
their economic development beyond the sectors which supply the
materials required by the rich countries. It could be argued that
growth in the poor countries would lead to competition for these
scarce materials and so operate against the economic interests of
the rich countries.

All countries, it may be said, have a mutual interest in the expansion of the world economy. The larger the world market the greater
are the possibilities of specialisation and division of labour and the

more likely it is that the fullest exploitation of economies of scale can be achieved. These are powerful arguments for the general dismantling of barriers to trade. The rich countries could benefit greatly from allowing the developing countries to produce labour-intensive manufactures for export to them, releasing resources which can be more productively employed in the relatively capital-intensive and skill-intensive industries in which their own comparative advantage lies. It is less clear that such a motive calls for deliberate policies such as aid and technical assistance to help more general economic and social development in the poor countries.

If governments in the rich countries are to operate strictly in terms of their own nations' long-term economic prosperity, one might expect them to try to see that the marginal social rate of return on their resources was equalised in all uses. If so, they would only invest (or permit their citizens to invest) abroad when rates of return after tax exceeded domestic rates, after allowing for external economies. They would select the countries where the returns were highest, which might or might not be the less developed countries. The chances are that they would in fact either be other rich countries such as Canada, Australia or Japan, or developing countries at the top end of that group such as Brazil, Mexico, Singapore, Malaysia, Tunisia or Yugoslavia. By concentrating their overseas investments in these countries where the necessary social overhead and co-operant facilities exist they could expect to obtain the highest direct returns.[9]

This could also be expected to achieve the fastest growth of the markets for their products, allowing an increase in the refinements of specialisation to satisfy increasingly sophisticated consumers and, through greater integration and further developments of the multinational corporations, increased component specialisation. It may be true that in most industries the existing markets are sufficiently large to allow for the achievement of all possible internal economies of scale in plant size, but there are a number of large and important industries where further economies of scale can be gained. In aircraft and vehicle production, petrochemicals, computers and other electronics industries, scale economies in research and development, technology, plant size, finance and marketing remain possible. These are much more likely to be achieved in the reasonably near future through further development of trade and investment among the industrially developed countries than through expenditure of a similar amount of effort and resources on developing the Third World.

Lower labour costs in developing countries do confer some attractions for assembly production in such industries as motor vehicles.

It is becoming increasingly difficult to persuade Germans, Swedes and Englishmen to work on these excruciatingly boring jobs, at least at existing wages. Firms are becoming dependent on immigrant workers from Greece, Turkey and Yugoslavia. But 'guest-workers' bring social problems. For these and other reasons, a few firms are shifting plants into some of the developing countries with a view to exporting from them, as opposed to merely producing for their home markets behind high tariffs.

It should be remembered that the time horizon for most investment decisions is short in relation to the time required for the developing countries to reach anywhere near the present GNP per capita standards of Europe today. Some simple arithmetic will make this very clear. Over the last ten years the developing countries achieved 2·5 per cent per annum increase in gross domestic product (GDP) per head. Suppose this is doubled by a combination of extraordinarily successful growth policies and control of population increase, this would mean that at a 5 per cent per annum compound growth the developing countries could double their average present standard of living in fifteen years. But this would only raise them to $400, which would remain far below present-day Western Europe. Even on these very optimistic assumptions, to catch up with present West European levels of per capita income would require fifty years.[10]

Any agency concerned with investment policy is likely to operate with a discount rate of at least 8 to 10 per cent when comparing alternative investments. This means that the present value of $100 twenty years hence is a mere $15. Fifty years hence it disappears into insignificance. This would suggest that, where the profitability of investments is related mainly to the general growth of demand through raised income levels, the rich countries generally represent by far the better bet to the prospective investor. When the political risks of investing in the Third World are added to the equation the result is even more biased against the poor and in favour of the rich.

Rise of OPEC and 'Commodity Power'

The events of 1973–4 added a new dimension to the issue. The combination of the 'commodity price' boom and the oil crisis increased the industrial nations' awareness of their vulnerability to interruption in supplies of raw materials and to pressure from producers' organisations. As far as oil is concerned, this change in the balance of power has been amply demonstrated. Finance ministers and trade delegations from the industrial nations scampered around the members of the Organisation of Petroleum Exporting

Countries (OPEC) in desperate attempts to win their favour. Offers of increased voting power in the World Bank and the International Monetary Fund (IMF) for the oil nations were soon forthcoming. At first, the Third World applauded without reservation and schemes were aimed to imitate the OPEC example in other mineral exports, but, for reasons set out in Chapter 7 below, none got beyond the drawing board. Third World nations such as Brazil and Mexico have increased their power through economic development and now have important markets to offer and attractive products to sell. Countries like Iran and Nigeria, on the basis of oil revenues and general economic development, are important military and economic powers within their regions.

How do these events affect relationships between the rich nations and the Third World? First, the raw material question can easily be exaggerated. Oil is unique in its suitability for cartelisation. For various reasons the dependence of the industrial nations on other minerals, although growing in a number of cases, is not as great since substitutes, both natural and synthetic, exist for them and often developed countries are themselves major producers. The rich countries cannot be held to ransom for these other materials in the way that OPEC can squeeze them on oil. Nevertheless, the risk that some producers of important raw materials may agree to restrict exports and raise prices is sufficient to extract some concessions from the rich, for even if such agreements fail in the medium to longer term, they can cause quite serious difficulties in the short term. If the OPEC nations give assistance to developing countries for such other producers' associations the risks are enhanced. This is why the United States and the European Community appear to have become more sympathetic to schemes to stabilise commodity export earnings. They have their own motives for wanting more stable prices and supplies. They even appear to be willing to see some transfers of resources to developing countries, via schemes such as the Lomé Convention's STABEX scheme or through liberalising the IMF's 'compensatory financing' arrangements, in order to ensure reasonable supplies.

How much further the rich nations will go to assist developing countries through commodity schemes depends on both the workability of the proposals and the solidarity of the Third World in backing such ventures as the 'Integrated Programme for Commodities' advanced by the United Nations Conference on Trade and Development (UNCTAD). That solidarity is suspect, for the Third World is a very diverse community of nations of all sizes, with varied political, religious and cultural systems and widely differing economic circumstances.

The industrially developed nations will undoubtedly seek strong trade and investment links with economically or politically powerful developing countries but that may still leave the vast majority of developing countries little better off. (The trade, aid and investment issues raised here are developed more fully in Chapters 6, 7 and 8 below.) Their preoccupation with a world slump, combined with high rates of inflation, leaves their governments little time for consideration of the even greater problems of many developing countries. They may quite reasonably take the view that the greatest help that they can give to the developing countries in these circumstances is to solve their own domestic problems of inflation and unemployment, and to restore the growth in world trade which has benefited everybody in the postwar era.

The upshot of this discussion is that, viewed simply in terms of the economic interests of the rich countries (excluding all moral and political considerations for the moment), the case that they should have a strong interest in the general development of the Third World is unconvincing. There are certain policies which in their own interests they ought to adopt and which would incidentally bring benefits to the poor countries. For example, they should end restrictions and taxes on imports of Third World manufactures and key commodities such as sugar, coffee, cocoa and tea. There are certain types of cooperation with developing countries which may be in their interest, such as international commodity agreements and the provision of capital and technology for the development of natural resources and certain food products in which developing countries possess an absolute or a comparative advantage. Provided there was confidence that political factors or domestic instability would not interfere with a steady supply of these commodities, investment in their development within developing countries should prove beneficial to both parties. There may, indeed, be a case here for official aid, or guarantees to private investors against certain types of risk, because the individual investing firms may be unable to spread their operations over a sufficient number of countries to reduce their overall risk. Also the social return to the rich countries in terms of better supplies of food and materials may be higher than the private rate of return to the investors if there are external gains to the economy which are not captured by the sale price of the commodities.

The rich countries and their industrial corporations undoubtedly have a commercial interest in the development of certain developing countries and in certain sectors of others, but that they have a straightforward commercial interest in the promotion of improvement in the general standard of living of the Third World is not at all clear. Indeed, if they became convinced by the prophecies of the 'eco-doomsters' they might see a general rise in the industrial production and consumption of the developing countries as a threat to their economic interests.[11]

In the last connection it can be seen that the rich countries do have an interest in seeing the developing countries reduce their rate of population growth. Rapidly expanding populations compete for food products, and increase environmental pollution and increase, too, the risks of epidemic disease. In the jet age world of the present this last is a serious problem. Diseases picked up in one country can be transmitted to a dozen others within a few hours. Policies to reduce fertility at the same time as policies to prevent infectious or contagious diseases are likely to attract support from the rich countries and are in everyone's interest. Incidentally, by reducing both birth and death rates they would bring about a much more efficient population structure in the developing countries, by reducing the ratio of dependent to productive members of the population. This should tend to accelerate improvements in the standard of living.[12]

Attraction of Skills

Many of the rich countries make use of skilled and professional labour from developing countries. It is often remarked that the United Kingdom's National Health Service would collapse were it not for the immigrant doctors and nurses drawn mainly from the Indian sub-continent, Africa and the West Indies. Teaching and research have also benefited from the notorious 'brain drain' of scientific and professional manpower from developing countries. It might be argued that this represents a benefit to the rich countries which stems in part from assistance to education and training provided by them in the past and could be regarded as an incentive to continuing such aid in the future. The issue, however, is clouded by a number of circumstances. First, many of these doctors and nurses working in Britain are trainees, some of them under technical assistance programmes, while others come on their own initiative to improve their expertise by study and experience in British hospitals. As with all such relationships they both give and receive. Secondly, it could be argued that the money and personnel provided for education overseas could have been employed domestically to improve the supply of such skills among British citizens and in improving rates of pay and working conditions, so as to make hospital employment more attractive to trained British workers, who have been migrating – voting with their feet – to the United States and to the rich Commonwealth countries. Finally, if a major result of aid and technical assistance to education and training of personnel from developing countries is to draw such people away from their own countries, it may damage rather than assist the development of the poor countries.

Keeping the Peace

The rich countries may have a strong commitment to the *status quo*. They have a very great deal to lose from serious wars. Clearly this gives them a strong motive to avoid being drawn into conflict with other powerful nations as a result of wars between developing countries. Even if they feel this to be a small risk, civil disturbances and wars between developing countries are, at the very least, a nuisance. They threaten the lives of citizens of rich countries resident in the belligerent countries. They disturb the normal flows of trade and investments and threaten supplies of raw materials. Revolutionaries are often radical – whether on the right or left – so that property owned by citizens and corporations in the rich countries is nationalised or damaged without compensation.

The belief that these are serious worries, that they stem from present poverty and the growing gap between the Third World and the rich countries, and that development in the Third World would help to reduce these risks is expressed in a passage from John P. Lewis's *Quiet Crisis in India*: 'Even if all Communist organisations were wiped from the face of the earth, the very poverty of the underdeveloped countries would represent a fundamental long-run threat to the security of rich countries, including especially the richest, now that the poor nations have become self-determining and have acquired massive appetites for material improvement. This threat, it is recognised, will grow at least as long as the welfare gap between the economically advanced and the economically backward countries continues to widen rather than narrow.'[13]

It would be fair to say that views similar to this have been widely expressed by supporters of the United States' aid programmes, but they are not self-evidently true. Precisely how are poverty and the welfare gap likely to produce a threat to the territories of the rich countries, given the distances involved and the enormous difference in military capability? It could be that there is a risk of embroilment in conflict with another major power because of alliances or other commitments to a developing country. There is also the risk of danger to property and citizens in the developing countries. There may be a risk of losing sources of important raw materials, especially oil and non-ferrous metals. Even such a large and richly endowed nation as the United States imports vast and growing quantities of raw materials. Until the late 1940s it was a net exporter of materials. By 1970 it had a net deficit due to imports of raw materials of $4,000m. In 1970 the United States imported all its requirements of chromite, columbium, mica, tantalum and tin; more than 90 per cent of its aluminium, antimony, cobalt, manganese and platinum; more than half of its asbestos, beryl, cadmium, fluorspar, nickel and zinc; and more than a third of its iron ore, lead and mercury.[14] The point was stressed in a staff report to the President's Council on International Economic Policy: 'Both from the viewpoint of our long-term economic growth and the viewpoint of our national defense, the shift of the United States from the position of a net exporter of metals and minerals to that of a net importer is of over-shadowing significance in shaping our foreign economic policies'.[15]

This may well be recognised as a possible reason for worry about political events in the developing countries. However, is the worry about temporary disturbance to the flow of materials or is it a fear that sources will be completely blocked off? The first can to a large extent be taken care of by strategic stockpiling of commodities, while ensuring that some supplies are available from secure places. Clearly a number of nations, including the United States, take this seriously and do hold substantial stocks. The idea of a total embargo on supplies of materials from developing countries is much less plausible. Since there always exists the threat of a particular material becoming obsolete, or at least largely replaced by changes in technology, rational owners of raw materials could be expected to try to sell them off at a fairly high rate and to invest the resulting funds in order to gain at least 10 per cent per annum with safety. The opportunity cost of sitting on unexploited minerals is really very high – even if one ignores the risk of technological obsolescence.[16] Moreover many jobs in developing countries are dependent on the production and export of raw materials, food and beverages. This, together with their need for foreign exchange, severely limits their ability to restrict supplies.

Local wars do not always disrupt supplies; and, even when they do, the disruption is often likely to be temporary. Since waging wars usually requires funds for munitions and soldiers, the side which gains control over mineral supplies is likely to market them. As far as the direct economic and political objectives of the rich countries are concerned it seems that revolutions, civil wars and limited wars in and between developing countries are likely to be more of a nuisance than a matter of vital importance.

Even if it were regarded by the rich countries as vitally important to minimise conflict, revolutionary change and wars in the Third World, would this be achieved by their attempting to foster a more rapid rise in the standards of living there?

First, it is by no means obvious that rising standards of living make for reduction in conflict and aid peaceful change. Economic development necessarily strains existing institutions, changes attitudes, raises expectations and breaks down the customs and habits which provide stability. Neither *a priori* reasoning nor empirical research has as yet established that economic development promotes political stability.

Secondly, it is by no means proven that attempts by the rich countries to foster improvements in the overall standard of living in the poor countries can make anything more than a marginal and uncertain contribution.[17] This is at least in part because few such attempts have really been made. For the major part of the bilateral aid programmes has had quite different objectives: strategic, political and commercial. Until recently few, if any, donors, whether bilateral or multilateral, have concerned themselves with the impact of aid or development policies on the distribution of income, a factor of more than a little significance in determining the standard of living of the mass of the people in the Third World. The will, knowledge and technical expertise have been lacking in most aid programmes to effect any real impact on economic growth. (The one possible exception to this is the World Bank's work, which has been aimed at development and within the limits of our knowledge of what promotes growth has been well directed towards that end.) The case is therefore not proven either way.[18]

It is undeniable that most of the rich nations of the West prefer political stability and peaceful social and economic changes within the Third World. Russia and East European countries may have less interest in this, but on the other hand seem quite willing to deal with right-wing governments in developing countries, and not particularly anxious to foment Communist revolutions outside Western Europe. China is the only leading power which is avowedly in favour of revolutionary change and her own standards of living are very little above those of India. But it may be of significance that these revolutionary socialist countries do not seem to regard economic aid as something which will run counter to their interests in radical change in developing countries.

A major difficulty in making any assessment of the public interest in policies towards less developed countries lies in the apparent irrationality which often characterises the behaviour of governments in both rich and poor countries. Actions are often taken which are against the welfare of their nations. A rational government must take into account the risk of irrational behaviour by another and make contingency plans for such eventualities. From the preceding analysis the major foreseeable risk to the rich countries in their relationships with the Third World lies in the possibility of inter- ference with supplies of key materials. Arising from this the main question is whether this constitutes a significant reason for the rich countries to have a self-interested motive for promoting general economic development in the Third World.

That question cannot be answered with any confidence. It depends on whether a more rapid rise in living standards in the Third World is likely to make for more stable and friendly political systems. But there is no evidence of correlation between poverty and aggressive action. If the rich countries were to think purely in terms of how they could safeguard their interests in stable supplies of materials at reasonable cost there are almost certainly cheaper ways of doing this than general aid policies to developing countries. These could include stockpiling, economising and finding synthetic or natural substitutes for materials where the risks seemed significant. In the last resort military intervention at specific points could be more certain in its effects than general economic aid in achieving strategic or economic objectives. Russian intervention in Hungary, Poland and Czechoslovakia or American intervention in Guatemala are cases in point.

All in all, the long-run enlightened self-interest motive for aid seems to depend more on faith than analysis or empirical evidence. Fortunately actions to promote economic development are not identical with financial aid. Dismantling of barriers to the exports of developing countries helps both rich and poor countries, even allowing for transitional difficulties in the protected sectors of the industrialised nations. International exchange of skills is also likely to benefit both areas. While there are certain dangers attached to foreign private investment for the host countries, provided certain precautions are taken it is likely to benefit both investing and host nations.[19]

While no single powerful motive for the rich countries to promote the development of the poor countries has been successfully identi- fied, a number of reasons for cooperation on specific issues, which could benefit both the rich countries and the development of the poor countries have been suggested. Population and disease control, and preservation of the environment, are examples of such common interest and these are not entirely unconnected with general econo- mic development. The rich may not feel *challenged*, but at least they may be willing to provide assistance for the attainment of these objectives.

Apart from these considerations, support for programmes to promote rising standards of living in the Third World may have to rely on educating the citizens of the rich countries and their leaders into recognition of an international morality which goes well beyond the economic calculus which has been considered up to now. Developing countries may also seek or foster support for their aims from special interest groups within the rich countries.

Interest Groups

Within any country there are important pressure groups for particular policies towards developing countries. Business firms whose products are or could be significant imports of the Third World are likely to lobby for aid tied to the supply of their goods. Transnational firms may have a broader interest in the development or preservation of goodwill between their nation and developing countries in which they operate and this leads them to support aid. Yet other firms see the encouragement of imports from the Third World to their country as a threat and are likely to campaign against such measures as preferential tariff removal for products such as textiles.

Various church organisations are vociferous supporters of aid programmes. Partly this stems from their old missionary links with colonial territories, partly from a belief in humanitarian action. They tend to support all aid and trade measures likely to confer benefits on developing countries. The trade unions are apt to be ambivalent. They have a general goodwill towards the underdogs of the world and a dislike of 'capitalist exploitation', but at the same time they have worries about the entry into American and European markets of goods produced with 'cheap labour' which may threaten the jobs of their members.

Political Challenge

As more and more of the peoples of the Third World have achieved independence and national sovereignty their numbers and influence in international fora have increased. This is particularly true within the United Nations General Assembly and certain of its subsidiary bodies. In these, votes are distributed simply on the basis of membership. The very smallest new African state has equal voting power with the mighty industrial nations such as the Soviet Union and the United States. India and China which have between them nearly a third of the world's population, have only the same votes as Ruanda or the Maldive Islands.

There were only 51 members of the United Nations when it was created in 1945. Of these only four were from Africa (one of them South Africa), three from Asia, six from the Middle East and twenty from Latin America. By 1969 there were 126 members and most of the addition had come from the developing nations of Africa and Asia. Over ninety of the present members are generally regarded as belonging to the developing countries and on many issues they act in concert, voting as a bloc. The political confrontation between the rich and the poor countries is thus a phenomenon of recent origin. In the eighteenth, nineteenth and early twentieth centuries they were mere pawns in the power game played between the European nations. Most of the Third World countries were still colonies up to the 1950s. Since their emergence as nation states what have been their main objectives? How have they sought to achieve them? What challenge has this posed both to themselves and to the rich industrial nations?

Objectives

Many in the developing countries have felt that the achievement of political independence was merely one step on the road to true national sovereignty. A major objective for them has been the achievement of 'true economic as well as political independence', which is seldom clearly defined. With some it appears to imply near-autarky; all trade, investment and aid relations with the industrially advanced countries are viewed with suspicion. The capitalist enterprises of the rich nations are regarded as naturally exploitative in all their dealings with poor countries and in such exploitation they are backed up by their governments and by those international institutions, such as the World Bank and the IMF, which display a strong preference for free enterprise in the organisation of production and distribution in the economies of the nations they assist.[20] Others, who take a less extreme position, nevertheless note the discrimination against their nations which results from a number of the trading activities of the rich countries. In the sphere of agriculture they find that temperate zone products such as wheat and other grains, beet sugar, meat, dairy products and wool are protected in the rich nations, thus reducing their demands for such goods from developing nations, frustrating their exports and lowering their earnings of foreign exchange.[21] They also see that excise duties, tariffs and quotas lower their earnings from exports of cocoa, coffee and tea. On the side of manufacture, they observe that the structure of tariffs in the rich countries discriminates heavily against the setting up of processing plants in developing countries to carry out even the elementary stages of processing of raw materials. In the European Community, for example, unwrought copper enters duty free, but copper bars, wire and plates bear a 10 per cent tariff and tubes and pipe fittings 15 per cent. Effective protection for the manufacturing processes in the rich countries resulting from this discrimination between crude and processed materials is substantial.[22]

They also observe that since most of their countries became independent in the late 1940s and early 1950s there has been, apart from during 1973–4, a downward trend in the prices of most of the products which they export, while the prices of manufactured goods, their major imports, have continued to rise. There is a widespread feeling that this is unfair, that someone is to blame for it and that consequently the trend ought to be reversed or that developing countries should be compensated for the loss in real export revenues.[23]

Discrimination against the countries of the Third World has also been seen in the charges imposed for transport by the shipping conferences. Such feelings of discrimination against them have led many developing countries to think that the existing institutions for considering matters of trade, aid and finance were loaded against their interests. This in turn led to the demand for the United Nations Conference on Trade and Development (UNCTAD). Such a conference, it was felt, would enable developing countries to make their voices and votes felt on such issues in the hope that the rich countries could be persuaded to agree to measures to improve the trade and aid prospects for the Third World. In the event their voice was heard but only in very small part acted upon.[24] Their continued dissatisfaction has found expression in their demands in the mid-1970s for a new international economic order, but, once again, the rich nations seem to see this as more of a challenge to their diplomatic skills than as a need to seek ways to change patterns of aid and trade.

Challenge to Science

Several factors connected with the growing disparity in living standards between the rich and poor countries represent serious challenges to science. It is not yet understood precisely what makes one nation grow fast while the economy of another stagnates. Factors which are associated with a rapid rise in the standard of living can readily be listed: high rates of saving and investment, improvements in technology, increases in general education and skill levels of the working force, a fall in birth rates. These are generally present, but the exact causal connections and the quantitative significance of each are not clear,[25] nor is the relative importance of social attitudes and institutions in determining the will and the capacity to develop. Government policies aimed at promoting economic development are still largely based on hunches about the fundamental determinants of growth, or on forecasts of savings, earnings of foreign exchange, import requirements and foreign investment which are at least as often seriously in error as they are approximately correct. Examination of the forecasts, targets and outcomes of a large sample of five-year development plans of the recent past should be a compulsory requirement for any aspiring economic planner.

Among the most pressing problems of the day, that of the burgeoning populations of the Third World, is probably the most crucial. It presents a food problem, an employment problem, a drag on immediately productive investment, an urban problem and in many parts of the world a severe pollution problem. If means can be found to cut population expansion in the developing countries from their present average levels of over 2·5 per cent per annum to, say, 1·5 per cent by the end of this century, an enormous improvement in the prospects for a rising standard of living would be made possible for the crowded nations of South Asia. It presents a great challenge to medical and social scientists.

The problem of urban unemployment and rural underemployment is already here. In recent years the expansion of manufacturing industry has done little to relieve it: changes in their structure and technology has made them more capital-intensive and demand for labour has risen much more slowly than the expansion of output. In some countries the labour force in manufacturing has been constant for several years in spite of rapid growth of industry.[26] The typical age structure of the populations in developing countries, where more than half are under twenty-one years old, means that the net addition to the labour force each year is very large. Young people drift from the land, where there is little for them anyway, in search of excitement and the possibility of a better job in the cities. But there they merely add to the unemployed citizens of the shanty towns with all the misery and social evils that implies.

Probably more waste, hardship, poverty, malnutrition and distress stems from unemployment than from any other factor. This is exacerbated by the fact that it is growing and for demographic reasons will continue to grow (even if birth rates decline sharply) for very many years unless jobs can be created faster than the youths enter the labour market.

The very basic problem of feeding the populations of the developing countries remains acute. Statements by the Food and Agriculture Organisation (FAO) of the United Nations, although less extreme than some of their past ones, still show this to be a major problem despite the Green Revolution. Many live on the brink of starvation and quite minor calamities can push them over the brink. This is specially true of the wives and young children of the poor.[27] The world food balance swings between surplus and deficit with alarming and unpredictable suddenness. Its unpredictability is not so surprising when huge potential buyers such as the Soviet Union and China conceal their production figures; and output everywhere is subject to the uncertainties of weather and disease. The shortage and high cost of chemical fertilisers due to the sharp increase in the price of petroleum, together with the setbacks of drought in 1972 and 1973, has made the prospect of desperate grain shortages in developing countries only too likely in the immediate future.

These, together with some of the more technical problems of foreign trade, aid and international liquidity present problems enough to the community of scientists and scholars. To find solutions to them is a major intellectual as well as a social and political challenge.

Conclusions on the Challenge

The first conclusion of this chapter is that the challenge of the Third World is primarily a challenge to the leadership of the nations of the Third World themselves. Without their will to develop, outside assistance will be of little avail. Moreover it seems unlikely that the rich countries have any genuine serious interest in promoting economic development in the Third World as a whole. There are particular areas of economic and social progress where they have interests in common with the Third World and these give scope for cooperation – as over population control, development and maintenance of the supply of non-renewable natural resources, international division of labour along lines of comparative advantage, scope for the sale of advanced technology or the development of subsidiaries, and joint ventures in developing countries by private firms. In addition to these specific areas for cooperation, the Third World can look to particular pressure groups within the rich countries to help to produce an atmosphere in which aid and cooperation in trade matters can continue and grow in importance. In the longer term it may be possible to persuade more and more of the citizens and leaders of the rich nations to adopt the value judgement that they *ought* to help to promote the economic and social development of their less fortunate fellow-citizens of the planet Earth.

NOTES

1. See W. J. Blum and H. Kalven, *The Uneasy Case for Progressive Taxation* (Chicago: University of Chicago Press, 1953), or R. A. Musgrave, *The Theory of Public Finance* (New York: McGraw-Hill, 1959) chs 4 and 5.

2. Military expenditure in developing countries is the fastest growing item in their budgets, as shown in the accompanying table. Their military spending reached about $30,000m in 1973, having risen from 6·6 per cent of world military expenditure in 1960 to 14·4 per cent in 1973. The Middle East and Africa have shown the fastest increase with 14·6 and 23·0 per cent respectively over the period 1949–71. The largest spenders have been India, Egypt, Israel and Iran. See *Stockholm International Peace Research Institute Yearbook, 1974*, p. 143 and Tables 7.1 and 8.1.

Average Annual Growth Rates, 1961–70

(Values in constant prices)	World	Developed	Developing
Military expenditures	3·2	2·6	8·0
GNP	4·8	4·8	4·7
GNP per capita	2·7	3·7	2·2
Public education	7·9	8·0	7·5
Public health	5·9	6·2	2·0
Armed forces	2·2	0·8	3·3
Population	2·0	1·1	2·4

Source: *Annual review of US Arms Control and Disarmament Agency, 1972.*

3. René Dumont, *False Start in Africa* (London: André Deutsch, 1966).

4. 'Foreign aid is a method by which the United States maintains a position of influence and control around the world, and sustains a good many countries which would definitely collapse, or pass into the Communist bloc', said John F. Kennedy in the Senate Committee on Foreign Relations, *Some Important Issues in Foreign Aid* (Washington: US Government Printing Office, 1966) p. 15. Also see Joan M. Nelson, *Aid Influence and Foreign Policy* (New York: Macmillan, 1968) p. 11; and Teresa M. Hayter, *Aid as Imperialism* (Harmondsworth: Pelican, 1971) pp. 87–98.

5. Mahbub ul Haq, 'Tied Credits: a Quantitative Analysis', paper to the Conference of the International Economic Association, July 1965. Also see Jagdish Bhagwati and R. S. Eckhaus (eds), *Foreign Aid* (Harmondsworth: Penguin, 1970).

6. The reasoning behind this is that capitalists are able to force wages down to a conventional subsistence level and appropriate all of the surplus value created by labour (profits). Competition between capitalists leads to a search for ways of cutting costs through innovation which saves labour. This increases the reserve army of unemployed and, since the goods have to be sold to workers, reduces the size of the market within the capitalist economies. This forces the capitalists to seek external markets and leads to

'colonialism' or 'economic imperialism'. A more sophisticated line of reasoning can be found in P. Patnaik, 'External Markets and Capitalist Development', *Economic Journal*, London, December 1972.

7. Brian Reddaway *et al.*, *Effects of UK Direct Investment Overseas: Final Report* (Cambridge: Cambridge University Press, 1968).

8. The 'Hickenlooper Amendment'. See *Legislation on Foreign Relations, with Explanatory Notes* (Washington: US Government Printing Office, 1955) p. 44.

9. In the international sphere, just as between regions within a country, the dynamic benefits associated with 'poles of growth' are likely to outweigh any tendencies towards diminishing returns to investment.

10. These crude estimates are based on data in *Statistical Yearbook* (New York: United Nations) which probably seriously exaggerate the differences in living standards because they make no allowance for differences in consumption patterns and in the real costs of non-traded goods, but they may do well enough here. See Dan Usher, *The Price Mechanism and the Meaning of National Income Statistics* (London: Oxford University Press, 1969).

11. D. H. Meadows *et al.*, *The Limits to Growth* (London: Earth Island, 1972).

12. Stephen Enke, 'Some Aspects of Slowing Population Growth', *Economic Journal*, March 1966, and 'Economic Consequences of Rapid Population Growth', *Economic Journal*, December 1971.

13. John P. Lewis, *Quiet Crisis in India* (Washington: Brookings Institution, 1962), quoted in R. F. Mikesell, *The Economics of Foreign Aid* (London: Weidenfeld & Nicolson, 1968).

14. *Material Needs and the Environment Today: Final Report of the National Commission on Materials Policy* (Washington: US Government Printing Office, 1973).

15. Quoted in H. Magdoff, *The Age of Imperialism* (New York: Monthly Review Press, 1970).

16. To postpone sales involves a sacrifice of income today for income tomorrow. Unless relative prices rise by more per annum than the discount rate the owner of the resource makes a loss.

17. See, for example, Lester B. Pearson *et al.*, *Partners in Development* (the Pearson Report) (London: Pall Mall Press, for the International Bank for Reconstruction and Development, 1969) p. 49. 'The correlation between the amounts of aid received in the past decades and the growth performance is very weak.' This document is cited hereafter as the Pearson Report.

18. A number of well-known academics, most notably Professor Peter Bauer, of the London School of Economics, have argued that aid is neither a necessary nor a sufficient condition for economic development and may even be detrimental. See Peter Bauer, *Dissent on Development* (London: Weidenfeld & Nicolson, 1971).

19. These arguments are expanded below in Chapter 8.

20. See Magdoff, *op. cit.*, and Hayter, *op. cit.*

21. Harry G. Johnson, *Economic Policies towards Less Developed Countries* (London: Allen & Unwin, 1968) pp. 87–8 and Appendix D. He estimates that the establishment of free trade in sugar would have increased developing

countries' export earnings by $897m. (This study for the Brookings Institution, in Washington, was first published in 1967.)

22. See Chapter 7 for further discussion of effective tariff rates.

23. See Raoul Prebisch, *Towards a New Trade Policy for Development* (Geneva: UNCTAD, 1964).

24. See Chapter 7 for discussion on the 'Challenge at UNCTAD'.

25. This is true despite the significant contributions by scholars such as Edward F. Dennison, *Why Growth Rates Differ* (Washington: Brookings Institution, 1967).

26. See R. B. Sutcliffe, *Industry and Development* (London: Addison-Wesley, 1971).

27. See the section on nutrition in Chapter 2.

CHAPTER TWO

Source of the Challenge

The economic distance between nations can be measured in many ways. The most widely used and probably the most misleading of these measures is that of annual income or gross national product per head. On the one hand it exaggerates the gap between rich and poor nations, making one despair of ever seeing that gap close significantly, and on the other it diverts attention from the real and tragic differences between the lives of the poor and the rich. What meaning can be attached to the statement that the national income per capita in the United States is $5,000 while in India it is $100?[1] Does it really mean that the average American citizen is fifty times better off than the average Indian? In one sense this is patently absurd. Merely to survive, to be able to buy enough basic food, clothing and shelter in the United States would cost over $1,000 while $100 would suffice for these in India, so that someone with $1,000 in America may be worse off than someone in India with $100. The fault lies in the fact that the international exchange rate between the Indian rupee and the American dollar does not reflect the domestic purchasing power of these currencies. In both of these nations foreign trade is a mere 5 per cent of total national product, yet only this tiny part affects directly the exchange rate.

There are other important reasons for the failure of GNP figures to measure adequately relative living standards. An obvious source of error lies in the acknowledged unreliability of both population statistics and calculations of national product in many developing countries, but apart from the human errors in collection of data and calculation there are systematic biases at work in estimating GNP in both poor and rich countries which tend to exaggerate differences in living standards. In most of the developing countries much larger quantities of output are not marketed, but are consumed within the family or exchanged directly for other goods or services. Much capital investment is in the form of direct construction by the family or community in building houses, farm buildings, breaking in new land, constructing minor irrigation channels, building banks for retention of irrigation water, terracing fields, and other rural tasks. Attempts to estimate the value of such unmarketed consumption and investment are generally inaccurate and probably seriously underestimate the value of subsistence production.

In the rich industrial nations, on the other hand, items which ought to be regarded as costs are treated as benefits consumed by citizens or government and so counted as part of national income. The Nobel Prize economist, Simon Kuznets, has stressed these problems in the following terms: 'If modern economic growth called for rapid urbanisation, it must be recognised that urban life required more resources to satisfy the countryside level of wants for food, sanitation, recreation, transportation from home to job, and so on. Furthermore, the greater complexity of industrial and other economic units may have required larger inputs into governmental regulation and adjudication. Many of these extra outlays, extra inputs of real resources, appear in national economic accounts under either household or government consumption, and are treated as *final* product, as a component of unduplicated aggregate output. But to the extent that the outlays, either by households or by government, are current expenditures necessary for the adequate participation in or smooth operation of the modern production process, they are intermediate, not final product; their inclusion represents duplication.'[2]

In addition to these roughly quantifiable adjustments which have to be made to correct conventional GNP estimates, there are all the other unconventional and environmental costs associated with higher incomes: the deaths and injuries resulting from the motor car, the noise and pollution due to all forms of transportation, the general pollution of the environment caused by the smoke and the waste disposal of industry, the crushing boredom of assembly line production in modern industry.[3]

In most societies income levels and requirements are correlated to a considerable degree with age. Most children have little or no income; older adults usually have more wealth and income than those in their twenties. In many underdeveloped countries more than half of the population are under twenty-one, whose requirements and actual incomes would be less than those of older people. This difference in age distribution alone accounts for an appreciable part of the differences in average incomes per head between the United States and developing countries.[4]

Different communities have very different life styles. Their customs, attitudes and tastes may differ greatly and this seriously weakens the usefulness of per capita national income figures as indicators of relative welfare. Both these social factors and the characteristics of their physical environment, especially its climate, affect the needs and desires of people. Obviously the requirements for clothing and housing are much affected by temperature so that in a warm climate needs for clothing and shelter can be met at much lower resource cost than in cold countries. Different attitudes to leisure and work confuse attempts to equate utility with per capita income figures. All in all differences in average per capita incomes are meaningful only where countries with rather similar social and environmental conditions are under comparison.

A final and most damaging criticism of the crude use of per capita income comparisons is that it conceals the way in which income is distributed within the population. If the major moral concern is with the sufferings of the poor then it is as well to concentrate on that issue. A relatively high national average per capita income may be the result of affluence for a few while abject poverty remains the lot of the many. A rapid rise in per capita income may be associated with a relative or absolute decline in the living standards of the bottom 20 per cent of the population. Recent studies reveal a shocking degree of inequality in many less developed countries and a very low absolute level of income among the bottom fifth of the population.[5] In a number of developing countries which have already attained relatively high per capita incomes – Brazil, Colombia, El Salvador, Jamaica, Lebanon, Mexico, Panama, Peru and Tunisia – a large proportion of the population still has a per capita income under $100, the official international 'poverty line'.[6]

The Pakistani economist, Mahbub ul Haq, has asked whether two decades of development have had any significant impact on the dire problems of poverty.[7] Even though the rate of growth as measured by the increase in GNP was respectable, did it even dent the problems of malnutrition, disease, illiteracy and homelessness? Such indices as he examined he found disquieting: 'A recent study in India shows that 40 to 50 per cent of the total population has a per capita income below the official poverty line where malnutrition begins. And what's more pertinent, the per capita income of this group has declined over the last two decades while the average per capita income went up.'[8]

In his own country, Pakistan, which was hailed as an outstanding success story of growth in the 1960s, he relates that 'unemployment increased, real wages in the industrial sector declined by one-third, per capita income disparity between East and West Pakistan nearly doubled, and concentrations of industrial wealth became an explosive economic and political issue'.[9]

The explosion which resulted from the tensions thus created is a matter of recent history and one whose repercussions still reverberate.

According to Robert McNamara, as President of the World Bank, Brazil's GNP per capita grew by 2·5 per cent per year, between 1960 and 1970, but the share of national income going to the poorest 40 per cent of the population declined from 10 per cent to 8 per cent. At the same time, the share of the richest 5 per cent of the population grew from 29 to 38 per cent. In Mexico the situation is similar and in India the poorest 10 per cent of the people may have become poorer.[10]

From all of the above it is evident that the GNP per capita measure is an extremely poor index of comparison of welfare between nations and may even conceal more than it reveals. This is not merely an academic debate about the possibility of precise measurement of things which are in any case obvious. True, no one would deny that there is a great gap between the standard of living of the vast majority of the citizens of the Third World (two-thirds of whom live in Asia) and the citizens of the industrialised nations; nevertheless, there are issues of fundamental importance here. To exaggerate the gap can lead to despair instead of constructive effort to improve the lot of citizens of developing countries. Over-concern with GNP can lead to faulty policies. It has led to the pursuit of high growth rates with too little concern for population control, employment, income distribution, agricultural production and quality in elementary education – factors which could have had a more direct impact on mass welfare.

Attempts at rapid industrialisation have often been seen as the way to rapid growth. Indeed, many developing countries have achieved increases in industrial production of 10 per cent per annum or more according to their official statistics, but, in terms of real growth, let alone social and economic development, this may have brought little real gain. The outputs of these industries were often sold in highly protected domestic markets or heavily subsidised for sale to export markets. In either case the benefits to the local community were seriously overestimated by the prices charged for their final outputs. Welfare is not improved by setting up a local industry to produce bicycles at twice the cost of an imported bicycle of similar or higher quality. But the national accounts will show an increase in local value added at local prices so that GNP rises while people are actually worse off. Only a few industrialists gain from monopoly profits, few jobs are created in this sector and sometimes at the expense of jobs elsewhere, and the real income of those who buy bicycles is clearly reduced.

The general impact of industrialisation in many of the largest developing countries has been to rob the poor in the rural sector – the vast majority of the people – in order to subsidise the rich in the shape of those industrialists fortunate enough to obtain licences for foreign exchange, high tariff protection and subsidies through export-bonus vouchers or multiple exchange-rate systems.[11] The failure of industrialisation to spread benefits throughout the community is one of the tragedies of two 'development decades'. While industrialisation has increased, so too has unemployment. Industry has failed to produce the needed jobs partly because it was often the wrong types of industries which were set up and partly because they robbed the agricultural sector of resources which could have created jobs and income there.

Alternative Measures of Economic and Social Progress

In human terms what really matters are the things which directly affect the lives of the mass of the people in the developing countries. Robert McNamara, as President of the World Bank, expressed this vividly in his address to the third UNCTAD, held in Santiago in 1972: 'What are we to say of a world in which hundreds of millions of people are not only poor in statistical terms, but are faced with day-to-day deprivations that degrade human dignity to levels which no statistics can adequately describe? – A developing world in which children under five account for only 20 per cent of the population, but for more than 60 per cent of the deaths. – A developing world in which two-thirds of the children who have escaped death will live on, restricted in their growth by malnutrition, a malnutrition that can stunt both bodies and minds alike. – A developing world in which there are 100m more adult illiterates than there were 20 years ago. – A developing world, in short, in which death and disease are rampant, education and employment scarce, squalor and stagnation common, and opportunity and the realisation of personal potential drastically limited.'[12]

Another dramatic way of looking at the problem, which gives some insight into the real impact of poverty, can be paraphrased from a statement by Paul Hoffman, of the United Nations staff. If we took a random sample of one hundred new-born children from the world's low income nations, the expectations would be that forty would be dead before they reached six years. Out of the sixty survivors another forty would suffer from serious malnutrition with its risks of irreversible physical or mental damage. Only twelve would complete an elementary education and only three a secondary education. When they reached adulthood, at least twenty out of the sixty would be unable to find work or would merely eke out a living with odd jobs.[13]

Some may consider these statements by committed leaders of international organisations to be overdramatised, but in the context they are at least as scientific as GNP statistics. The characteristics they describe are directly relevant indicators of the kind of life an infant in a typical community in Asia or Africa can expect. In principle the indicators they mention can be measured with reasonable accuracy. They can be objective and they can be directly comparable between countries. We can list a number of such indicators of social and economic performance and if the data are available they can give a much more accurate picture of current living standards and of progress in developing nations than can the blunt instrument of the GNP. If we make the broad value judgement that human beings should be adequately nourished, that their lives should be as free as possible from sickness and disease and not ended prematurely by avoidable catastrophe, that they should have clothing and housing, that they should be able to find employment at reasonable wages, and that there should be opportunities for the acquisition of knowledge and skills through the availability of education, we should in fact be in accord with objectives which are laid down in the preambles to most national economic plans and in the objectives of most of the international organisations under the United Nations.[14]

The rich countries already publish such data and many of the developing countries collect and publish estimates for several of these indicators. For indicators of nourishment it is already possible to set up norms for a minimum adequate diet which command some measure of agreement among experts. The FAO has calculated the calorie and protein requirements of the average citizen in most countries, allowing for differences in sex, body weight, age structure of the population, and climate. For other indicators it may be possible in future to define internationally acceptable norms, but for the present the very diversity of developing countries, differences in their basic resources and their objectives, makes this too difficult. With agreement on norms for each indicator and agreement on the weight to be attached to each indicator an index of national economic welfare alternative to the per capita GNP or per capita consumption index could be obtained. Without such agreement the best that can be done is to set out the data on each and leave the individual reader to make his or her own judgements.[15]

Nutrition: Disappointment of Green Revolution

Nutrition is a basic component of the level of living. Among low income groups, food is inevitably the largest item of consumption expenditure. The quantity and quality of the food which they consume is a major factor in personal satisfaction and in the health of the population, and in the ability of the people to work efficiently and to enjoy life. Quantity can be measured in terms of the energy (calorie) content of the food, and the protein content of the diet is a good indicator of the quality. Normally, if the calorie requirement is met, the protein supply will also be adequate. Lack of certain essential elements – iodine, vitamins and minerals – can lead to certain deficiency diseases, but much less information is available on these items.

The potential food supply can be calculated from production data and net imports. This has to be adjusted by deducting requirements for seed and for feeding livestock, an allowance for wastage and spoilage and the net change in stocks. The apparent food supply can under-estimate or over-estimate the actual supply because of a number of factors: (i) the diet in primitive societies is often supplemented by food gathered in the wild; (ii) the food value may be reduced by poor methods of preparation, over-sophisticated processing, as, for example, the polishing of rice or refining of sugar may reduce the nourishment from the basic food; and (iii) the macro approach to estimation is again subject to the problem that it fails to indicate the distribution, which is especially worrying because certain groups in most developing countries – for example, children within the crucial age period of six months to two years and pregnant women or young mothers – are particularly at risk in terms of the inadequacy of their diet. The bulk of deaths occur among such children,[16] and it appears that 'studies of mental growth similarly indicate that malnutrition-caused debilitation, where it occurs, traces back to this critical eighteen-month period'.[17]

Recognition of these difficulties stresses the need for national governments and international agencies to develop more detailed sample surveys of nutrition linked with medical studies of deficiency diseases. They exist for a small number of countries, but are too few and insufficiently standardised for comparative studies at present. Some comfort can be drawn from the fact that deviation from the average is much less for the consumption of food than for other items of consumption. As incomes rise the proportion spent on food tends to decline. Consequently a rise in food consumption, particularly in terms of calories, is more likely to stem from an improvement at the lower rather than the upper end of the income scale. Table 2.1 below sets out nutritional levels in various areas of the world as revealed in United Nations studies.

In most of the regions the populations appeared to have an average diet in terms of calories below, but only a little below, what is considered adequate by international experts. Over the decade 1960–70 the food balance seems to have improved in all regions. 1972/3 saw a major setback with drought in the Sahel and failures of the monsoon in parts of India. Table 2.11 shows how food production stagnated in developing countries in these years. In terms of protein the situation is only slightly worse. There is little margin for emergencies and of course the bottom 10 per cent of the population in many of these countries would be much worse off, particularly the young children and mothers. The problem may be much more one of providing an income to these groups than of increasing total output of food.

Table 2.1

Calorie Supply Per Capita as a Percentage of Established Standards, 1959/61 and 1970

Region	1959/61	1970
Developed Regions	115	117
Developing Regions		
Central America	91	92
South America	90	96
Centrally Planned Asia	76	86
South Asia	92	97
of which India	85	88
Middle East	96	99
North Africa	94	99
East Africa	98	102
West and Central Africa	103	105

Source: *Trends in Developing Countries* (Washington: IBRD, 1973).

Figures on food requirements have been challenged, notably by Colin Clark, while Director of the Institute of Agricultural Economics at the University of Oxford. His attacks on some of the earlier estimates of world hunger emanating from the FAO were valid. The more recent estimates, though, are based on the best available nutritional advice and command a wide measure of agreement among experts.[18] Even making allowances for some exaggerations, the situation depicted by Table 2.1 is dismal. Large numbers of the populations of the Third World – 300m to 500m according to the Director of FAO – remain poorly fed, and there has been no significant improvement in the situation in recent years.

The much heralded Green Revolution in agriculture – new seed varieties and other technological advances – is far from solving the problems of hunger. In some ways it has actually made it worse.

Robert McNamara, in his address to the Board of Governors of the World Bank in 1972, commented that 'the miracle of the Green Revolution may have arrived, but for the most part the poor farmer has not been able to participate in it. He simply cannot afford to pay for the irrigation, the pesticide, the fertilisers – or perhaps even for the land itself on which his title may be vulnerable and his tenancy uncertain.'

The medium or large farmer who can afford to take the risk of innovation, can pay for sinking a tubewell, can afford to buy fertilisers and can attract help from government servants is the one who gains the main benefits from the new varieties of wheat and rice which form the core of the Green Revolution. Their gains have sometimes been at the expense of the small tenant farmer and have led to his losing his farm to become a landless labourer. If jobs were available this might be no great change for the worse, but unfortunately farm machinery is being introduced by many of the larger farmers and reducing their need for hired workers.

Even apart from these adverse side-effects the Green Revolution does not appear to be living up to its promise in terms of sheer food production. India and the Philippines, two of the main areas for the new grains, have been facing shortages and high grain prices. India, Bangladesh and China are frequently in the international market to buy grains. In the early 1970s India seemed to be on the verge of another serious famine. In developing countries with a population totalling over 1,100m, food production per capita actually declined between 1961–3 and 1971–3, according to the World Economic Survey for 1974 by the United Nations.

As Table 2.1 shows, there is considerable variation between the regions of the world, but even within each area experience varies enormously. In Asia, people in Israel and Taiwan have very adequate diets, while those in India, Indonesia and Iraq achieve only about 85 per cent of the calories and 75 to 85 per cent of the protein regarded as adequate.[19]

It is worth underlining, however, that even on the statistical evidence the amount by which diets have to improve to become adequate is not great and the statistical gaps are probably overestimated. If efforts to improve could be concentrated on the vulnerable groups, as China appears to have done, the task of improving this key element of welfare might not be so formidable.

Health: General Improvement

The incidence of disease and ill-health must affect the well-being of a population. It will also affect their capacity for work, showing up in absenteeism and lack of physical stamina. In the absence of detailed data on death and illness from particular diseases the general death rate, life expectancy and changes in these statistics may serve as rough indicators of the state of health. Because of differences in the age structure of the populations, inter-country comparisons of crude death rates cannot be used to rank countries' health status. Age-specific rates would be required for such a purpose. Nevertheless, bearing in mind the fact that the populations of developing countries are generally much younger than in the rich countries the higher crude death rates generally experienced in the Third World do suggest significantly worse health. Table 2.2 shows average death rates for the main regions of the world.

Table 2.2

Crude Average Rates of Death (per 1,000 population), 1965–73 around 1968

Region	Average
Developing Countries (Total)	17
Western Hemisphere	10
Africa	21
Asia	16
Rest of the World[a]	9·4

Source: *Demographic Yearbook, 1973* (New York: United Nations, 1974) Table 1.
[a] Developed market economies and centrally planned.

One age-specific rate widely available is for deaths before one year old. Rates for this are about four times higher among the populations of developing countries than in the rich countries. Again there is a wide spread between the areas, with Africa and Asia averaging about 123 infant deaths per 1,000 live births while Latin American countries recorded 81 per 1,000.[20] In Asia 80 per cent of the population live in countries where infant mortality rates exceed 120 deaths per 1000 live births. In the industrially developed countries the infant mortality rates range from under 15 per 1,000 in Northern Europe to over 50 in parts of Southern Europe.

In this sphere at least there has been a significant improvement over the decade. According to the United Nations 'about 90 per cent of the thirty-seven developing countries for which two estimates are available, and an even higher proportion for the rest of the world, recorded a decline. Some of the most notable reductions occurred where high rates had prevailed in the 1950s: in Chile, for example, the rate declined from 125 per 1,000 live births in 1960 to 92 in 1968, in Burma from 200 to 114, in the Philippines from 99 to 72 . . .

even in countries with more moderate infantile losses, substantial reductions were achieved.'[21]

This fall in infant mortality was the main factor in the overall decline in crude death rates experienced in the Third World. It does represent an improvement in welfare in the sense that bereavement through the loss of young children is a universal cause for sorrow in most communities. It is also the major cause though of the high rates of population growth which explain the slow growth of per capita incomes and act as a brake on future development.[22]

The demographic effects of the decline in infant mortality show up in increased life expectancy and higher natural increase in population growth as shown in Table 2.3.

Table 2.3

Life Expectancy and Rate of Natural Increase of Population

Region	Life expectancy at birth Around 1968	Rate of natural increase of population (percentage per annum) 1970–3
Developing countries (total)	45	2·5
Western Hemisphere	61	2·9
Africa	40	2·8
Asia	44	2·3
Rest of the World	70	0·9

Source: *World Economic Survey 1969–70* (New York: United Nations, 1971) Table 14; and *Demographic Yearbook, 1973* (New York: United Nations, 1974) Table 1.

The survival, in increasing numbers, of young children increases the dependency ratio – the ratio of unproductive to productive members of the population. It also increases the need for social overhead capital in the form of housing, schools, hospitals and sanitation. These are investments which have no immediate impact on the capacity of an economy to produce more goods and services and at the same time make it harder to save because these additions to the population only consume. Improvements in life expectancy and reductions in infant mortality would be unambiguous indicators of economic and social advance if birth rates could also be significantly reduced.

So far only four or five developing countries, and these rather small ones, have shown any decline in birth rates. India has a fairly massive programme of population control, but has so far attained only very limited success. It is estimated that by 1975–6, after twenty years of government programmes, births will be only 2·9m fewer than the 25·9m that would be expected in the absence of control. This is nowhere near official targets for population policy.[23] The birth rate in India in 1968 was 42·8 per 1,000 compared with rates ranging from 13·3 in West Germany to 18·2 in the United States for the rich countries.[24]

Medical Facilities

While it is true that the availability of doctors, trained nurses, well equipped hospitals and other medical facilities clearly affect the level of living, difficulties of comparing quality and poor statistics on these matters weaken the usefulness of these indicators for cross country comparisons. The general picture, however, shows that physicians are few and far between in most of the Third World. According to the United Nations' World Economic Survey of 1969–1970, 'less than 2 per cent of the population live in countries with less than 1,000 persons per doctor, while a fourth live in countries in which each doctor has over 14,500 potential patients and in a number of African countries there are over 50,000 persons per doctor.'[25]

Nurses are rather more available. But the definition of a nurse differs considerably between countries. There is a sharp contrast between the availability of hospitalisation, as indicated by the availability of hospital beds. The vast majority of the Third World live in countries where there is less than one hospital bed to over 600 people, while in the industrially developed countries most live in countries where there is one hospital bed (with attendant back-up services) to less than 150 people. For most of the 85 developing countries studied there was an improvement in the ratio of registered medical practitioners between 1960 and 1966. Over the same period there was some worsening of the situation with regard to nurses, but in aggregate hospital beds increased more or less in line with population.[26]

In fact, these figures tell us little about the health of the population. Data on the incidence of particular diseases would be much more useful, but it is not available. We know, however, that since the early 1950s various preventive measures have reduced the incidence of malaria, cholera, smallpox and tuberculosis in many areas of the Third World. Apart from some resurgence in Indo-china and Sri Lanka, malaria has been practically eliminated and dramatic reductions in deaths from epidemic diseases have been achieved.

World Health Organisation (WHO) statistics show that between 1951 and 1966 deaths from plague fell from 17,000 to 47, from cholera 63,700 to 4,400, and from smallpox 226,000 to 12,700.

What emerges very clearly from this brief survey of health indicators is that, despite some improvement, the average citizen of the Third World is very much worse off on practically all counts than his counterpart in Western Europe or North America. It is also evident that the developing countries of the Western Hemisphere, mainly Latin America, do much better than Asia or Africa in most indicators, although this too conceals wide variations within a continent including countries as different as Argentina and Haiti.

Housing: Shanty Towns

Housing needs and standards vary enormously as a result of differences in climate, available construction materials, customs and practices. No international standard is practicable. Few countries in the developing world have conducted adequate censuses of housing. Faced with these difficulties, all that can be done is to discuss this aspect of living standards in qualitative terms, making use of existing indicators, however inadequate.

It is well known that developing countries have experienced high rates of population growth and that urban populations have expanded much faster as a result of inward migration from the rural areas. Rates of increase of 10 per cent per annum or greater have been experienced in a number of African towns. Most developing countries show rates of urban population increase of between 5 and 8 per cent.[27] These facts are bound to have created great social needs for increased investment in urban housing. The available indicators of house construction, such as the issue of permits to build and data from national accounts on gross fixed capital formation in dwellings, suggest that in most countries the rate of increase of urban housing was insufficient to keep up with needs in the 1960s.[28] This accords with the general reports of pavement sleepers in India and shanty towns on the outskirts of most cities in the Third World.

Standards of urban housing in most developing countries are of course much lower than in the rich nations: they have fewer rooms, occupational density is much higher, and fewer have piped water, electricity or flush toilets.[29]

Most people in the developing world still live in the rural areas in small villages and hamlets, but statistical information on rural housing is entirely lacking for Asia or Africa and fairly sparse even for Latin America. From a mass of observation, albeit casual, we know though that most such families live in crowded village huts with only one or two rooms, with none of the facilities regarded as normal in most of Western Europe and North America.

Employment and Wages

As countries develop, more of their labour force tends to move from self-employment to wage-earning employment, so that un-employment becomes a major cause of poverty and social aliena-tion. Unemployment has a significant and increasingly important influence on the living standards of the mass of the people. Accurate data on this would therefore be an important indicator of welfare. So far few developing countries have accurate statistics of unemploy-ment and those which they have tend to be biased towards the urban areas and industrial occupations. In those countries for which there are statistics, unemployment appears to have increased over the period from 1962 to 1974. Table 2.4 summarises data from the Inter-

Table 2.4

General Level of Unemployment ('000s)[a]

Region	1962	1966	1972	1974
Asia				
Ceylon	151	225	440	485
India	2,081	2,610	5,928	8,202
Indonesia	116	72	90	84[b]
Korea	715	578[c]	499	401
Malaysia (West)	51	106	161	140
Pakistan	–	–	157	182
Africa				
Egypt (UAR)	118	–	135	–
Ghana	16	11	31	23
Nigeria	15	27	15	22
Tunisia	14	42	32	35
Zambia	–	16	13	8
Latin America				
Chile (Gran Santiago)	40	47	41	–
Jamaica	–	145[d]	185	–
Puerto Rico	86	96	111	105

Source: *Yearbook of Labour Statistics* (Geneva: International Labour Organisa-tion, 1972) and 1974, Table 10.

  [a] Most of these statistics are for registered applicants for work.

  [b] = 1973.

  [c] = 1967.

  [d] = 1968.

  – = not available.

national Labour Organisation (ILO). That the situation in Sri Lanka has caused sufficient concern to attract a large high-powered ILO mission to make recommendations to deal with the problem is borne out by the figures. Kenya is another country whose problems of unemployment have attracted the ILO's attention, but the statistical series for this country is too brief to record in the table. India has also shown a substantial rise in unemployment.

In reality these figures represent the mere tip of the iceberg. Unemployment is much larger than the recorded figures indicate, for who bothers to register when it is clear that no jobs are available? In addition the urban areas in many countries are now characterised by large-scale disguised unemployment in the form of petty trading, shoe cleaning, car polishing, car minding and other odd services. The governments openly employ excessive numbers of messengers and clerks who appear to do little of a productive nature, and such employment must be regarded as a form of social security benefit. Household servants are employed in extraordinary numbers by the rich and the small middle class.[30]

Most of the serious cases of starvation in the Indian sub-continent have been due to lack of income to buy food, because the failure of the monsoon deprives the landless labourer of employment. It is the families of these groups, rather than the small farmers or the urban workers, who have suffered most in recent famine situations.

Wages in Manufacturing

In most developing countries real wages in manufacturing appear to have been rising in the 1960s but in most developing countries this affects directly only a small percentage of the total labour force: about 13 per cent on average in Latin America in the early 1960s and about 9 per cent in Asia and Africa at the same time. In Latin America the range was from a rise of 8 per cent in real wages in manufacturing in Honduras to 25 per cent in Argentine. In Africa, with the exceptions of Southern Rhodesia and Mauritius (both 15 per cent), the figures were 9 per cent or less. In Asia (excluding Israel), the range ran from 3 per cent in Thailand to 16 per cent in South Korea. India and Ghana were notable exceptions to the general experience of rising real wages in manufacturing. In India real wages fell by 2·2 per cent per annum between 1961 and 1967. In Ghana the decline was 0·5 per cent per annum during the years from 1960 to 1967.

To sum up on the crucial issue of unemployment: it is clear from the figures in Table 2.4 that in a number of developing countries unemployment was growing even before the effects of the world recession of the mid-1970s had made themselves felt. Tentative figures suggest a worsening of the situation. Increasingly, commentators on the general situation of the developing countries have been pointing to prospects of rising unemployment as perhaps one of the most dangerous aspects of their immediate future in the late 1970s. Large numbers of young people emerging from schools to find no prospects of employment could cause an explosive situation.

For reasons developed in Chapter 3 below, rapid industrialisation has so far provided no solution. The continuing growth of population, and the high proportion of it concentrated in the under-21 age groups, with many young people drifting to the cities either because the pressure on scarce land leaves no room for them in the rural areas or because city life attracts them, gives rise to great social problems when no jobs are available. Large crowds of deprived and jobless youths are a threat to the stability of any government. The constant turmoil in Calcutta derives partly from the crowds of jobless, but politically active, youths.

Such threats to political stability may be the real reason why the problem has attracted so much official attention from the international community in recent years. Whatever their reasons, rising unemployment is a powerful negative factor in the welfare equation. Not only does it mean great personal dissatisfaction, loss of self-esteem and physical hardship for the unemployed. It is also a major cause of maldistribution of income, starvation and malnutrition.

Education and Literacy

Education contributes to living standards through the provision of direct consumer satisfaction and by providing a means for self-improvement and enhanced earning power. From the viewpoint of society the latter aspect is important as adding to the stock of human capital. An educated or trained workforce is much more productive than an unskilled one. Most recent research on economic growth has stressed the importance of investment in education as a major determinant of growth.

The focus here, however, is on its contribution to personal satisfaction, not that all education contributes to such an end. For many children years of humiliation, abuse and even ill-treatment at the hands of intolerant schoolteachers may be a poor trade-off for a minimum knowledge of the 'three Rs'. Nevertheless, since education represents one possible escape route from poverty, and can give access to entertainment and pleasure, it is a much sought-after commodity in most developing countries. In Tunisia, for example, an attempt around 1970 to restrict entry into secondary schools led to such indignation and strife on the part of parents that the govern- ment had to back down and recruit teachers directly from France to meet the demand. Most people seem to feel that to deny human beings the means, through education, to develop their full human potential leads to personal frustration and unhappiness. The avail- ability of education is widely regarded as an important index of social progress.

Two principal measures of progress in this field are possible for at least some countries, namely levels of literacy or formal educa- tion in the population, and changes in enrolment at various educa- tional institutions. Like most of these indicators of levels of living, literacy rates are a tricky statistic to interpret. Definitions are apt to vary between countries and the data are collected infrequently, usually at the time of a major census. Most of the data refer to the 1960s. While detailed international comparisons are impossible, the evidence does support generalisations on the contrast between the Third World and the more advanced countries, and between the three developing regions. At least half of the developed countries had literacy rates in excess of 90 per cent, while only Argentina, Barbados and Uruguay among developing countries attained this level. No advanced country had a literacy rate of under 30 per cent but almost half the developing countries were under this. Among the Latin American and Caribbean countries only one, Haiti, fell below this level, but in Asia over a third and in Africa four out of five had literacy rates of less than 30 per cent.[31]

As for formal education, it appeared that in only two of the reporting countries in Europe (Albania and Turkey) were over 70 per cent of the population without any formal schooling, and both of these are claimed by the OECD to be developing countries. In Latin America 40 per cent of the countries were in this category, in Asia 60 per cent and in Africa practically all. In all the more advanced countries (save Albania and Turkey) at least 5 per cent of the population had received education beyond the primary stage, whereas this was true of only a third of the developing countries and most of these were in the Western Hemisphere and Asia, with only one in Africa. In a quarter of the developed countries over 20 per cent of the adult population had completed secondary or higher levels of schooling. Among the developing countries this was so only for Israel.[32]

The general picture which emerges from a study of enrolment data is that most of the developing countries made progress in the 1960s. By the middle of that decade the proportion of developing countries with less than 30 per cent of children enrolled in primary school had been reduced to a fourth, most of them in Africa. How serious efforts to improve the situation can be frustrated by rapid population growth is well illustrated from the circumstances in Latin America where the proportion of children not in school was lowered from 52 per cent to 43 per cent. 'Despite this, the actual number of children not provided for expanded by three-quarters of a million. The requirements in the way of new schools and teachers were far in excess of actual performance so that at the Punta del Este Conference in 1967 the goal of universal primary education was deferred to the 1970s.'[33] Efforts to catch up have proceeded apace as shown in Table 2.5, but the actual levels remain well below those of the rich nations.

Table 2.5

Growth in School Enrolment and Teaching Staff in Developing Countries, 1960–71

| | 1971 index (1960 = 100) in education at the | | | | | |
| | Primary level | | Secondary level | | Tertiary level | |
Region	Enrol-ment	Teachers	Enrol-ment	Teachers	Enrol-ment	Teachers
Developing countries	174	159	249	226	320	218
Latin America	168	181	297	262	315	277
Africa	177	174	252	222	270	308
Asia	162	144	179	194	300	270
Arab countries	185	219	297	235	299	311
Rest of world	114	129	142	174	239	225

Sources: Centre for Development Planning, Projections and Policies of the United Nations Secretariat, based on data furnished by the United Nations Educational, Scientific and Cultural Organisation. *World Economy Survey, 1974* (New York: United Nations, 1975) Table 31.

In the sphere of education, as in the other indices of level of living, the Third World falls well below the standards of the more advanced countries. Within the Third World the African countries and Haiti appear to be particularly backward.

Conclusion on Living Standards

Imprecise and scattered though they are, these non-monetary indicators of the level of living do give a more comprehensive impression of the comparative standards in rich and poor countries.

Perhaps the most useful are the mortality and life expectancy figures and the nutrition data. These are likely to be strongly affected by factors influencing the living standards of the bottom 20 per cent in most societies. Consequently they will reveal whether economic progress is spreading down to the groups in greatest need or is accruing solely to the better off sections of the community. Incidentally, the indicators observed in the foregoing do delineate some important characteristics of developing countries – characteristics which influence not only current living standards but also the prospects for future development. In the next section of this chapter attention is turned directly to those attributes of the countries of the Third World which affect their development.

Constraints on Economic Growth

The capacity of a nation to produce output which may be either consumed or invested to augment future production is determined by a complex of factors whose interaction is as yet only rather imperfectly understood. The major factors involved include: (i) human resources, the quantity and quality of a nation's labour force; (ii) material resources, both in the form of non-renewable natural resources, such as available cultivable land or minerals,[34] and in the form of the man-made resources, such as stocks of capital, communications and transport systems, power plants, buildings, machinery and inventories of raw materials and intermediate goods; (iii) the institutional organisation of the society; and (iv) the social attitudes and customs of the society.

Productive Capacity

Apart from climate and to a lesser extent natural resources, most of the factors which determine productive capacity are the result of activity in the past and are subject to change by current and future human endeavour. The basic resources have always been there; it is the evolution of human knowledge, technical skill and the accumulation of capital which have rendered their exploitation for man's benefit possible. The main differences between most of the developing countries and the countries currently regarded as developed which could explain the wide gap in the levels of output per head probably lie in the different stocks of physical capital and human capital in the form of trained minds. These are instrumental variables in the growth equation. The rate of accumulation of human and physical capital are to a large extent subject to the control of government policy. It is therefore natural that economists should pick these out as the main factors for analysis and policy proposals, but others should not be neglected.

The simple factor of climate may also provide a significant difference between the countries of the Third World and the presently developed ones. Certainly almost all the underdeveloped countries are located in or near the tropics and there are some *prima facie* reasons why climate should affect development. Anyone who has worked in the tropics can testify to the difficulties of physical or mental labour in conditions of high temperature and humidity. Heat and humidity also contribute to deterioration of the soil through erosion, leaching and salination, and to spoilage of stored crops and other material goods. The risks of drought and of flood damage in areas dependent on the monsoon greatly increase the risks of innovation and investment in Asia. Ill-health, absenteeism and low levels of work efficiency can be partially attributed to a tropical environment. Clearly climatic factors can be an obstacle to development. The disadvantages can be ameliorated to some extent by planning and investment, and of course a tropical climate brings some advantages. Many valuable crops require it and it can be a bonus for a tourist industry. Probably planners should pay more attention to climate than they have in the past, but the developmental successes of places like Israel, Hong Kong, Singapore and Taiwan would suggest that climate is not a crucial obstacle.

Differences in the basic natural resource endowment of a nation must also affect its capacity to develop, but apart from the extreme contrasts between a nation like the Yemen, with a desert for countryside and no minerals beneath it, and a nation like Canada or Sweden, with vast natural resources, this factor does not seem to be crucial. Countries such as Japan, Switzerland, Norway and Denmark have achieved very high levels of per capita output with poor resource bases. Among the developing areas Hong Kong and Singapore demonstrate remarkable growth with negligible natural resources. On the other hand, no one can deny that it is an enormous advantage to any country to be sitting on an oilfield. The per capita income of Kuwait or Abu Dhabi now exceeds that of the United States. Such immense wealth makes possible the rapid economic and social development of its society even if that development lags somewhat behind its growth.

The institutional requisites for economic efficiency are difficult to define. Highly centralised governments of an undemocratic nature, such as Nazi Germany and Soviet Russia, appear to be compatible with rapid growth in per capita product or other economic objectives of their societies. But *laissez faire* societies like the United States, Switzerland and Hong Kong seem even more successful.

Almost all systems of political government from dictatorship to near anarchy are represented in the nations of the Third World. The one common element, at least in most of Asia and Africa, is that their political systems are very new and in many cases are initially modelled closely on the institutions of their former colonial rulers. Their boundaries, drawn at independence, were highly artificial, cutting across ethnic groups and thrusting together people with considerable differences of language and culture. This has produced great internal stresses and conflicts between Chinese, Malays and Indians in South-East Asia, between Hausa and Ibo in Nigeria, between Kikuyu and Luo in Kenya and between Asian and African in all of East Africa.

While at the time of the industrial revolution in Europe most of the presently developed nations were consolidated nation-states, few of the developing countries of Africa and Asia have yet achieved that position. This circumstance adversely affects their prospects for development in many ways. It makes it difficult for them to pursue national policies effectively. It induces disproportionate expenditures on military and para-military police forces to maintain external and internal security. It affects industrial location policy to satisfy regional jealousies. It increases their difficulties in attracting foreign investors.

Political stability, legal enforcement of contracts, freedom from dispossession by either the state or rival groups, and freedom from discrimination are the minimum requirements essential for the successful operation of economies based on private capitalism, and most developing countries are largely market economies with most enterprises in both agriculture and industry remaining in the hands of private individuals or companies. As economies grow, other institutions, like banks and capital markets, become increasingly essential.

The different history of Latin America means that the countries there have a much longer period of political independence. They were heavily settled by Europeans in a way much more like the United States and the British dominions. Their cultures – particularly the culture of their ruling class – are European. They do not have an inheritance of centuries of a traditional society to inhibit the adoption of modern techniques and attitudes. In the early 1900s Argentina's per capita income was not significantly different from Europe's, and it is not surprising that per capita incomes in most of the Latin American countries are substantially higher than in Asia or Africa. Several of them surpass certain countries of Europe in per capita product, but the distribution in most is particularly skewed. Their slums are surpassed in horror only by the worst of Asia.

The presently developed countries started their period of accelerated development from a rather higher economic base as well as a better political state. Calculations of per capita products for countries in the eighteenth century are naturally fraught with difficulty, but there is a great deal of historical evidence which points to this conclusion.[35] Starting from a higher base is a considerable advantage. If two countries have the same per capita growth rate of 3 per cent per annum, but one starts from a base of $400 per head and the other $200, the first would reach the quite respectable level of $1,600 in 40 years while the other would have attained only $800.

Population

A much more important obstacle to raising GNP per head than any of the foregoing is the rate of growth of population. This is a crucial difference between the circumstances of developing countries and the circumstances facing the present developed countries in their experience of growth throughout the nineteenth and early twentieth centuries. For them population expansion was of the order of one per cent per annum as compared with the 2 and 3 per cent common in most of today's developing countries. This high rate of growth of population has meant that developing countries have had to run very hard just to stand still. To make any progress they have had to increase GNP by more than 3 per cent per annum.

As was indicated above, this fast growth of population has increased the ratio of dependants to productive population, forced countries to spend more on housing, education and medical services rather than on more immediately productive investment, and has made it more difficult to generate surpluses for further investment. Table 2.3 shows the regional breakdown of population growth rates. Table 2.6 sets out total populations and population growth rates for several of the largest developing and developed countries.

Perhaps the problem of rapid population growth has been sufficiently dramatised in both the literature of development and in discussions of environmental crises. We need not labour the point here but merely make the following notes. If the present trends continue, the Asian population in the year 2000 would be higher than the 1970 world population of 3,635m.[36] There would be 3,778m people in an Asia which is already overcrowded, out of a world total of 6,515m. These trends may of course change. Asian couples may decide to have only two or three children rather than five or six, but it would be exceedingly optimistic to assume that this will happen. Much more needs to be done to encourage a reduction in family size.

Population is one area in which social attitudes and institutions are of strategic importance. High birth rates are socially and economically justified in economically primitive societies where high death rates require many pregnancies and births to ensure surviving children to provide labour in primitive agricultural and rural occupations and to provide support for the parents in their old age or in periods of incapacity. When death rates fall and investment in the education and training of children for skilled, higher paid employment becomes a paying proposition, the need and the economic motivation for many children declines.

Table 2.6

Population (mid-1970) and Average Annual Growth Rates, 1960–70

Country	Population ('000s)	Growth rate (percentage per annum)
Developing Countries		
China (Mainland)	863,000	2·0
India	538,129	2·3
Pakistan and Bangladesh	130,166	2.7
Indonesia	115,567	2·0
Brazil	92,764	2·9
Nigeria	55,070	2·9
Mexico	50,670	3·5
Philippines	36,850	3·0
Developed Countries		
USSR	242,768	1·2
United States	204,800	1·2
Japan	103,390	1·0
Germany (Federal Republic)	61,560	1·0
United Kingdom	55,730	0·6

Source: *World Bank Atlas* (Washington: IBRD, 1972).

Unfortunately there tends to be a lengthy time-lag between the fact and its appreciation by the relevant people. Also as with many religious and other taboos which once made sense but have become obsolete, people hang on to their old practices and beliefs. Prestige continues to be attached to large family size. Priests of various religions condemn the practice of contraception. These social factors delay the adjustment of birth rates to the new situation. In Europe it took about 25 years for birth rates to decline in response to lowered death rates. In Africa and Asia the obstacles are probably much greater even although the available technology of contraception is now vastly better than even a few decades ago. Birth rates are already falling in a number of developing countries but population growth rates remain too high because of the increased numbers in the child-bearing age groups and because death rates are still falling and have a long way to go to reach European levels.

Social and Institutional Obstacles

Response to economic incentives is often alleged to be much weaker in developing countries than in Western Europe or North America. A good deal of writing in colonial times, and reports by businessmen today, focus on differences in attitudes to work and earnings as between, say, European and Asian workers. An early academic statement of this view can be found in a study based on Indonesia by the Dutch sociologist, J. H. Boeke, where he claims that 'anyone expecting Western reactions will meet with frequent surprises. When the price of the coconut is high, the chances are that less of the commodities will be offered for sale; when wages are raised the manager of the estate risks that less work will be done; if three acres are enough to supply the needs of the household a cultivator will not till six.'[37]

Another sociological study, this time of Indian agriculture, *Blossoms in the Dust* by Kusum Nair, reports a chaotic variety of attitudes and responses to the agricultural policies of the Indian Government among Indian villagers.[38] There have been many reports of apparently perverse responses to agricultural prices.

It is not possible, in the face of so much impression of differences in attitudes, to simply deny them. A number of careful statistical tests of particular cases of alleged non-economic behaviour have shown though that, in respect of them, the allegations were ill-founded. Often the original commentators have failed to notice key factors in the situation described. When noting, for instance, that a rise in the price of cotton led to a reduction of cotton acreage, they have failed to observe that wheat or some other crop competed for cotton acreage and that wheat prices had risen still further.

Over the last ten years there has built up a great deal of empirical evidence in support of rational profit-maximising behaviour on the part of peasants.[39] Often when their actions appear perverse there is a sound reason for it. The small farmer may not adopt new techniques because for him the cash outlay in relation to the risk of a crop failure is too great. He is quite rationally minimising his risks because his margin above subsistence is too slender to gamble with.[40] Fertiliser sales, in an area where there are high returns on fertiliser use, may fall off and appear to testify to the conservatism of farmers, but further investigation often reveals that distribution was at fault. Government organisations failed to get the fertiliser to the local distribution points in time for sowing.

Social and institutional arrangements in the agricultural sector do, however, inhibit economic change. This is partly because these arrangements have a distinct rationale. The extended family system, the Hindu *jajmani* system, share-cropping and other social systems do provide some measure of social insurance against personal calamities. But they do inhibit change. The extended family may expect to benefit from the improved fortunes of any enterprising farmer and this may so reduce his returns from innovation or hard work as to be a serious disincentive. Share-crop systems, where they do not compensate *pro rata* the providers of the new inputs, may inhibit investment and innovation. 'In West Pakistan, landlords failed to persuade tenants to adopt intensive Japanese methods of rice cultivation. On examination, the tenant's crop share return for the extra work involved was found to be worth less than could be earned by casual employment off the farm.'[41]

But share-cropping does not necessarily militate against efficiency.[42] The system of land tenure, the division of land between large landlords, small farmers and tenant farmers, the customary method – communal or legal individual tenure – can have effects on the productivity of agriculture. Land reform is often a part of the policies of governments or opposition parties in developing countries. Frequently this is in response to general feelings of social justice, but it is also in part aimed at raising the productivity of land and agricultural labour.

Where the existing system involves holdings which are fragmented and dispersed, measures to consolidate land holdings are almost bound to raise physical productivity, but they may also increase the farmers' risks. His ability to grow a variety of crops over a longer period of the year in varied soil conditions and in places subject to different flood risks is reduced. Breaking up large estates may or may not increase productivity. If the previous landlords were absentees with little or no interest in the land, then the small farmers who gain the land will almost certainly raise output per acre. In general small farms do have higher yields per acre in developing countries but their output per man-hour is usually low.

Since land is the main constraint and under-employment common in most of Asia, this would argue for relatively small farms. The whole issue of land reform, however, and its effects on productivity differ so greatly from region to region that it is much too complex a problem for simple prescription.

Other social and institutional factors inhibit development: the caste system and other rigid barriers to social and occupational mobility, discrimination against the employment of women, tribalism, obsolete dietary inhibitions, poor law enforcement through weak government, the existence of widespread corruption among officials. Many of these are characteristics widespread in the Third World and there is no doubt that they act generally as obstacles to development. Most development literature and government policy has paid insufficient attention to them. To be successful economic planning must take them into account. It is not that they are an absolute barrier to progress but that they have implications for the effectiveness of economic policy. For example, the recognition that the interaction between the social system of villagers and the methods of traditional agriculture are intimately linked in complex ways means often that a single innovation such as the provision of new improved seeds will not be adopted. A whole carefully designed package of new methods may be required before the benefits of modernisation will outweigh the costs of abandoning traditional ways.

Human and Physical Capital

Education and Training

Earlier in this chapter education was treated mainly as a consumption good. In national accounting terms most of the current expenditure on education, such as teachers' salaries, is treated as consumption. Nevertheless, most basic education, all vocational education and most higher education are investments in raising the level of skills in the community. The trained and educated manpower of a nation represents a stock of human capital which can explain a substantial part of the differences in productive capacity between nations.[48] We have already shown above (pp. 42–44) that on literacy and general educational provision, developing countries, especially in Africa, fall far below the standards of the richer nations. At secondary and higher levels the differences are even greater, despite rapid expansion since the 1950s. In Africa, although some 50 per cent of the appropriate age group are in primary schools, only 7 per cent receive any form of secondary education and less than one per cent attend a university. Drop-out rates are high at all levels so that enrolment rates exaggerate the educational provision in most developing countries and the quality of instruction is often poor by the standards of the rich nations. Moreover, the sad part is that a great deal of the education in developing countries is inappropriate, irrelevant or even harmful to economic and social development. Instead of providing practical skills the schools are often too academic, too concerned with Western litera-ture, history and culture. Unconcerned with local problems, they appear to inculcate or encourage a distaste for practical work in agriculture or industry.[44]

As Table 2.7 shows, the quantitative provision of education is also much lower in developing countries, particularly in higher education. The enrolment of students in the 5–19 age group runs from 46 per cent in Latin America to 6 per cent in Africa. The percentages of those enrolled in tertiary education were 2 for Latin America and 0·8 for Africa.

Table 2.7

Comparison of Educational Provision (around 1966)

	Developed	Underdeveloped	Africa
Students enrolled in age group 5–19 (per cent)	79	36	6
Students enrolled at tertiary level (per cent of all students)	6·2	1·9	0·8

Source: Gerald Meier, *Leading Issues in Developing Economics* (London: Oxford University Press, 1970) Table 1, pp. 21–2.

A substantial part of vocational training takes place through apprenticeships and on-the-job training but there is a dearth of statistical information on this aspect of education. Since most of it takes place in industry and the industrial sector remains small in most developing countries, it must be assumed that in relation to their age group the proportion of apprentices is also much smaller there than in the industrially advanced countries.

Capital

It is impossible to quantify the existing capital stock of the developing countries. To measure the value of capital is in principle difficult, if not conceptually impossible. What is undoubted is that the stock of capital – equipment and social overheads together – is enormously greater in the industrially advanced countries than in the Third World. This is probably the major proximate reason for differences in productivity. Since equipment requires energy to run it, we can gain some idea of the services provided by capital goods from the amount of energy consumed. The United Nations publishes statistics of per capita energy consumption and these are summarised by region in Table 2.8. North America consumes over a third of the total energy produced in the world. On a per capita basis, the average consumption of energy in North America is over thirty times that of Africa, but these extremes reflect the cheap energy available historically to the United States and a huge consumer expenditure on petroleum for automobiles and gas for domestic heating.

Table 2.8

Total Energy Consumed per Capita (annual kg of coal equivalent)

Region	1967	1970
World	1,644	1,889
Less Developed Countries		
Africa	290	312
Central America	1,017	1,119
South America	613	706
Asia (Middle East)	542	775
Asia (except Middle East)	376	480
Developed Countries		
North America	9,708	10,944
Western Europe	3,140	3,784
Oceania	3,633	4,031
Centrally Planned Economies	1,450	1,693

Source: *Statistical Yearbook* (New York: United Nations, 1972) and for 1973, Table 137.

As a measure of industrial capital probably the consumption of electrical energy forms a better index. Table 2.9 sets out the total and the per capita consumption of electrical energy in 1970. The differences remain enormous.

In all the other items of capital which contribute to the efficiency with which goods can be produced and distributed, the rich countries are much better off. In roads, railways, rolling stock and commercial vehicles the numbers possessed by the developed countries greatly surpass those in developing countries. The United States alone has nearly 18m commercial vehicles compared with a mere half million in India. Apart from the oddity of Liberia, the developing countries' merchant fleets are tiny in comparison with those of North America and Western Europe.

Table 2.9
Consumption of Electrical Energy

Region	Total consumption (*m kW*) 1953	1972	Approximate per capita consumption (*kW*) 1970
World	1,264,100	5,646,700	
Africa	20,600	103,300	250
South America	25,400	125,500	380
Asia (excluding Japan)	29,505	206,500	120
North America	595,300	2,156,400	8,320
Europe	387,000	1,585,400	3,030

Source: *Statistical Yearbook* (New York: United Nations, 1972) and for 1973, Table 139.

Recent Economic Progress

In most of the foregoing sections of this chapter the main concern was with the differences in the current situation between the Third World and relatively advanced countries and between the countries of the Third World themselves. Changes over time have been noted in a number of the variable factors examined and this section gives a brief review of economic growth and development since the early 1960s.

By historical standards the postwar growth of GNP in the developing countries has been very fast, much faster on average than the rates achieved by any of the rich countries until recent years. When allowance is made for increases in population the performance still remains apparently respectable. On average developing countries have been achieving per capita rates of growth of GNP of about 2·5 per cent per annum since 1950.

Experience since 1965 shows that on the whole the largest and poorest countries have not been doing as well as the smaller and the less poor, whose per capita incomes have risen fast. Mainland China, India, Pakistan and Bangladesh, Indonesia, Brazil and Nigeria between them have over 1,750m people, almost half of the world's population. Their per capita growth was 1·5 per cent (1·7 per cent when weighted by population) while in 1971–3 India and Bangladesh have seen an actual decline in per capita income. Only Brazil showed real success with growth rising from 3·2 per cent to 7·9 per cent per annum. Apart from Brazil the above rank among the poorest of the world's nations. Few of the spectacular successes in the growth league are large or poor. Countries from among the fifteen developing market economies, accounting for less than 150m people, which exceeded 4 per cent growth are often quoted as the success stories for modern development. Some of the statistics for these fifteen are shown in Table 2.10.

Table 2.10

Growth Rate, GNP Per Capita and Population of Fifteen Rapidly Growing Developing Countries

Country	Growth rate 1960–70 (*per cent*)	GNP per capita 1970 (*$US*)	Population (*millions*)
Libya	20·4	1,770	1·9
Hong Kong	8·4	970	4·0
Saudi Arabia	7·4	440	8·0
Zambia	7·1	400	4·1
Taiwan	7·1	390	14·0
Korea (Republic)	6·8	250	32·0
Iran	5·4	380	28·7
Singapore	5·2	920	2·0
Thailand	4·9	200	36·2
Sierra Leone	4·7	190	1·4
Ivory Coast	4·5	310	4·9
Mauritius	4·5	140	1·1
Papua	4·5	300	2·4
Mali	4·4	70	5·0
Panama	4·2	730	1·5
Total population for the group			147·2

Source: *World Bank Atlas* (Washington: IBRD, 1972).

Most citizens of the Third World still live in countries where progress has been comparatively slow. Between 1971 and 1973, growth was negative or under one per cent in countries accounting for 48 per cent of the population of developing countries, most of them countries where the annual per capita income was under $200.[45]

An examination of the more basic indicators shows that progress is still rather slow. Table 2.11 shows index numbers for food production per capita from 1963 to 1973. The gains appear to be rather small and subject to the vagaries of weather; this is also true of total agriculture.

Table 2.11
Per Capita Food and Agricultural Production (1961–5 = 100)

	Region			
	Per capita food production		Per capita total agricultural production	
	Developed	Underdeveloped	Developed	Underdeveloped
1963	101	101	102	101
1964	102	101	102	101
1965	102	99	101	99
1966	105	97	103	97
1967	109	99	106	99
1968	110	101	108	100
1969	109	102	106	102
1970	108	103	105	102
1971	113	101	110	101
1972	112	99	109	99
1973	113	99	110	99

Source: *Production Yearbook* (Rome: FAO, 1973).
Note: Developed = Europe and the Soviet Union, North America and Oceania.
Underdeveloped = Latin America, East Asia (excluding Mainland China), Africa.

Industrial production has grown rapidly from a very small base in the 1950s, but employment in industry has expanded at a much lower rate, as shown in Table 2.12.

Table 2.12
Index Numbers of Industrial Production and Employment (1963 = 100)

	Developing countries		Industrially advanced countries	
	Production	Employment	Production	Employment
1955	56	74	70	87
1958	69	82	73	90
1965	118	109	115	103
1966	125	112	124	106
1967	131	115	127	106
1968	142	117	136	106
1969	155	118	147	109
1970	166	123	150	110
1971	178	125	152	108
1972	192	n.a.	163	107

Source: *Statistical Yearbook, 1972* (New York: United Nations, 1972) and for 1973, Tables 9 and 10.

As argued above on p. 30 some of the figures showing extremely rapid growth in the value of industrial production are spurious because of distortions in the value of industrial goods resulting from heavy protection of import substituting industries and subsidies to exports. Perhaps more worrying from the viewpoint of welfare is the slowing down in the rate of increase of industrial employment. This may be due either to changes in the composition of industry, such as a trend towards heavy industries which require less labour inputs per unit of output, or to improvements in labour productivity in existing industries. Probably both have been occurring. Certainly heavy industry has been expanding faster than light industry. Taking 1963 as the base year (1963 = 100) the index numbers for employment in heavy and light manufacturing industries had grown to 134 and 117 respectively.[46] Given the rapid growth in the urban labour force characteristic of developing countries in recent years, this means high and rising levels of unemployment.

In terms of the social indicators which we examined earlier there has been some progress. Endemic diseases have been substantially reduced. Infant mortality rates have fallen. Education in terms of numbers attending school and numbers of years of education completed by the workforce has improved, but the quality of so much of this educational provision is so poor that it is difficult to estimate the benefits likely to flow from it.

Concluding Remarks

The precise division of the world between developing and developed countries is the result of statistical convention with an overtone of political cynicism. By the United Nations convention the poorer European economies such as Portugal (660), Spain (1020), Greece (1080) and Turkey (310) are excluded, as are all of the centrally planned economies of Eastern Europe such as Yugoslavia (650) and Albania (600), while countries in Latin America such as Argentina (1160) and Venezuela (980) and in the Middle East, Libya (1770), are included. (The figures in brackets are per capita incomes in American dollars in 1970.) The Organisation for Economic Cooperation and Development (OECD) includes the Southern European countries in its category of developing countries. Clearly nations at this upper end of the income scale are likely to be much more similar to Italy or Ireland in the kinds of problems they face rather than to India, Nigeria or China.

In fact the diversity of developing nations should be stressed. They range from arid deserts to lush tropical islands, from the gigantic nations of China and India to the tiny Tonga. Nearly 70 of the developing countries have populations under one million, while over two-thirds of the population of the Third World live in a few huge countries: China, India, Pakistan, Bangladesh, Indonesia, Brazil and Nigeria. Every system of government is represented among them and they differ in religion, culture and tradition. With such heterogeneity it is hardly surprising that few generalisations fit. No one should expect policies for India to be suitable for Malawi or vice versa.

Economic progress among this assembly of nations has ranged from the spectacularly successful to the abysmally poor, but unfortunately it has been among the largest and poorest that progress seems to have been so slow. For most of the nations, probably even for most of the people, there has been progress. Most of the indicators point that way. Nevertheless, in terms of improvement in the lot of the least fortunate 20 per cent very little progress seems to have been made. The main weakness lies in this failure to ensure that a fair share of the benefits of economic growth has gone to the really poor. Major factors in that have been failures to curb population growth sufficiently and to create enough opportunities for employment. To achieve success in these is probably the main challenge to leadership in the Third World today.

NOTES

1. *Yearbook of National Accounts Statistics, 1973* (New York: United Nations, 1975) Table 1B.

2. Simon Kuznets, *Economic Growth of Nations* (Cambridge, Mass.: Harvard University Press, 1971) p. 76.

3. Edward G. Mishan, *The Costs of Economic Growth* (London: Staples, 1967) gives a lively account of some of these factors. Also see Usher, *op. cit.*

4. A. Krueger, 'Factor Endowments and Per Capita Income Differences Among Countries', *Economic Journal*, September 1968.

5. I. Adelman and C. T. Morris, *An Anatomy of Patterns of Income Distribution in Developing Nations*, Report from USAID, 12 February 1971.

6. John H. Adler, 'Development and Income Distribution', *Weltwirtschaftliches Archiv*, No. 108, 1972, p. 330.

7. Mahbub ul Haq, 'Employment in the 1970s: New Perspective', *International Development Review*, December 1971.

8. *Ibid.*, pp. 10–1.

9. *Ibid.*

10. Robert McNamara, Address to the third UNCTAD, Santiago, 1972, p. 4.

11. See Chapter 4. Studies on industrialisation in developing countries by several distinguished economists suggest this conclusion: see references in Chapter 4.

12. The third UNCTAD, Santiago, 1972.

13. Reported in statement by Rudolph Peterson, Administrator of the United Nations Development Programme, to the United Nations General Assembly, 'Dimensions of the Decade', 1972.

14. It is not only in the context of the Third World that there is a weakening of faith in the value of GNP statistics as indices of economic progress. Japanese economists have recently sought to construct a 'happiness index' or indicators of Net National Welfare (NNW). This concept was introduced by Naomi Marno in a publication *Kutabare GNP* ('To Hell with GNP'). Economists of the Sanwa Bank published a 'happiness index' based on 33 indicators in six groups: satisfaction with society, personal satisfaction, safety and a sense of security, working conditions, irritant factors and the feeling that life is worthwhile. See Häkan Hedberg, *Japan's Revenge* (London: Pitman, 1972) pp. 106–7.

15. Most of the following data and some of the methodology is drawn from an excellent discussion in the *World Economic Survey, 1969–70* (New York: United Nations, 1971) Chapter II.

16. John B. Wyon and John E. Gordon, *The Khanna Study: Population Problems in the Rural Punjab* (Cambridge, Mass.: Harvard University Press, 1971).

17. F. James Levinson, 'Facilitating Effective Investment in Nutrition', *International Development Review*, No. 4, 1972, p. 19.

18. See P. V. Sukhatme, 'The World's Food Supplies', *Journal of the Royal Statistical Society*, London, Vol. 129, No. 2, 1966, and comments by Colin Clark and others in the same issue.

19. *World Economic Survey, 1969–70, op. cit.*, Appendix, Table 8 gives data for individual countries around 1967.

20. *Ibid.*, Table 14.

21. *Ibid.*, p. 41.

22. See Enke, 'The Economic Aspects of Slowing Population Growth', *Economic Journal*, March 1966; *Economic Journal*, December 1972; and George B. Simmons, *The Indian Investment in Family Planning* (New York: Population Council, 1971).

23. Simmons, *ibid.*, quoted in a review by Enke, *International Development Review*, No. 3, 1972, p. 26.

24. *World Economic Survey, 1969–70, op. cit.*, Table 14.

25. *Ibid.*, p. 43.

26. *Ibid.*, pp. 44–5.

27. *Ibid.*, Table 17.

28. *Ibid.*, pp. 53–7.

29. *Ibid.*, Table 18.

30. The concept of disguised unemployment – a situation in which many are employed in ways which add little or nothing to total production – has been applied mainly to the agricultural sector. There it has been alleged that labour could be removed without any fall in agricultural output, in technical terms the marginal product is zero. In the context of agriculture there is much criticism of the concept and little empirical support for it.

31. *World Economic Survey, 1969–70, op. cit.*, Appendix, Table A10.

32. *Ibid.*, p. 61.

33. *Ibid.*, p. 63.

34. The non-renewable natural resources are only a fixed stock in terms of given technology, existing knowledge and prices. Uses and demands change as society progresses; what was merely a popular medicinal panacea in the United States in the nineteenth century has become the world's major energy source. The known reserves of oil change each year as the oil companies extend their exploration and rising prices justify heavies investment in extraction.

35. Kuznets, *op cit.*

36. Staff Report by the United Nations Economic Commission for Asia and the Far East (ECAFE) for the Asian Population Conference in Tokyo, 1972.

37. J. H. Boeke, *Economics and Economic Policy of Dual Societies* (New York: Institute of Pacific Relations, 1972) p. 40, quoted in Walter Elkan, *An Introduction to Development Economics* (Harmondsworth: Penguin, 1973) p. 35.

38. Kusum Nair, *Blossoms in the Dust: Human Factor in Economic Development* (New York: Praeger, 1962).

39. See, for example, Theodore W. Schultz, *Economic Growth and Agriculture* (New York; McGraw-Hill, 1968); W. P. Falcon, 'Farmer Response to Price in a Subsistence Economy: Case of West Pakistan', *American Economic Review*, May 1964; and Robert M. Stern, 'The Price Responsiveness of Egyptian Cotton Producers', *Kyklos*, Vol. XII, Fasc. 3.

40. Michael Lipton, 'The Theory of the Optimizing Peasant', *Journal of Development Studies*, Vol. 4, No. 3, 1968; and Leonard Joy, 'Strategy for Agricultural Development', in Dudley Seers and Joy (eds.), *Development in a Divided World* (Harmondsworth: Penguin, 1971) p. 182.

41. Joy, *loc. cit.*, p. 183.

42. See P. K. Bardhan and T. N. Srinivasan, 'Cropsharing Tenancy in Agriculture: Theoretical and Empirical Analysis', *American Economic Review*, March 1971; and S. N. S. Cheung, *The Theory of Share Tenancy* (Chicago: Chicago University Press, 1969).

43. Studies such as Dennison, *op. cit.*, and Robert Solow, 'Technical Change and the Aggregate Production Function', *Review of Economics and Statistics*, August 1957, attribute the major part of growth in countries like the United States to educational inputs.

44. Richard Jolly, 'Manpower and Education', in Seers and Joy (eds.), *op. cit.*, pp. 207–13. He also points out that education in developing countries is relatively expensive. For the expenditure of a similar share of GNP they purchase a smaller share of real resources, mainly because relative to average incomes in their economies the wages of teachers and educational administrators are too high. See also Gunnar Myrdal, *Asian Drama: Inquiry into the Poverty of Nations* (Harmondsworth: Penguin, 1968).

45. Data for 1971–3 from *World Economic Survey, 1974, op. cit.*, Tables 3 and 4.

46. *Statistical Yearbook, 1972* (New York: United Nations, 1973) Table 10.

CHAPTER THREE

Response to the Challenge:
the Role of the State

Chapter 2 has sketched the dimensions of the development problem. Most developing countries face the same unholy trinity – rapid population growth, unemployment and inequalities of income and economic opportunity. The very coexistence of the rich and the poor nations has in some ways aggravated the development problem. Western capital-intensive technology has not always been conducive to employment creation. Although modern medicine has lowered death rates, the absence of parallel developments in controlling birth rates has aggravated the population problem. International demonstration effects have been more powerful in the sphere of consumption rather than production. This has in some ways aggravated the income distribution problem.

Severing international links, however, is not the solution. Going it alone is unlikely to work in an era of increasing international interdependence. The challenge is to integrate the developing countries into the international economy. The task is to harness aid, trade and foreign investment to further the mutual interests of the developed and the developing countries.

This is admittedly a complex task. It calls for intricate commercial diplomacy and concessions on the part of both the developed and developing countries. First steps in this direction are being taken. The Generalised System of Tariff Preferences (GSP) for the exports of the developing countries is one such. The United Nations declaration on a New International Economic Order is another. It is at least a statement of intent if not a concrete agenda for action.

The noises of ideological warfare, however, often swamp the real issues. Popular imagination is fired by ritualistic debates on capitalism versus socialism and the merits of public as opposed to private enterprise. Comparative studies on the economic success of countries subscribing to differing ideologies have become fashionable. 'China versus India' is almost a regular fixture at the annual meetings of economists. 'Ghana versus the Ivory Coast', 'Malaysia versus Indonesia' have also been played. These studies, though not without their merits, scarcely provide any conclusive evidence on the value of one ideology as opposed to another. The conclusions reached often depend on the ideological predilections of the writers.

The choice of a particular type of economic organisation is complexly related to political and historical factors. It is more important to analyse and understand these complex forces than pontificate on the course that the Third World ought to follow. The success of the proposed new economic order largely depends on mutual trust and understanding. Such understanding can hardly materialise in an atmosphere of ideological warfare polluted by preconceived notions of the superiority of one '-ism' to the other. Be it 'socialism' or 'capitalism', it cannot be thrust upon countries whose approach to economic organisation is as yet undergoing an evolutionary process. As Alvin Hansen put it, 'the task of the outside critic is not to persuade underdeveloped countries to do something fundamentally different, but to help them think more realistically about what they are trying to do'.[1]

It is in the spirit that understanding is more important than prescribing that this chapter addresses itself to the forces that have shaped economic philosophy in the different countries of the Third World. It is the role of the state that symbolises the economic philosophy pursued. It is the extent, nature and manner of state participation in economic activity that is often the focus of debate. The first part of the chapter analyses the general factors that have thrust the state into the forefront of economic activity. The second part discusses the historical and political forces that have shaped the economic philosophy of the different countries of the Third World. The last section dwells briefly on the mechanics of state participation in the different countries of the Third World.

Impact of Western Experience and Ideology

The tendency to look to the state for economic progress is in fact world-wide. The Harvard economic historian Alexander Gerschenkron's masterly survey of nineteenth-century European industrialisation highlights the role of the state.[2] In the absence of financial institutions like the banks of mid-nineteenth-century Germany, the state had to play the role of a financier in Russia. In Britain the state was instrumental in abolishing the corn laws and promoting the enclosure movement. These reforms solved the food problem and created a labour supply for industry. In Japan the state not only provided the infrastructure but was also a tireless innovator, later on disposing of the industries to the private sector.

Historically the reasons for state action in these countries have been various. In the countries of the Third World today the political and economic reasons for state intervention have been even more compelling. Yesteryear's colonial domination still casts long shadows. Capitalism and private enterprise are seen as the major instruments of colonial exploitation. *Ipso facto* private enterprise should be bridled by the state if not eliminated.

Western economic and political ideology has also had an impact. Since the 1930s most Western governments have been committed to pursuing policies of full employment and economic equality. The heavy hand of Keynes and Beveridge rests on the leaders of the Third World too. As is often the case, whether in theology or economics, the converted are more bigoted than the perpetrators of a doctrine. The Nehrus, Bhuttos and Nyereres of the English-speaking Third World have usually been educated at British schools and universities, and they also came under the charismatic influence of Harold J. Laski, Bernard Shaw and Kingsley Martin. The imprint of their education is all too clear in the economic manifestos.

Jawaharlal Nehru, the first Indian Prime Minister and architect of Indian development plans, was an early exponent of the philosophy of a mixed economy. His conception of a mixed economy consisted of a regulated private sector, a fast-expanding public sector in strategic and key industries, and a cooperative sector in agriculture, with the overall direction of the development by the state, through its control of the commanding heights of the economy involving resource mobilisation and allocation. Progressive socialisation of the economy and the avoidance of concentration of private economic power were the cornerstones of this philosophy. In Nehru's words, 'the main thing is that power, economic power, should not be concentrated in private hands, that vested interests should not grow up in regard to any important matter, strategic or socially important matter, that there should be a dispersal of economic power, and therefore should be avoidance of monopolies of any kind'.

Economic Rationale for State Participation

Traditionally certain spheres of economic activity are regarded as the exclusive responsibility of the state. Provision of public 'goods' such as defence and education is an example. The social rate of return to investment in such 'goods' is likely to exceed the private rate of return. Consequently private enterprise may fail to provide such goods. As such state intervention is justified.

The failure of the market to provide certain types of goods is a well orchestrated theme.[3] The novel arguments for state participation, however, question the very ability of free enterprise and market forces to initiate and sustain development. Private enterprise may have neither the will nor the resources to embark on the task. The state may have to substitute for private enterprise or at least provide the stimulus for private entrepreneurial activity. Above all there is the general presumption that private enterprise is by its very nature wedded to the pursuit of its own interests, rather than that of the common wealth.

A powerful economic rationale for state intervention was also provided by several strategies of development formulated in the early 1950s. The best known of such theories, most widely debated and somewhat shopworn, are the 'balanced' and 'unbalanced' growth strategies.

Both theories share one feature; the need for a massive initial investment effort. They disagree, however, on how best to deploy it. The balanced growth theorists see the small size of markets in developing countries as a major bottleneck. The world markets for primary products are none too buoyant. Low levels of income delimit the domestic market. The solution in the words of Ragnar Nurkse, an early exponent of balanced growth, is 'a balanced pattern of investment in a number of industries, so that people working more productively, with more capital and improved techniques, become each other's customers'.[4] Some advocates of the strategy also see gains on the supply side. Interdependence of industries may result in cheaper inputs and cost-reducing innovations.[5]

This thesis has been challenged on many grounds. The most controversial aspect, however, relates to the role of the state. The strategy implies coordination and the need for a massive investment effort or the 'big push'. It is the government that has to be the coordinator. Indeed some commentators equate balanced growth with balanced planned growth.[6] Shortages and bottlenecks that may arise in different parts of the economy need to be foreseen and catered for. Private enterprise may have neither the information nor the foresight. Moreover, no individual entrepreneur would be able to take account of the gains arising out of interdependence of industries in his calculation of costs and benefits. These gains may accrue to the society as a whole rather than to individual private profit-making entrepreneurs. This is the so-called 'external economies' argument. Hence the need for state participation.

These arguments, however, have not gone unchallenged. Peter Bauer and Basil Yamey, both of the London School of Economics, while conceding the external economies argument contest the need for state participation. The externalities argument may provide a justification for the provision of information by the government but not for direct state participation.[7] But, as S. K. Nath points out, 'a hesitant investor in industry A does not merely want to know that if industry B is established, investment in A will be more profitable, but also that industry B will be established'.[8] It is necessary for the government to guarantee that industry B will be established.

The antithesis to balanced growth was provided by the Yale economist Albert Hirschman. Aptly enough the strategy is called 'unbalanced growth'.[9] The world of balanced growth is one of tranquillity, where supply and demand are evenly balanced. Economic activity is coordinated by design and conscious effort. The realm of unbalanced growth is, however, one of tensions, bottlenecks and disequilibrium. A state of disequilibrium prompts action. Action promotes development. According to Professor Hirschman the lack of 'decision-making capacity' or entrepreneurial talent is the main limiting factor. Investment decisions are to be induced by deliberately creating imbalances. These imbalances will set up stimuli and pressures needed to induce investment decisions.

This can be done by massive investment in a few carefully chosen industries. These are the industries with strong complementarities; the setting up of certain projects should give rise to a need for others. Their creation should result in investment opportunities elsewhere. They should create tensions, bottlenecks and obstacles resulting in 'group pressure on public authorities' and 'complaints'. There is, however, no set sequence in which industries are to be set up. As Stephen Enke puts it 'the important thing is that a "self propelling" sequence be started; whether it runs by profit steam or political gasoline doesn't matter so long as there is a maximum increase in useful national product'.[10]

The significant aspect of the thesis is that it is the state that has to induce disequilibrium. Private horizons may be too narrow to do the job. Furthermore, the state may have to step in to repair the disequilibrium.[11] The shortages and tensions created by the strategy may result in vested interests and monopoly gains. The state has to repair these damages. The proper sequence of investments and the degree of imbalance required need to be determined. All this necessitates planning and state planning at that.

Development economics is rife with theories. Many excite the taste buds but fail to give sustained nourishment. Such has been the fate of these two theories. As Gerald Meier, of Stanford University, puts it, 'each approach has become so highly qualified that the controversy is now essentially barren . . . it may be concluded that while a new developing country should aim at balance as an investment criterion, this objective will be attained only by initially following in most cases a policy of unbalanced investment'.[12] These two much debated strategies, however, highlight the crucial role of the state in the development process.

Yet it all appears to be a question of tastes and preferences. Economic history, theoretical models, and the socio-political structure and heritage of the developing countries all attest the need for state participation in economic activity. Yet the precise nature and extent of state participation is the matter of a debate which has been inconclusive, and invariably clouded by political ideology and preconceptions. Every weighty argument in favour of either government control or free enterprise is countered by an equally weighty argument against it. One can sympathise with the MIT economist, C. P. Kindleberger, who, after a review of the merits and demerits of government organisation, concludes that 'whether public enterprise is good or bad in a country is an empirical question, rather than a matter for doctrine, and turns on the advantages and disadvantages of private enterprise and government in general, and the particular circumstances'.[13]

Despite this admirable attempt at impartiality even Professor Kindleberger appears not to be able to quell his proclivities for private enterprise. His objectivity takes a hard knock when he recommends 'reserve government for what private enterprise with decentralised decision making cannot do'.[14] Would any hard-nosed advocate of free enterprise concede that there is anything that decentralised decision making cannot do? Again, 'development from below can be private or public, but the spontaneous private is clearly easier to organise, when it exists, than the contrived public'.[15] Where is the need to organise that which is spontaneous? Even so it can be organised only when it exists. What if it does not? 'The presumption of external diseconomies to centralised decision-making is probably stronger than the likelihood of positive economies to big push.' This may be so. But it may be too much to claim, as Professor Kindleberger does, that this statement is an accepted principle which favours decentralisation.[16] Accepted by whom? Certainly not by the advocates of big push.

Morphology of State Participation in Developing Countries

Discussions on the mechanics of state participation in economic activity are inevitably influenced by value judgements and subjective considerations. The issue often tends to be cast in terms of 'socialism' versus 'capitalism'. But these labels are often misnomers.

Debates conducted on these lines amount to fighting windmills; perhaps an intellectually rewarding pastime, but futile for understanding the development problem.

Indeed, socialism is a term which means all things to all men. Sir Arthur Lewis, the West Indian economist, distinguishes between three different sets of interpretations of the term. The first set relates to the degree of equality of distribution of income; the second to ideas of ownership of property; and the third to the power of the state. Within each of these three broad divisions there is room for at least three different types of interpretation of socialism. For example, equality of distribution of income may mean equality of opportunity or equality of reward or opposition to profits as a form of income. As Professor Lewis remarks, if we just take three possibilities from each set there are twenty-seven different types of socialists, and since there are more than three possibilities in each set, the actual number of concepts can run into several dozens.[17]

Evidently it is difficult to box and label developing countries as 'socialist' and 'capitalist'. Moreover, the economic policies they pursue in practice often blatantly belie the public pronouncements. Political constraints and economic compulsions often impede the implementation of the best-intentioned of policies. India for instance has an impressive volume of land reform legislation on the statute books. Ceilings on land holdings are specified and provision for redistribution made. Yet by the end of 1970 the area distributed was only 0·3 per cent of the total cultivated land.[18]

On a more general plane, even the most avowed and fiercely socialist countries have either been unable or found it impractical to totally suppress the private sector. They may have regulated it and exercised operational controls over it, but they have not done away with private ownership of property as such. In most countries where the state has directly participated in manufacturing activity it has been out of necessity rather than ideology. As the Secretariat of the Economic Commission for Asia and the Far East (ECAFE) put it, commenting on the countries of South-east Asia, 'except . . . in the centrally-planned economies, where state control of almost the entire productive apparatus has been adopted on ideological grounds, the countries of the region have left both agriculture (constituting the bulk of the productive economy) and handicrafts and small-scale industry in private hands. Even in large-scale industry, the state has stepped in less on grounds of doctrine than of necessity, since private enterprise was either unwilling or unable to start off.'[19]

Although most developing countries have a substantial private sector they differ from each other in the specific role they have assigned to the state and in their professed economic philosophies. They present a broad spectrum in this respect. At one end are countries which have primarily relied on private enterprise for their development. The state does play a role, perhaps a vital role, even in these countries. But it is confined to creating the climate for private enterprise to flourish. Malaysia, Kenya, the Philippines and to an extent Thailand and Pakistan fall under this category. At the other extreme are countries like Burma, Indonesia, Egypt and Yugoslavia. In so far as they have extensively nationalised industrial activity, banking and commerce they can be categorised as 'socialistic' for want of any other term. But even in these countries the agricultural sector, and in Burma and Indonesia a sizeable proportion of the manufacturing sector, remain in private hands. Indeed, there are few countries outside the Sino-Soviet orbit which have completely expropriated private property and where the state exercises absolute control over the economy, and even there much private enterprise is permitted to continue.

In between these two extremes are the countries which have adopted the 'middle path', or the so-called mixed economy philosophy. Strictly interpreted all economies are mixed, in the sense that there exists both a public and a private sector. But the mix varies from country to country. They differ in the extent and intent of public sector participation. Some of the Afro-Asian countries regard extension of state activity as a first step towards socialism. Others, like Mexico, look upon state participation as a means of strengthening and facilitating the growth of the private sector. The main feature of the mixed economy type of economic structure, however, is direct participation of the state in productive activity and regulation of private enterprise by the state.

The countries of the Third World are thus very much a mixed bag in their approach to economic organisation. Moreover, most developing countries are undergoing a 'learning process'. Their approach to the development problem is in a sense 'evolutionary' in nature. They have not hesitated to change horses in midstream. Major changes in the balance of political power are bound to bring in their wake changes in economic philosophy. But variations in emphasis to much less radical changes in the political balance of power have occurred. For instance Burma, which began on a fiercely socialistic note, accommodated itself to free enterprise when circumstances dictated it in the late fifties. Again, when a major change in the balance of power took place, in the form of the generals taking over the reins of power, it swung back on to a so-called socialist path. More than two decades of experimenting with all sorts of operational controls over the private sector and international trade has also not been without its lessons for some of the developing countries. Major swings in economic policy towards a more liberalised attitude to international trade and exchange rate policies have occurred in India, Pakistan and Indonesia. Benjamin Cohen and Gustav Ranis, the Yale economists, have called this change the Second Post-war Restructuring.[20] The initial impulse to follow a particular course of action of the countries of the Third World can be explained only by their past history.

Legacy of History

Most developing countries have shed the yoke of colonialism comparatively recently. Their economic philosophy appears to have been largely conditioned by the manner of their reaction to foreign domination.[21] Countries which did not react violently to foreign domination appear to have subscribed to a free enterprise philosophy. And those that reacted violently to such domination have been inclined to adopt a relatively a hostile attitude to private enterprise. They have expressed such hostility by extensive nationalisation of foreign enterprises and trade and commerce. Some of these countries have also assigned a more positive role to the state in manufacturing activity.

The manner in which they have reacted to foreign domination has in turn been conditioned by two major factors: the ease with which they attained political independence and the type of economic and social structures they inherited from their colonial masters.

Free Enterprise-oriented Economies

Malaysia, Singapore and, to an extent, Thailand and the Philippines in South-east Asia, and Kenya in Africa provide examples of countries which are largely free-enterprise-oriented. All these countries have assumed a more or less benign attitude towards foreign private capital. They have by and large confined the role of the state to providing social overheads, promoting exports and assisting the development of manufacturing industry by tax concessions and subsidies.

This is not to say that the state has not actively intervened at all in the development process in these countries. But where it has done so it has been motivated by social and economic necessity rather than ideology. Moreover, such interventions have been within the framework of the market and in conjunction with private enterprise. Thus Malaysia has followed a policy of granting tax holidays to 'pioneer industries' as a part of her attempt to develop manufacturing industry. She has also had various schemes of financial assistance and state subsidies directed at helping the Malay section of the population to catch up with the economically dominant Chinese section.

In Thailand there has been a tradition of state monopolies. But as the Swedish economist, Gunnar Myrdal, remarks: 'it is the impulse to exploit political position for personal gains, and not any ideological principle, that accounts for the existence of a large public or quasi-public economic sector in Thailand'.[22] The Philippines has also established some state enterprises. But this is regarded as a regrettable interim measure to be abolished eventually.

The Kenyan Government has also actively participated in economic activity, but here again only within the framework of a free enterprise economy. The activities of the Kenyan Development Finance Company, founded in 1964, primarily to provide share capital for productive enterprises, was to be confined to fill marginal gaps in private project finance. Indeed, the Kenyan Government's policy of confining the role of the state to the provision of social overheads was explicitly stated in the Kenyan Development Plan, 1964–70.[23] Of late, however, the Kenyan Government has been actively participating in the banking and financial sector. It has also subscribed to the share capital of cement, sugar and petroleum industries. A few joint ventures, however, and state intervention in industrial financing do not amount to 'winds of change' in economic organisation. As yet they appear to be only a modest flutter.

None of these countries, perhaps with the exception of Kenya, had to wage a bitter struggle for independence. In fact Thailand is unique in this respect. It has escaped the dubious distinction of being colonised. There were no resistance or independence movements. There have been changes of government brought about by military coups, but a strong central government under one kind of military dictatorship or the other has prevailed. The concern of the ruling élite appears to have been to shield the masses from disruptive influences. As Professor Myrdal remarks, the ruling oligarchies appear to have been motivated by a selfish desire to hang on to their spoils of power. They seem to rest content with a private enterprise system, largely dominated by the Chinese, which provides them with a large share of the fruits of industry.

The passage to independence was relatively smooth for Malaya and the Philippines. This is not to say that there was no desire for political independence or opposition to foreign rule. There were insurrectionist movements, especially in Malaya. But there was no prolonged and bitter struggle for independence, such as those experienced by India, Indonesia or Vietnam. In any case their fight for freedom has not merited historical treatises, provided grist for doctoral dissertations or, for that matter, even attracted the attentions of Hollywood.

Malaya is a clear-cut example. As Gunnar Myrdal states, 'Malaya engaged in no real struggle for independence and was only galvanised into purposeful political activity after the Second World War by the fact that the British clearly intended to withdraw as quickly as possible'.[24] Moreover, the social set-up of the country was such that there was no real interest in either dislodging the British or in comprehensive plans of economic and social change. The indigenous Malays did not want British rule to end until they could fortify their economic and social position. Furthermore, the Malayan élite, composed of the wealthy and privileged members of the Malay, Chinese and Indian sections of the population, looked upon any change as a threat to their vested interests. Again to quote Myrdal, 'state planning would almost inevitably involve taking land away from the Malay aristocracy or interfering with the industrial enterprises of the Chinese business class'.[25]

Malaya may even have been nudged towards independence by the British. But in the case of the Philippines it appears to have been thrust upon them by the Americans. True to its 'professed' liberal traditions the United States had always disclaimed territorial ambitions and President Wilson had confirmed his country's intention of granting independence to the Philippines even before the United States entered the First World War. Though laudable, such liberalism was not entirely devoid of economic self-interest. The most enthusiastic supporters of the independence of the Philippines were the senators from the States affected by competition from Filipino sugar. It may have been no mere coincidence that the granting of independence after a ten-year transitional period was made conditional upon that sugar entering the United States bearing the full rates of customs duty.[26] There was no need for the Philippines to engage in a struggle for independence when her colonial masters were only too eager to grant her political freedom.

The philosophy of free enterprise pursued by the Philippines is largely a legacy of the American colonial rule. The American public school system may also have significantly nourished the ideals of individual freedom and dignity. F. H. Golay remarks: 'Largely through the public school system there slowly permeated through Philippine society awareness that individual dignity, security and welfare were dependent upon the efforts of the individual to realise his capacities as well as upon birth and vagaries of nature.'[27]

Kenya fits the thesis being argued rather loosely, perhaps as a reminder that there do not exist comfortable generalisations. Kenya has had a history of nationalist movements or stirrings dating back to the 1920s. The first attempts were aimed at obtaining redress for their grievances within the framework of the settler-oriented colonial state. After the Second World War nationalism took the form of petition and constitutional protest. Its culmination was the violence-ridden 'Mau Mau' movement. Whether or not the 'Mau Mau' was a genuine nationalist movement remains a matter of debate. To many it represents no more than a psychological aberration on the part of the Kikuyu people who were unable to cope with the demands of modernisation. As such it is adjudged regressive and atavistic and the decision to suppress it by violent methods is condoned.[28] But the thesis that it was an integral part of an ongoing, rationally conceived nationalist movement has also been vehemently argued.[29]

Kenya's penchant for private enterprise is perhaps explained by its socio-economic set up. The 'Mau Mau' was largely spearheaded by the Kikuyu tribe. The European land settlement affected the Kikuyan much more than the other tribes. It is conceivable that though the other tribes shared the desire for independence they had little reason to struggle against the colonial pattern of economic organisation. Moreover it is fascinating to note that the social organisation of the Kikuyu emphasised individual ability and achievement. Entry into the warrior grade and the attainment of the status of an elder in the community were based on economic achievement. Elder status was not based on age but on the ability to pay the bride price in livestock and to establish a homestead. A relative absence of authority and emphasis on initiative and achievement was characteristic of the social organisation.[30] Such a societal structure may have influenced the type of economic organisation that Kenya adopted after independence.

Indeed, in some of the developing countries their social structure may have significantly influenced the prevailing types of economic organisation. A characteristic of most developing countries is the non-homogeneity of their populations. Significant in this context is the sizeable immigrant communities they possess. Kenya has had a largely middle-class-oriented Indian community in the vanguard of trade and commerce. Equally well known is the dominant role played by the Chinese communities in most of the South-east Asian countries. These communities acted as a buffer between the European colonialists and the native population. More often than not they identified their interests with those of the colonialists rather than the native population. In Kenya the Indian community claimed equality with the Europeans. If at all they played only a marginal role in the expanding conflict between the European power élite and the African population. The presence of these communities may have been a factor inhibiting an organised independence movement. It may also have been a factor influencing the type of economic organisation that some of these countries have opted for.

The immigrant communities tend to be close-knit groups wedded to the pursuit of efficient production and money-making rather than social intercourse with the native population. They are a totally commercialised people. To use Trotsky's expression, they are 'Belgianised', worthy, industrious and stable, but a people who have renounced all national ideals and visions. In this sort of a plural economy, competition tends to be keener than in the western world. As the Dutch social anthropologist, J. H. Boeke, put it, 'there is materialism, nationalism, individualism, and a concentration on economic ends, far more complete and abstract than in homogeneous western lands; a total absorption in the exchange and market, a capitalist world with the business concern as subject, far more typical of capitalism than one can imagine in the so-called capitalist countries, which have grown slowly out of the past and are still bound to it by a hundred roots'.[31]

The political and social characteristics of the countries cited above are conducive to the adoption of a free enterprise philosophy. A smooth passage to political independence obviated the need to galvanise the masses by attacking the manifest symbols of colonialism, capitalism and free enterprise. The presence of immigrant communities in the vanguard of trade and commerce also facilitated the adoption of a free enterprise philosophy.

'Socialist' Economies

The presence of immigrant communities may not always favour the adoption of a free enterprise philosophy. It also depends on the ability of the ruling élite to make use of immigrant communities to further the development process. Malaysia provides an example of a country which has by and large attempted to redress the economic balance without forfeiting the entrepreneurial and business talents the aliens provide. But where such abilities are absent or the immigrant communities hold too dominant a position, it may provoke radical reactions. Add to this a bitter and prolonged struggle for political independence and one has a recipe for extensive nationalisation, expulsion of alien communities and mongrel varieties of socialism. The Indonesian, Burmese and Ugandan experience is illustrative.

Indonesia and Burma provide examples of countries where state intervention in economic activity has been extensive. Both these countries began their independent existence with a commitment to socialism.[32] There was a brief interlude in Burma in the late fifties when it retreated from its radical programme of nationalisation and came out in favour of free enterprise. But with the assumption of power by the army in 1962 there ensued an extensive programme of nationalisation. The 'Burmese way to socialism' was in fact heavily cloaked in Marxian terminology. At the outset of Indonesia's independence, banking and rail and air transport were nationalised. After the 1957 West Irian action, Dutch enterprises were taken over and the public sector was considerably enlarged. In the spring of 1965 British and American companies were taken over and import trade nationalised.

These two countries neatly fit the thesis that the economic philosophy pursued is largely a function of the manner of their reaction to 'foreign domination'. Both these countries reacted violently to foreign domination. And with good reason. The passage to independence was far from smooth for them. Burma had been occupied by the Japanese during the Second World War. During this period there developed more than one type of underground movement and resistance group. Japanese occupation fanned the flames of nationalism.

More galling to the Burmese nationalists was the Indian domination of the economy. Until 1937 Burma was ruled by the British as a subordinate and relatively backward province of India. Even after 1937, when Burma was accorded the status of a separate entity, Indians predominated in the professions and the civil service. Much of the modern and quasi-modern sector of the economy was in Indian, and to a lesser extent, in Chinese hands. As in the case of Dutch rule in Indonesia to be discussed below, Britain ruled Burma indirectly through the Indians. As a result, Burma did not possess a Western-educated élite, capable of assuming the reins of power. It is not surprising that Burmese nationalism should have been directed as much at the 'alien' Indian community as at the Europeans. In the event, Burmese economic policy was directed at nationalising Indian interests, even expelling them.

These elements also characterise Indonesia. It had to wage a protracted struggle for independence. There was no voluntary transfer of power by the Dutch. It had to be wrested from them by armed rebellion. Further, the Dutch favoured a policy of governing Indonesia indirectly, through hereditary local rulers. This meant an even more pronounced policy of divide and rule than is natural in every colonial regime. Consequently it did nothing to promote social cohesion or break down the compartmentalisation of Indonesian society.[33] The Dutch style of colonial policy also failed to foster an

élite, educated and trained along Western lines, who could successfully implement economic policy. As Benjamin Higgins, writing in
1957 remarks, 'the problem is less one of formulating appropriate
economic policy and having it accepted at cabinet level than it is of
getting policies through parliament and administering them once
adopted. Below the top ranks of the civil service there is an almost
complete absence of administrative training, experience and
ability.'[34]

It is only the British who can boast of a civil service, a *lingua
franca* and a trained corps of army officers which they have be-
stowed on their ex-colonies. The British favoured a system of direct
rule. Their style required a corps of civil servants trained along
Western lines to implement their policies. In the event, British ex-
colonies like Malaya and India were better prepared for self-
government than Indonesia.

In the absence of a trained indigenous élite the 'alien' elements of
the population rushed in to fill the vacuum created by the existence
of the colonial powers. In Burma it was the Indians and in Indonesia it was the Chinese who controlled the commanding heights of
trade and commerce. Resentment of this alien control was reflected
in radical policies of nationalisation and expulsion of the aliens in
both these countries. The presence of an educated administrative
élite may have made a difference to the type of economic policies
pursued by these countries. For instance, Malaysia also has a sizeable Chinese population. The Malays also resent the economic
superiority of the Chinese. But Malaysia has tried to tilt the balance
of economic power in favour of the Malays by providing subsidies
and financial incentives of various sorts to Malay entrepreneurs. It
has tried to solve its ethnic problem within the framework of a
market-oriented system. As Hla Myint, of the London School of
Economics, argues, this policy of setting up subsidised infant institutions may prove burdensome to the economy in the long run.[35]
Nevertheless it is a positive and pragmatic approach to the ethnic
problem. This contrasts with the negative policy of supplantation
pursued by Indonesia and Burma with its consequent adverse effects
on their economies.

Burmese and Indonesian socialism was more a reaction to foreign
domination, capitalism, liberalism and everything associated with
colonialism, than a deliberate strategy of development. Their economic philosophy at least in the early years of independence appears
to have been more concerned with distributive justice than increased
production. The concern was with cutting equal or more or less
equal slices out of a small pie rather than baking a bigger pie.

Thus socialism, or what these countries purport to call socialism, far from being a deliberate and reasoned choice appears to be a nationalist reaction to alien domination of their economies. They may have in the process sacrificed economic efficiency for the sake of narrow nationalist aims. No doubt they desire development, but their commitment to development may be subordinate to achieving other goals. Under these circumstances policies which assign a high priority to development are likely to flounder. A failure to grasp the relationship between politics and development is particularly damaging to development planning. It may result in the discrediting of planning itself.[36]

Philosophy of a 'Mixed Economy'

As stated earlier, strictly speaking all economies are mixed. But some are more mixed than others. The mix of course refers to the coexistence of public and private sectors. While private enterprise is not discouraged the public sector is assigned a prominent place in the economy. Public sector participation is justified both by egalitarian ideals and economic necessity. In a sense it represents a compromise between the socialist ideology and the capitalist creed. India provides a good example of this approach and because of its sheer size and political importance deserves close attention.

India's approach to economic organisation is widely held to represent the mixed economy philosophy. The state owns and manages key industries such as iron and steel. Certain sectors of manufacturing industry are reserved for the state. However, most economic activity including agriculture is in private hands. Foreign private investment, though fettered by various restrictions and regulations, is not altogether shunned. The public sector has expanded by establishing new enterprises rather than by state take-over of existing enterprises. Exceptions are the nationalisation of the life assurance business and the nationalisation of key segments of the commercial banking system.

The interplay of political and economic factors, the influence of the intellectual and business élite, and the impact of the colonial legacy are all too clear in the Indian approach to economic organisation. It is instructive to dwell at some length on the Indian experience.

India also waged a protracted struggle for independence. Indian historians trace the first stirrings of a liberation movement back to the so-called Sepoy Mutiny of 1857. Latter-day Indian historians regard the mutiny as the first war of independence – although Churchill disputed such claims.[37] The movement for independence waged in this century in all its elaborate detail, and the disputations as to whether or not it was a non-violent struggle, are well-documented history. But the point is that India, unlike Malaya and the Philippines, had to struggle for her independence.

Again, unlike the other South Asian countries, India was not saddled with separate ethnic entities well entrenched in privileged economic positions. She did, however, inherit a large and highly educated class of thoroughly Westernised intellectuals. All these three elements, the long struggle for independence, the absence of 'alien' communities and the existence of a Western-educated élite have influenced the type of economic organisation that India has chosen.

Indian nationalism derived its motivating force as much from a desire to control and direct the country's economic and social welfare as from concrete political objectives. The indifference and apathy of the British Government in dealing with the economic problems of the country were always major targets of attack of the Indian nationalists, especially of the Indian National Congress. The British, especially in the nineteenth century, were wedded to an economic philosophy which espoused free trade and free enterprise. They practised this creed with a religious fervour in the colonies. This is illustrated by the reaction of the British authorities to the famine that gripped the province of Orissa in 1866. So tenacious was their adherence to the philosophy of *laissez faire* that they opted to do nothing. Philip Woodruff's comment, in *The Men Who Ruled India*, is apt: 'At Haileybury, every one had learnt that political economy was a matter of laws, that money and goods would move by themselves in ways beneficial to mankind. The less any government interfered with natural movements the better. If there was real scarcity in Orissa, prices would rise, grain-dealers from elsewhere would be attracted and hurry grain to where it was needed. If the government tried to anticipate this process, they would cause waste and incur loss ... By the time relief came a quarter of the population were dead.'[38]

The twentieth century has not witnessed any dramatic change in British economic policy. The absence of an overall economic policy was the main target of attack by the Indian nationalists. The great depression of 1930 lent additional stimulus to the fast-gathering opposition to British rule. Although the great depression affected all countries, India had to suffer its effects for a longer duration, almost until the outbreak of the Second World War. The Indian nationalists were most vocal in criticising the failure of the Government to take steps to relieve the distress of the people. The lack of a consciously designed economic policy on the part of the Indian Government drew fire from all quarters – even from the Indian business community. It was a leading Indian industrial and business magnate, G. D. Birla, who articulated the need for government intervention: 'We cannot improve our lot, until we decide to take mass action, well thought out, well planned, as part of a scheme of coordination launched with the necessary authority to make it a success. Government intervention thus became necessary ... The Government knows the evil of drifting without a plan. But it would not think of taking planned action. Probably the apathy on the part of the Government is due to the fact that the head of every department in the Secretariat has a five-year plan of ruling and then retiring ... the one object of men in authority in New Delhi is to maintain law and order and balance budgets and of the Clive Street Burra Sahib to retire leaving things as he found them.'[39]

The Indian nationalists were thus not only highly critical of British economic policy, but also conscious of the need for positive government intervention in economic affairs. Of even greater significance was the powerful influence wielded by Western-educated intellectuals in the Congress Party. Foremost among them was Jawaharlal Nehru, a product of Harrow, Cambridge and the Inner Temple. Natural scientist by training, lawyer by profession and a historian and man of letters, his ideas of socialism appear to have been deeply influenced by his sense of history. To him socialism was the natural outcome of an ongoing historical process. In this Nehru was profoundly influenced by the Marxist theory of historical determination. He viewed the decline of capitalism and the disappearance of economic imperialism as a world-wide phenomenon. India's problem was therefore a part of a world-wide phenomenon and socialism the inevitable course she had to follow. But Nehru did not accept the Marxist ideology *in toto*. It was his conviction that Marxism was to be reviewed in the light of new developments, such as political democracy and technological advance, both of which Marx did not foresee.[40] To Nehru socialism meant pursuit of egalitarian objectives in conjunction with political democracy. Socialism is interdependent with modernisation and industrialisation and is equated with planning. The motive force of economic development is the state.

Perhaps if Nehru could have had his own way he would have favoured large-scale nationalisation of industry and collectivisation of agriculture. In this he was heavily influenced by the Soviet approach to economic development. But there were forces within the Congress Party which bridled Nehru's radicalism. Nehru's penchant for socialism was not all that palatable to the financial and industrial interests that were influential in the Congress Party. Moreover, the economic philosophy of the other leading light in the

Indian Nationalist Movement, Mahatma Gandhi, was often at variance with that of Nehru. Gandhi was no doubt an egalitarian. In principle he was for complete economic equality, but he was fundamentally opposed to any violent means of achieving social revolution. His method of achieving economic equality, as everything else, was through moral persuasion. Thus his famous theory of social trusteeship,[41] according to which 'the rich man will be left in possession of his property for his personal needs and will act as a trustee for the remainder to be used for society'. In this he assumed that the trustees would use their wealth to promote the common good without regard to their self-interest. Gandhi also demanded a moral revolution, a change of heart on the part of the wealthy.

The thesis of trusteeship may sound bizarre to a socialist, and it did to Nehru. If only the privileged few could be trusted to act in the interests of the common good it would be a primrose path to socialism. But Gandhi above all was a pragmatist. India unlike the other South Asian countries had a well developed indigenous business class. They were a force in the Congress Party. Their coffers were essential to finance the Party. Moreover, their managerial skills were necessary if India were to progress. Above all compromises between the different ideological factors of the Party were imperative to wage a concerted struggle for independence.

The philosophy of a mixed economy pursued by India is a result of these political and ideological considerations. The Industrial Policy Resolutions of 1948 and 1956 gave clear indication of the ideological compromises that had been arrived at. They testify to the compromises that had been forged between various factions. They also underscore the pragmatic approach of the leadership to economic philosophy. There was not much that was denied the private sector. In fact the fields reserved for the public sector were those in which the private sector may not have the resources to invest. Nehru himself, perhaps a much mellowed Nehru in the post-independence era, was quick to recognise the costs involved in replacing the private sector. In his statement to the Indian Parliament in 1956 he said, 'I can understand "prevent that, control that, plan for that"; but where there is such a vast field to cover, it is foolish to take charge of the whole field when you are totally incapable of using that huge area yourself. Therefore, you must not only permit the private sector, but, I say, encourage it in its own field.'[42]

Despite all this pragmatism, however, India has not been able to completely avoid conflict between economic efficiency and political considerations. These came to the forefront in the sixties at the beginning of the third five-year plan. It became increasingly difficult to demarcate and separate out spheres of activity for the two sectors. On the one hand the public sector had 'learnt by doing' and the problems of starting from scratch were no longer important. On the other hand the private sector could not be excluded from 'socially necessary' investments on the ground that it was incapable of doing so. The financial and protectionist policies of the government itself had made such investments both possible and profitable. The private sector could not be kept out except on strict ideological grounds. The inevitable result was a compromise in the form of a slackening of the public sector's share in investments combined with numerous restrictions on the growth of the private sector.

These developments in the Indian economy have important lessons. As Bhagwati and Desai argue, the compromises forged by India represent the triumph of pragmatism over ideological imperatives. But they also reflect the futility of depending on a gradualist approach to a Marxist state. In a mixed economy, where the private sector plays a major economic role, it would be naïve to expect that there would occur a democratic liquidation of capitalism.[43]

The foregoing underscores the complex interplay of social and political factors that have shaped the economic philosophy of the countries of the Third World. The pursuit of a particular type of economic organisation appears to be more a result of historical accident than a deliberately chosen course of action to achieve stated economic and social objectives. It would therefore be naïve to pass judgment on their choice of economic philosophy.

Mechanics of State Participation

It would be more pertinent to examine the impact of state participation on the development process in the different developing countries. But this is an even more daunting task than accounting for the course of action they have chosen to follow.

The state influences economic activity in a myriad of ways. Quantitative exercises relating the size of government expenditures to rates of growth or the extent of public ownership of industry to growth of industrialisation cannot capture the full impact of state on development. More than the extent of government participation, it is the nature, composition and timing of government intervention that influences development. Indeed, if the timing and nature of intervention are wrong it may impede rather than promote development.[44] It is, however, worth dwelling on three major spheres of state participation in economic activity: government expenditures, mobilisation of resources for development, and direct state participation in industrial production.

Extent and Pattern of State Participation in Economic Activity

Data inadequacies are a perennial problem in development economics. Data on national income and public expenditures are readily available. However, they are not comprehensive enough and there are problems in comparing them across countries. Despite these deficiencies an attempt is made in this section to analyse the extent of state participation in some of the countries of the Third World. Table 3.1 shows government expenditures as a percentage of GDP.

Table 3.1

Government Expenditure as Percentages of GDP, 1970–2

Brazil	13·2	India	14·0	Pakistan	20·3	Kenya	22·0
Chile	25·1	Sri Lanka	29·8	Burma	18·0	Ghana	23·8
Colombia	16·3	S. Korea	22·8	Philippines	9·4	Egypt	21·0
Mexico	11·0	Malaysia	33·9	Thailand	18·0	Average	19·9

Source: *Statistical Yearbook, 1974* (New York: United Nations, 1975).

For the fifteen countries listed in Table 3.1 the average of total government expenditures to GDP is around 20 per cent. There are, however, wide variations around this figure. In avowedly free-enterprise-oriented economies like Malaysia and Kenya the proportion of government expenditures to GDP is above the average. In the case of India, a country committed to a socialistic pattern of society, it is well below the average.

There are also wide variations in the pattern of public expenditures in these countries. Table 3.2 shows the percentage share of principal categories of expenditure to total public expenditures.

The category 'other current expenditures' bulks large in the case of most countries listed in Table 3.2. With the exception of Malaysia and the Philippines this high figure is to be accounted for by administrative expenditures. This is especially so in the case of Brazil and Ghana which have swollen bureaucracies. In the case of Malaysia and the Philippines expenditure on transport and communications is included in this category. A large proportion of public expenditure in the case of these countries which are avowedly free-enterprise-oriented is in fact for infrastructure development.

Defence accounts for a relatively high proportion of the total expenditures in the case of Burma and Pakistan followed by Thailand, Brazil, Malaysia and India. For the year 1965 for a group of

22 developing countries military expenditures as a percentage of GDP is reported to have been around 3·8 per cent. For most of the countries listed in Table 3.2 with the exception of Kenya this figure was well above the average.[45]

Table 3.2

Percentage Share of Major Categories of Public Expenditure, 1970-2

	Education	Health	Defence	Other current expenditures	Capital formation
Brazil	5·0	1·7	19·7	58·4	–
Chile (1970–1)	18·5	9·0	9·0	33·5	30·0
Colombia	16·9	7·7	13·2	18·4	43·8
Mexico	22·0	5·6	8·5	35·0	16·0
India	7·8	3·2	13·6	31·4	13·0
Pakistan (1969–70)	7·2	4·3	23·0	12·4	15·2
Malaysia	18·0	6·1	15·7	29·0	–
Philippines	26·0	–	11·4	40·0	21·6
Burma	13·9	5·5	32·4	30·0	11·5
Thailand	17·0	3·0	18·8	33·0	26·2
Kenya (1970–1)	17·7	5·9	4·5	49·0	9·2
Ghana	18·0	5·9	7·3	44·2	13·6

Source: *Statistical Year Book, 1974* (New York: United Nations, 1975).

A high proportion of these administrative and military expenditures are obviously non-productive. There may be scope for economising in expenditure on bureaucracy. Reduction in military expenditure is subject to international cooperation and understanding. Measures designed to control international trade in arms and armaments, much of which may be illicit, is one positive step that the developed countries can take in this direction.

Some countries like India, Burma and Pakistan spend much less on education and health than they spend on defence. In view of the population problems these countries face and the need to improve the quality of their population the expenditures they incur on these categories appear to be very low.

Role of the Government in Capital Formation

The data on capital formation reported in Table 3.2 understates the true extent of government investment in the case of some of the countries. As stated earlier, in the case of some countries like Malaysia and the Philippines expenditures on infrastructure development are included under the category of other current expenditures. In fact obtaining comparable data on capital formation is a major problem. However, it is significant that countries like India and Burma which are avowedly socialistic spend relatively less on capital formation than other countries.

It is, however, significant that in most countries the government irrespective of professed economic ideology plays an important role in capital formation. Although in recent years some reaction has set in against the emphasis on capital to the neglect of other factors, capital still holds the centre of the stage in development economics. Professor Arthur Lewis's contention that the central problem of development is rapid capital accumulation, and that it is therefore crucial to understand the process by which savings and investment increase from 4–5 per cent of national income to 12–15 per cent is well known.[46]

Most developing countries have achieved a rate of investment of much more than 10 per cent of national income. The share of the government in total investment varies between different developing countries. It is, however, substantially higher than that prevailing in the developed countries when they were in a comparable stage of development. Table 3.3 shows the relevant data for selected developing countries for the year 1965.

All of the countries listed in Table 3.3 had achieved the Rostow-Lewis magic investment figure of 10 per cent and above. In most countries government investment as a percentage of GDP was around 3 to 5 per cent. More revealing are the data on the share of the government in total investment. The average figure for the fifteen countries for which data are available was around 36 per cent. For India, Pakistan and Egypt this figure was well above the average. India, more than any other developing country, has established several public enterprises. The government owns and operates industries manufacturing iron and steel, machine tools, heavy electrical equipment and telephones. Pakistan had made substantial public outlays on water, power, and transport and communications – a case of a free-enterprise-oriented economy with the accent of government investment on infrastructure. The exceptionally high figure for Egypt is indicative of its commitment to socialism. It is also of interest to note that socialist Burma and free-enterprise-oriented Malaysia have roughly similar shares of government investment in total investment.

These figures indicate that, irrespective of professed economic ideology, the government plays an expanding role in capital formation in most developing countries. Indeed, the share of government investment to total investment in the present-day developing countries is much higher than it was in the developed countries at a comparable stage of development. At present the share of government investment in total investment in most developed countries is around 25 to 40 per cent compared to the 25 to 45 per cent range for developing countries. But the developed countries have progressed to this figure over a relatively long period of time.[47] This difference partly reflects the tendency on the part of the developing countries to look to the state to provide the infrastructure for development. The fact that foreign funds to finance capital formation are mostly channelled through the state and the weakness of the incentives to private investment may also be contributing factors.

Table 3.3

Investment as a Percentage of GDP and Share of Government Investment in Selected Developing Countries, 1965

Country	1 Total investment	2 Government investment	3 Share of government investment in total investment
Argentina	17·2	5·4	27·7
Brazil	10·7	4·4	48·3
Colombia (1964)	15·9	3·1	18·3
Chile	15·9	9·0	–
Mexico	15·7	2·8	41·8
Burma (1961–6)	18·1	8·3	46·0
Ceylon (1961–6)	13·1	4·8	38·1
India	15·8	5·3	61·0
Malaysia (1964)	17·0	7·1	44·0
Pakistan (1961–6)	14·7	5·8	50·3
Taiwan	16·3	5·3	34·6
Thailand	21·8	5·6	32·4
Philippines	20·0	5·0	11·9
S. Korea	14·7	3·2	22·0
Egypt (1964)	17·8	–	80·7
Kenya	16·0	3·3	25·5
Ghana	16·2	–	–

Source: Cols. 1 and 3 from Angus Maddison, *op. cit.*, pp. 307 and 165. Col. 2: Estimated from data in *National Income Accounts for Less Developed Countries* (Paris: OECD, 1970). Figures relating to 1961–66 from L. G. Reynolds, 'Public Sector Saving and Capital Formation' in Gustav Ranis (ed.), *Government and Economic Development*, (New Haven: Yale University Press, 1971).

The composition of government investment in most developing countries is heavily oriented towards infrastructure including power, transport, and communications and services. Table 3.4 shows the planned distribution of public investment for selected developing countries for which data are available.

Table 3.4

Planned Distribution of Public Investment in Selected Developing Countries, mid-1960s

Country	Commodity production	Basic facilities	Services
Egypt	55	25	20
India	48	42	10
Pakistan	48	29	23
Ceylon	47	30	23
Malaysia	30	39	31
Burma	27	37	36
Philippines	24	69	7
Kenya	21	35	45
Chile	15	43	42
Colombia	6	52	42

Source: R. B. Sutcliffe, *Industry and Underdevelopment* (London: Addison-Wesley, 1971) p. 305.

With the exception of the first four countries in Table 3.4, all others have a relatively high proportion of planned public invest-ment in basic facilities and services. India, Egypt and Ceylon place greater emphasis on manufacturing within the commodity produc-tion category. Pakistan's planned investment is oriented more towards agriculture where the state-established Pakistan Industrial Development Corporation has invested in sugar, fruit canning and fertilisers. The Philippines places great emphasis on power and transport and communications. The services sector which includes banking and trade claims a relatively high proportion of government outlays in Burma, Kenya and the two Latin American countries. In the case of Burma this reflects the Government's policy of national-ising certain sectors of trade and banking. The other countries have actively engaged in promoting state-established development banks and finance corporations. These organisations mobilise finance for private enterprise. Save in the case of a few countries like India and Egypt, most developing countries appear to subscribe to the idea that the government should act as a catalyst to private enterprise. Even India has established several industrial financing corporations and development banks to assist mainly small-scale industries.

Role of the State in Resource Mobilisation

The state influences not only capital formation in the public sector but also private sector savings and investment. Its taxation and borrowing policies may affect private incentives to save and invest and so can its monetary and credit policies. In some of the developing countries the state-established financial institutions play a significant role in financing private industry, especially the small-scale industries. The state can also exert an influence on the flow of external financial resources of public aid and foreign private investment. These two aspects are discussed in later chapters.

Table 3.5

Sources of Public Sector Capital Formation, Selected Asian Countries, 1961–66

	Total public investment		Percentage of public investment financed by		
	Percentage of GNP	Percentage of total investment	Government savings	Domestic borrowing	External sources
India	7·4	63·7	20·0	45·8	34·2
Pakistan	5·8	43·0	15·1	26·7	58·2
Ceylon	6·8	46·1	8·3	75·1	16·6
Malaya	7·1	37·7	32·0	44·8	23·2
Thailand	5·8	26·9	44·9	35·9	19·2
Philippines	–	–	12·4	47·1	40·5

Source: Gustav Ranis (ed.), *Government and Economic Development* (New Haven: Yale University Press, 1971) p. 536.

Among the major domestic sources of finance for the government are taxation, public borrowing, profits of the public enterprises and savings directed from the private sector by increased monetisation or inflation. Each of these aspects merits a separate dissertation. The discussion here is confined to the major issues. Taxation and income from the operation of public enterprises is often referred to as public sector savings. Except in the case of a few developing countries, government savings do not contribute very much to public sector revenues. The gap between government revenues and expenditures is made up mostly by domestic borrowing and external finance. Table 3.5 shows the contribution of different sources to public sector capital formation for selected Asian countries for which data are easily available.

Such data are unfortunately not available for all developing countries. But some individual country studies also point to the relatively low contribution of government savings to total public sector capital formation.

This poor showing of government savings and the heavy dependence of developing countries on domestic borrowings have been widely discussed. The pertinent issues are the inappropriate tax structures of the developing countries, their inability to collect taxes, and the inefficiencies associated with the operation of public enterprises. Further, there is a wide-ranging debate on the propriety of large-scale resort to domestic borrowing. The most controversial aspect in this area relates to the role of inflation as a source of development finance.

Tax Structure

Two aspects of the tax structure of developing countries are often pointed out. First, the proportion of tax revenues to gross national product is typically much smaller than in developed countries. While the developed countries collect around 25 per cent of their GNP in taxation, most developing countries collect only 8 to 15 per cent. Out of a total of thirty-three developing countries only fifteen were found to have a tax revenue exceeding 15 per cent of gross domestic product. In no case was the figure higher than 28 per cent.[48]

Secondly, the bulk of the tax revenues of the developing countries are accounted for by indirect taxes. A majority of developing countries collect 70 per cent or more of their tax revenues from indirect taxes compared to about 35 to 50 per cent in the case of developed countries. In export-oriented economies like Malaysia and Ceylon, customs duties account for a major share, nearly 40 per cent of the total tax revenues.

Countries relatively less dependent on trade have also resorted to taxation of international trade besides purchase taxes on consumer goods and services. This is a reflection of the ease with which taxes can be levied and collected on goods moving in international trade. It must, however, be noted that taxes on international trade, especially import duties, are also levied with a view to affording protection to domestic industries from international competition.

The low incidence of taxation in the developing countries cannot be easily explained away in terms of their relatively low levels of per capita income. It may be the pattern of income distribution rather than the level of per capita income that is a good guide to taxable capacity. If the income and wealth distribution are highly unequal and the upper income groups indulge in inessential and luxury consumption, the potential for taxing them could be considerable. This thesis has been persuasively argued by the Cambridge economist Nicholas Kaldor in the context of the tax policies of developing countries.[49]

A recent study by the World Bank and the Institute of Development Studies at Sussex has shed more light on the relatively unresearched aspect of income distribution.[50] According to this study, the share of the lowest 40 per cent of the population in total income is around 9 per cent for nearly half of the developing countries. This contrasts with a 16 per cent share for the lowest 40 per cent of the population in the developed countries. What is more relevant is the fact that in nearly eighteen of the 46 countries for which data are reported, the top 20 per cent of the population had more than a 60 per cent share of income. Even in the case of those countries which the study categorises as low inequality countries, the top 20 per cent had a 40 to 45 per cent share in total income. The so-called middle class appears to be only a thin wedge between the low-income and the upper income groups.

Comparable data are not available on the consumption patterns of upper income groups. But that they do indulge in ostentatious consumption is well known. The contrasting sights of mud hovels by the side of luxury mansions and Mercedes competing for road space with bullock carts are all too common in these countries. The existence of industries producing luxury goods, such as air conditioners and refrigerators, in countries with low average per capita incomes can only be explained by the demand for them by the upper income groups. Indian economists refer to the upper income groups as the U sector, after the huge U-shaped houses they live in.

But paradoxically enough, the uneven distribution of incomes which holds promise of higher tax revenues also impedes their collection. The oligarchic power exercised by the upper income groups may be an important factor explaining the relatively low tax revenues of developing countries. Direct taxes which fall on wages and salaries are collected easily enough at the source under the pay-as-you-earn schemes. But typically wage and salary earners tend to be in the low income groups. It is the upper income groups who derive income from property, and self-employed professional classes like lawyers and doctors who are in a position to evade the taxes. In India one million people were assessed for income tax in 1956, and only half of these paid tax, out of 200m in the labour force. In Pakistan, income tax is paid by only one-tenth of one per cent of the total population. Maintaining two sets of accounts, one for the tax man and the other for one's own use, and disguising consumption expenditures as business expenses are favourite gambits of tax avoidance. Low public morality is often compounded by administrative inefficiencies and corruption.

Administrative inefficiencies may be overcome by training and the borrowing of technical expertise from abroad. But what of low public morality? Can one upbraid the business community and the ill-paid tax collectors when the top administrative élite and those in seats of power fail to practice what they preach? This is a recurring theme in the Indian press. It may be of little consolation that it is debated and discussed. The Indian Parliament devoted more time to discussions of the so-called import licence scandal involving members of the Parliament than to economic policy.

More serious than the low levels of tax revenue collected are the regressive effects of the tax structures of developing countries. Indirect taxes often impinge heavily on many basic consumption goods. Taxes on such items as sugar, tobacco and kerosene oil figure in every government budget as they are characterised by low price elasticities of demand. Even the income tax, as pointed out above, fails to hit the well-to-do and falls largely on the middle-income salary and wage earners.

The heavy dependence on indirect taxes also results in a lack of buoyancy in the tax structure. In other words tax revenues do not increase proportionately with income as the commodities subject to tax tend to have a low income elasticity of demand. Therefore, if the share of tax revenue in total income is to be maintained, frequent revisions of the rate structure would be required. Most developing countries, however, display an elasticity of tax revenue with respect to GDP of greater than unity.[51] In other words, government tax revenues appear to increase faster than income. This may have been achieved by frequent revisions of rate structure of indirect taxes. Further, the elasticity of government expenditures with respect to income tends to be higher than the elasticity of tax revenue.

Another issue which has attracted wide attention is the relatively low levels of tax revenue collected from the agricultural sector. Though contentious, several virtues of agricultural taxation have been pointed out. It is agriculture that contributes the major share to national income. Agricultural taxation is a means of adding to total savings. It can also be an instrument for augmenting the marketable surplus of agricultural output. Further, income inequalities tend to be high in rural areas also. In most developing countries nearly 50 per cent of the agricultural income is reputed to accrue to only twenty per cent of the population.

The arguments in favour of taxing agriculture are strong, but there are practical problems involved in doing so. It may be difficult to assess agricultural incomes. Taxation of land may involve problems of assessing the land values. Ingenious schemes of land taxation incorporating the virtues of progressiveness, equity and administrative ease have been suggested,[52] but none implemented. The major impediment again appears to be politically oriented. The rural oligarchy commands a considerable number of votes. Political parties in power in democratically-oriented countries like India are loath to tax the agricultural sector for fear of losing votes. Even military dictatorships are dependent on the support of the landed aristocracy. Moreover, the landed aristocracy may be indifferent to development itself, especially when it disrupts the traditional rural structure and poses a threat to their privileged positions. The major obstacle to raising tax revenues thus appear to be mainly political. This lesson has been brought home to many outside experts. Professor Kaldor's ingenious tax schemes for India and Ceylon appear to have foundered on the bedrock of politics.

Public Borrowing

Governments of many developing countries have resorted to public borrowing to bridge the gap between their expenditures and revenues. When such borrowing takes the form of issuing public debt it may serve a useful function. By providing acceptable government instruments it may discourage consumption and promote savings. But it is the merit of imposing forced savings on the community by monetary expansion that is debatable. That a moderate degree of inflation is an inevitable price to pay for development is generally accepted. In fact a moderate degree of inflation may help to reallocate resources from the traditional sectors to the developing sectors. But should a country deliberately use inflationary policies to mobilise resources for development?

The weight of the theoretical arguments appear to be against a deliberate use of inflationary policies. Harry Johnson, of the University of Chicago, has made out a lucid case against such policies.[53] He distinguishes between two schools of thought on the issue: the Keynesian and the monetarist.

According to the former school, inflation promotes savings by redistributing income in favour of groups with a high propensity to save and invest. Further, by raising the nominal money rate of return on investment relative to the rate of interest, it promotes investment. But these propositions rest on two assumptions. First, that only entrepreneurs realise that inflation is occurring and that other groups will be blissfully ignorant of it and refrain from pressing for higher prices for their services. Secondly, that nominal rates of interest on interest-bearing assets will not rise with inflation. But neither of these assumptions appears to be empirically valid.

The 'monetarist' interpretation of the process which is analytically interesting is that inflation is a form of indirect tax. It is a tax on the holders of money balances whose real value or purchasing power steadily depreciates with inflation. The attempt to restore the real value of money balances they hold results in their relinquishing command over real resources. These resources accrue to the government which issues the money. But there is a collection cost attached to this form of taxation. This consists of the waste of real resources and reduction in income that results from an attempt on the part of the money-holders to evade the tax by substituting real goods for cash and other means of economising on cash.

This form of taxation may have its attractions, but the advantages of such a policy may be far outweighed by its drawbacks. To begin with there is the 'collection cost'. Further, inflation may retard development by increasing uncertainty and reducing incentives for innovations. Moreover, sustained inflation may adversely affect the balance of payments which in turn may foster inefficient protectionist and exchange control policies. On strict economic grounds the weight of the argument appears to be against inflationary financing. As Professor Johnson puts it, inflationary financing may represent the only way of bridging deep political divisions. In the absence of agreement on the taxation required to finance development and on the division of national income among claimants to it, countries may resort to inflationary financing.[54] Politics thus appears to bedevil every aspect of development.

The weight of the available empirical evidence on inflation in the developing countries appears to support the foregoing theoretical prognostications. The annual average compound rate of change of the domestic price level for a group of 22 countries over the period 1952–65 was 8·7 per cent – modest perhaps by recent standards even in developed countries. There is though a wide variation around this figure. For Argentina, Brazil and Chile this figure was around 25 to 33 per cent. At the other end of the spectrum were Malaysia, Thailand and the Philippines with only a 1·4 to 1·8 per cent change in the price level. For most other countries the figure was around 5 to 8 per cent.[55]

Most of these countries have followed a policy of generating excess demand. The Latin American countries have adopted inflationary financing almost as a creed. The debate between the so-called 'structuralists' and 'monetarists' in Latin America is well known. To put it briefly, the structuralist thesis is that permissive monetary and credit policies are imperative to break the structural rigidities characterising the economies of Latin-American coun-tries.[56] Especially important among these structural rigidities are inelastic agricultural output and exports. Inflationary policies according to this view are an inevitable necessity in the face of exogenously imposed constraints on development. The monetarists favour an environment of monetary stability and attribute inelasti-cities and rigidities to policies of inaction on the part of the govern-ment. Structuralism appears to have influenced the policies pursued by Brazil, Argentina and Chile. Mexico appears to have been more pragmatic in this respect. She appears to have resorted to inflation as a temporary expedient in the face of an initially weak fiscal position of the government. The experience of Taiwan, Greece and Israel is similar.

India and South Korea among the Asian Countries have resorted to inflationary financing. In the Indian case it appears not to be reflected in the price level data which registered only a 2·3 per cent increase over the period 1950–65. But due to the rationing and licensing devices employed by India, inflation may have been of the suppressed variety. Since the late 1960s, however, India has experi-enced substantial increases in the price level.

It cannot be totally denied that inflationary financing has had no positive impact on development. The Mexican experience is illus-trative of the benefits to be had from resorting to it as a temporary expedient. But its blessings have not all been unmixed. Brazil, Argentina and Chile have all experienced serious misallocation of resources and balance of payments problems. It had serious political and economic consequences especially for Argentina. Although Brazil experienced a big push in industrial development over the period 1951–61 under the impetus of inflationary financing, it had to spend the years between 1964 and 1967 in relative stagnation while it attempted to stabilise the economy. Meanwhile it also acquired a military regime. This appears to have been the fate of most Latin-American countries that attempted to engineer a struc-tural revolution by means of inflation.

India has suffered the consequences of suppressed inflation. Her experience with controls over resource allocation and the resulting inefficiencies have become classic textbook examples. There has been much discussion of a so-called parallel black money economy in operation in India. This refers to the black market or grey market operations of private businessmen and traders in commodities like cement and steel which are subject to price and quantity controls by the Government. This presumably extends to trade in import licences also. Exercise of rationing and controls inevitably result in black market operations. But it is the extent and scope of such a market that makes it glaring in India. A highly profitable black market in controlled products can only exist in the face of a relatively high demand. That it does exist is presumably a consequence of the excessive increases in money supply that have occurred in recent years. Some economists have recently been arguing for a so-called programme of 'semi-Bambla' or demonetisation of certain denominations of the currency, to counter the operations of the black money economy.

Direct State Participation in Production

Most governments of developing countries have attempted to participate in industrial production by setting up public enterprise. These are owned, controlled and managed by the state. In some cases existing private enterprises have been nationalised. In others the state has established new production units. The rationale for their establishment and their economic efficiency is a much debated issue. We dwell on some of the major aspects here.

Empirical evidence on the rates of return on capital is scanty. Available data for India show that the performance of public enterprises was mixed. In certain industries like machine tools the rates of return compare favourably with industries in the private sector. But in the case of several other industries they recorded either substantial losses or showed dismal rates of return. Although there are exceptions, by and large the rates of return of public enterprises do not compare favourably with those of the private sector industries.[57] The case of Turkish public enterprises, where the rate of return on capital was found to be as low as 1 per cent in 1963[58] is similar.

But do rates of return reflect economic efficiency? That they may not be a valid criterion for judging the performance of public enterprises has often been emphasised. There is first of all the ubiquitous argument that public enterprises are more than mere commercial entities. They are often regarded as instruments of social change and public policy. They may provide new stimuli and new social structures. To use the economists' pet jargon they confer externalities. For example, they may provide relatively cheap inputs for other industries. But why should such externalities be specific to public investment and public enterprise? Of course, any investment can generate externalities. But the point is that private enterprise is concerned with private profits and cannot foresee such externalities. Even if it does, its concern is with profits it can capture for itself, not with profits that accrue to others. In other words even if private rates of return are low, the social rates of return could be high. It is a question of recognising interdependence and internalising the externalities. As the well known writer on Soviet economics, Alec Nove, has said, 'one of the principal arguments for public operations and control of any sector of the economy is that it permits the internalisation of externalities. And internalisation of externalities is what taking public interest into account means.'

The performance of public enterprise could not be judged by rates of return on capital alone. Moreover, the low rates of return may reflect not inefficiencies of operation but government interference. Both in India and Turkey the government has intervened in the operation of public enterprises. The major area of such interference is in the formal and informal control it exercises over prices. Such policies often result in below market prices for output. But at the same time they are forced to pay competitive wage rates. Such pricing policies may have been dictated by political considerations and social objectives. But increasingly economists in developing countries are questioning the rationale for such pricing policies. It is urged that public enterprises should be run on the same lines as other commercial concerns. And the no-loss, no-profits philosophy should be abandoned in favour of making profits.

A policy of underpricing the output of public enterprise may also have other distorting effects on the economy. It may lead to sub-optimal and excessive use of inputs supplied by the public enterprises to other final-goods-producing industries. These may be industries in the private sector. To the extent that the end users price their products at the market clearing price, they would be making profits at the expense of the public sector. If these profits lead to additional consumption in the private sector, the pricing policies of the public sector will only have militated against the government's efforts to raise savings.[59]

The meagre empirical evidence on the operation of public enterprises in India and Turkey suggest that their operations have not been an unmixed blessing. They appear to have been heavily dependent on external sources and domestic borrowing for financing their investment. James Land argues that the expansion of public enterprises in Turkey since the 1950s was at a heavy opportunity cost to the private sector.[60] Further, a host of inefficiencies in project selection, inventory control, and choice of techniques of production in Indian public enterprises have been pointed out. Several instances of bad planning and project selection have been cited. Often no calculations of costs and benefits of proposed projects were made. In fact, *ex post* social cost-benefit analysis of some of these projects revealed that they would have dismal rates of return when their outputs and inputs are valued at international prices.

Studies on public enterprises in Ghana and Nigeria also tell the same story. Lack of managerial, supervisory and administrative talents have been the major causes of inefficiency.[61] It is, however, important to recognise that all such inefficiencies stem from the political milieu in which these enterprises operate. It is political influence that is the root cause of such inefficiencies. National prestige rather than economic considerations may influence the decision to set up certain enterprises. Top managerial appointments may be the result of political patronage rather than proven executive ability. Inefficiency may thus not be the result of public ownership as such, but of political interference.

That such enterprises can be profitable in the absence of political interference is exemplified by the Ugandan experience. Prior to independence from Britain, public enterprise in Uganda had reached a high degree of prestige and importance. This was mainly due to the principles of non-interference and autonomy established by the colonial regime. It is, however, impossible to say whether these principles have survived under General Amin. The essential point is that it is political interference rather than the fact of public ownership that is the root cause of the poor performance of public enterprises.

Public enterprises thus pose a major challenge to the ability of the political system to adapt itself to the demands of economic efficiency. Such adaptation extends beyond political non-interference and guarantees of managerial autonomy. Novel methods of organisation need to be explored. The Mexican device of promoting joint ventures between public capital and foreign and domestic private capital is one such. In fact Charles Frank's case studies – while at Princeton University – of Nigeria, Ghana and Uganda show that joint state / private enterprises are more often profitable than wholly-owned state enterprises. India has also been contemplating the promotion of a joint sector. Public enterprises can be significant instruments of development policy. Their contribution in terms of public interest and externalities are difficult to quantify. But such benefits can be potentially significant. The future of such enterprises obviously depends on the ability of the developing countries to accommodate themselves to economic realities without compromising their social objectives.

Conclusions on the State's Role

The state plays a multi-faceted role in the development process. State participation in economic activity in the present-day developing countries is much more extensive than in the developed countries at a comparable stage of development. The precise scope, extent and manner of state participation differs between the countries of the third world. The specific role they have assigned to the state is largely conditioned by their past history and social and political influences. There seems to be no point in being theological and dogmatic about the role of the state in the development process. Despite professed ideologies most developing countries themselves have not hesitated to change horses in mid-stream in response to changing economic and political conditions. A lack of awareness of the political and social factors influencing the development process has often resulted in meaningless debates on the virtues of rival ideologies and high-handed pontification on the course developing countries ought to follow.

Political factors appear to be a key constraint in most spheres of economic activity in which the state engages. This is clearly so where taxation is used as an instrument for mobilising resources, especially so in the field of agricultural taxation. Again political expediency rather than economic efficiency may explain the recourse that some countries have had to inflation as a method of financing development. Political problems are more obviously prominent in the operation of public enterprises. Here again economic efficiency may sometimes have been sacrificed for political objectives. The ability to ride simultaneously the horses of economic efficiency and political expediency is one of the major challenges facing the developing countries. This dilemma is also manifested in the other crucial choices that they face, such as the relative emphasis they have had to place on agriculture and industry. Politics permeates not only mobilisation of resources but also allocation. The following chapter is largely devoted to this issue.

NOTES

1. A. H. Hanson, *Public Enterprise and Economic Development* (London: Allen & Unwin, 1970).

2. A. Gerschenkron, *Economic Backwardness in Historical Perspective* (New York: Praeger, 1962) pp. 16–21 and 353–5.

3. See M. Bator, 'The Anatomy of Market Failure', *Quarterly Journal of Economics*, August 1958.

4. R. Nurkse, 'The Conflict between Balanced Growth and International Specialisation', *Lectures on Economic Development* (Istanbul: Faculty of Economics and Political Sciences at the University of Istanbul, 1958).

5. See P. Rosenstein Rodan, 'Problems of Industrialisation of Eastern and South Eastern Europe', *Economic Journal*, September 1943.

6. S. K. Nath, 'The Theory of Balanced Growth', *Oxford Economic Papers*, Vol. 14, 1962.

7. Bauer and B. S. Yamey, *Economics of Underdeveloped Countries* (New York: Nisbet, 1957) p. 249.

8. Nath, *op. cit.*

9. A. O. Hirschman, *Strategy of Economic Development* (New Haven: Yale University Press, 1958).

10. Enke, *Economics for Development* (London: Dennis Dobson, 1964) p. 325.

11. Paul Streeten, 'Balanced Versus Unbalanced Growth', *Economic Weekly*, Bombay, 20 April 1963.

12. Gerald Meier, *Leading Issues in Economic Development: Studies in International Poverty* (London: Oxford University Press, 1970) p. 332.

13. Charles P. Kindleberger, *Economic Development* (New York: McGraw-Hill, 1965) p. 126.

14. *Ibid.*, p. 133.

15. *Ibid.*, p. 128.

16. *Ibid.*, p. 128.

17. W. A. Lewis, *Some Aspects of Economic Development* (London: Allen & Unwin, 1969) pp. 57–9.

18. Pranab K. Banadhan in Hollis B. Chenery (ed.), *Redistribution with Growth* (London: Oxford University Press, 1974) p. 254.

19. Quoted by Myrdal, *op. cit.*, p. 845.

20. Benjamin I. Cohen and Gustav Ranis, 'The Second Postwar Restructuring', in Ranis (ed.), *Government and Economic Development* (New Haven: Yale University Press, 1971).

21. This thesis is also argued by Hla Myint, *South East Asia's Economy* (Harmondsworth: Penguin, 1972).

22. Myrdal, *op. cit.*, p. 394.

23. Charles P. Frank, Jr., 'Public and Private Enterprise in Kenya', in Ranis (ed.), *op. cit.*, p. 89.

24. Myrdal, *op. cit.*, p. 383.

25. *Ibid.*, p. 383.

26. *Ibid.*, p. 148.

27. F. H. Golay, *Public Policy and National Economic Development* (New York: Cornell University Press, 1961).

28. John Strachey, *End of an Empire* (London: Victor Gollancz, 1961) p. 256.

29. See G. Rosberg, Jr. and John Nottingham, *The Myth of 'Mau Mau': Nationalism in Kenya* (New York: Meridian, 1970).

30. For a detailed discussion of this point see Rosberg and Nottingham, *ibid.*, pp. 147–50.

31. Quoted in Arnold J. Toynbee, *A Study of History*, abridgement by D. C. Somervell (London: Oxford University Press, 1957) Vols. vii–x, p. 224.

32. This section on India and Burma draws heavily on the account of Myrdal, *op. cit.*

33. *Ibid.*, Vol. 1, p. 163.

34. J. B. Higgins, *Indonesia's Economic Stabilisation and Development* (New York: Institute of Pacific Relations, 1957) p. 108.

35. Myint, *op. cit.*, pp. 38–9.

36. Colin Leys, 'Political Perspectives', in Dudley Seers and Leonard Joy (eds.), *Development in a Divided World* (Harmondsworth: Penguin, 1971) pp. 111–2.

37. For a synoptic account of the mutiny see Winston S. Churchill, *A History of the English-speaking Peoples* (New York: Dodd Mead, 1966) Vol. 4, pp. 80–90.

38. Philip Woodruff, *The Men Who Ruled India* (London: Jonathan Cape, 1963) Vol. 11, p. 101.

39. Quoted by K. N. Chaudhuri, 'Economic Problems and Indian Independence' in C. H. Philips and Mary Doreen Wainwright (eds.), *The Position of India, Policies and Perspectives 1945–1947* (London: Allen & Unwin, 1970) p. 298.

40. R. K. Karanjia, *The Mind of Mr. Nehru* (London: Allen & Unwin, 1960) pp. 30–1.

41. For a detailed discussion see Myrdal, *op. cit.*, p. 755.

42. Quoted in Bhagwati and P. Desai, *India Planning for Industrialisation* (London: Oxford University Press, 1970) p. 141.

43. *Ibid.*, p. 146.

44. The case of Ghana, where the colonial government concentrated on specific commodities at the expense of general development, is illustrative. Even then, it chose to back gold and rubber when cocoa turned out to be the winner. See Stephen Hymer, 'The Political Economy of the Gold Coast and Ghana', in Ranis, *op. cit.*, pp. 133–78.

45. Angus Maddison, *Economic Progress and Policy in Developing Countries* (London: Allen & Unwin, 1970).

46. W. A. Lewis, 'Economic Development with Unlimited Supplies of Labour', *Manchester School*, May, 1954.

47. L. G. Reynolds, 'Public Sector Saving and Capital Formation', in Ranis (ed.), *op. cit.*

48. *Mobilisation of Internal Resources by the Developing Countries* (Geneva: UNCTAD, 1967).

49. Nicholas Kaldor, 'Will Underdeveloped Countries Learn to Tax?', *Foreign Affairs*, Vol. 41, No. 2, January, 1963.

50. Chenery (ed.), *op. cit.*

51. Meier, *op. cit.*, pp. 203–4.

52. See Bhagwati, *The Economics of Underdeveloped Countries* (New York: McGraw-Hill, 1966) pp. 120–1.

53. H. G. Johnson, 'Is Inflation the Inevitable Price of Rapid Development or a Retarding Factor in Economic Growth?', *Malayan Economic Review*, Vol. XI No. 1, April 1966.

54. H. G. Johnson, *Economic Policies Toward Less Developed Countries* (New York: Allen & Unwin, 1968) p. 76.

55. Maddison, *op. cit.*

56. A good exposition of the debate is found in Roberto de Olivera Campos, 'Economic Development and Inflation with Special Reference to Latin America', in *Development Plans and Programmes* (Paris: OECD Development Centre, 1964).

57. Data from Maddison, *op. cit.*, p. 79.

58. James W. Land, 'The Role of Public Enterprise in Turkish Economic Development', in Ranis (ed.), *op. cit.*, p. 72.

59. Bhagwati and Desai, *op. cit.*, p. 157.

60. Land, *op. cit.* However, see note of dissent on J. W. Land's paper by R. Rockwell in Ranis (ed.), *op. cit.*

61. Frank, *op. cit.*

CHAPTER FOUR

Growthmanship and Industrialisation

The christening of the 1960s as the First Development Decade by the United Nations has proved apt in many respects. It was a decade marked by promise and misgivings. It was also a decade of intense debate on the development strategy which has yielded rich insights.

The average rate of growth of GNP of developing countries was around 5 per cent per annum over the 1960s. Rapid population growth, however, held down the rate of per capita increase in income to around 2·5 per cent per year. Yet, as the Pearson Commission remarks, even this represents by any historical standard of comparison a remarkable acceleration.[1]

More impressive is the rate of growth of manufacturing output. The average rate of growth of industrial output for seventeen principal countries is estimated to have exceeded 7 per cent per annum over the years 1960–7.[2]

All these averages do conceal wide variations in growth rates between the countries of the Third World. Some have experienced virtual stagnation while others have registered dramatic increases. But the rapid rates of increase achieved by most and the dramatic performance of some holds out the promise that the challenge of underdevelopment can be effectively met.

This promise is, however, heavily punctuated by misgivings. The record of most developing countries in income distribution and employment is none too encouraging. The impressive strides made in manufacturing output have not been matched by growth in employment. In fact employment in manufacturing has not even grown as rapidly as the labour force. Inequalities in income have often widened.

This is not to say that growth has everywhere and anywhere resulted in increasing inequalities. There is no such causal relationship between growth and inequalities and employment. Among both high- and low-income countries some have experienced improvements and some deterioration.[3] But in general the record of most countries in terms of growth rates is not matched by that of other indicators of development. These dimensions of the development problem have been dealt with in Chapter 2.

The puzzle is why has growth not resulted in development? A spate of studies appeared in the sixties on this issue.[4] These studies have provided rich insights into the development problem. Especially significant is their analysis of the dangers involved in a philosophy of import-substituting industrialisation. This philosophy, pursued by most if not all of the developing countries, may have significantly contributed to the problem of unemployment and increasing inequalities.

This is not to imply that the pursuit of industrialisation as such is a folly. In fact, not even the pursuit of import-substituting industrialisation can be questioned. It is not the general philosophy, but the strategies and instruments deployed to attain the goal that are to be questioned. The panoply of restrictions on international trade and exchange rates, ill-conceived regulation of investment allocation, the choice of industries to be set up, the squeezing of agricultural incomes, 'forced savings' through inflation and a host of other instruments have been employed to attain the goal of industrialisation. It is this zeal to industrialise at any cost that appears to have aggravated the development problem though it has produced impressive growth rates.

This excessive concern with growth and enchantment with industrialisation are, however, not mere aberrations of amateurs tackling the development problem. Deep rooted political and social factors have influenced this myopic concern with growth and industrialisation. No less to blame is the firm grip of postwar economic wisdom and newfangled economic arguments favouring industrialisation as the *primum mobile* of development.

Politics of Industrialisation

Many of the new nation states see economic advancement as a prerequisite for guarding their political independence. Their relative position in the growth league tables appears to have a symbolic value of its own. It has become important for these countries to stand up and be counted in international power politics. A recent commentator has observed that 'many of the developing countries began their careers by looking upwards and outwards and it is only recently that they have begun to look downwards and inwards. Upwards because imitating the advanced countries of the West was the fashion; outwards towards fronts of anti-imperialism and global causes that got them nowhere.'[5] It is not unreasonable that many developing countries feel that political independence does not necessarily imply the end of 'economic colonialism'. Even the developed countries have expressed such concern in the context of the burgeoning growth of American-based multinational enterprises.[6]

The success story of the Soviet Union in attaining the status of a world power by apparently pulling itself up by its own bootstraps may also have been an influential factor. In addition, the political tensions prevailing within the Third World have been responsible for their excessive concern with industrialisation and, too, with defence build-up.

Industrialisation as a Collective Good

Industrialisation is regarded as symbolic of economic achievement. It is also a means by which nationalist sentiments can be gratified. As Harry Johnson puts it, the psychic taste for nationalism can be gratified by providing a collective consumption good.[7] A collective consumption good is one where consumption by one individual does not preclude consumption by another. Apart from the benefits enjoyed by the participation in the production process, industrialisation may act as a collective good. The society as a whole can pride itself in the achievement of industrialisation as such. It becomes a matter of national pride, an image of the country that can be projected abroad.

Further, as Professor Johnson elucidates, 'nationalistic economic policy will tend to foster activities selected for their symbolic value in terms of concepts of national identity and the economic content of nationhood; in particular, emphasis will be placed on manufacturing; and within manufacturing, on certain industries possessing special value symbolic of industrial competence (such as steel and automotive industries)'.[8]

Nationalism also implies discrimination in favour of nationals or national interests as against foreigners or the community of nations as a whole. This endeavour of nationalistic economic policy is to create an independent economy which relies little on the international economy for its existence.

It is thus that most countries emphasise import-substituting industrialisation. The noteworthy examples in this context are the Indian and Pakistani industrialisation programmes. Rapid industrialisation with emphasis on basic and heavy industries was one of the major objectives of the second five-year plan of India. In the early years of planning Pakistan stressed the need to reduce dependence on external sources. The following except from the industrial policy statements of Pakistan illustrates this point: 'To meet the requirements of the home market, efforts will be made to develop consumer goods industries for which Pakistan is at present dependent on outside sources. Some of the heavy industries might have to come at a later stage of the industrial programme, but no opportunity should be lost to develop any heavy industry which is considered essential for the speedy achievement of a strong and balanced economy.'[9]

The main considerations governing the planning of industrial growth were set out to be the use of indigenous raw materials, the reduction of imports, particularly of essential items in which the country should have a minimum of indigenous productive capacity, the maximisation of productivity and employment, and net social and economic advantage to the country. The considerations of social and economic advantage to the country as Stephen R. Lewis has pointedly noted, come at the bottom of the list, the emphasis being on domestic production.

Heavy Hand of Conventional Wisdom

The conventional wisdom of economic theory, as propounded and practised has often supplied the intellectual basis for the zealous pursuit of growth and industrialisation by the developing countries; postulating causal relationships between variables is a favourite pursuit of social scientists. Economists who have been hankering for their discipline to be considered as a science have been in the vanguard of this pursuit. This is especially true of the recent *genre* of model builders. While they may have achieved a good measure of success in establishing causal links between the various factors affecting growth in developed market oriented economies, they have also unthinkingly attempted to transfer their intellectual apparatus to analyse and prescribe for the problem of underdevelopment. The development plans of many of the developing countries are built on the foundations laid down by 'growth models' of the post-Keynesian variety.

The Harrod-Domar model is the most celebrated of the type of model which underlies the plans of most developing countries. The procedure employed in these models is to set out targeted rates of growth of money income and output, estimate capital-output ratios and then calculate the required levels of savings and investment to achieve these growth rates. Conversely, given capital-output ratios and a savings function postulating the amount of savings that can be expected from both domestic and external sources, the maximum feasible growth rates are estimated. The Harrod-Domar formula or versions of it like the Mahalanobis model, which formed the basis for the second five-year plan of India, have been employed by most of the developing countries.

These models assign pride of place to the role of capital in the development process. Technical conditions exhibited in the estimated capital-output ratios and the propensity of the community to save become the key determinants of growth. Apart from leaving out of the reckoning the factors that determine the decision to save and invest, it has little to say about the problem of income distribution. Indeed, this savings-concentrated approach might actually favour an uneven income distribution. Far less has it got to say about the dynamic factors relevant for development like technical progress and institutional change. It is no wonder that the celebrated Cambridge economist Joan Robinson has remarked that this formula (the Harrod-Domar formula) has made a great negative contribution to the development of economics.[10] This may be even more so in the case of development economics. Even so, the formulation of plans with a conceptual framework may be useful in certain respects, for they may help to identify – as is their purpose – the consistency of the different objectives and show whether targeted growth rates are feasible. But they serve little purpose in improving understanding of the causes of underdevelopment and assisting the development process.

The phenomenon of underdevelopment being so complex, it is understandable that the Western economists who have advised the developing countries have been led to think that what works in their countries should work for the developing countries too. It is only recently that economists have been giving more attention to the sociological and cultural factors of underdevelopment. It may be easier to draw up a plan based on mechanistic relationships between savings, investment and growth rates than understand the complex socio-cultural factors and institutional constraints that bind the developing countries. In an interesting article Dudley Seers, an economist from the Institute of Development Studies at the University of Sussex, shows how an inability to understand the socio-political structure of a developing country inhibits the success of visiting economists.[11]

But why does the leadership of the Third World unthinkingly accept and adopt the conventional wisdom of economic theory? As already stated, the achievement of high growth rates has a political charisma of its own; thus the advice tendered to developing countries is geared to maximising growth rates. Also, models oriented towards savings and capital formation provide a rationale for increasing the role of the government and the public sector. Moreover, the leadership and intellectual élite of the Third World is mostly cast in the same mould as that of their Western advisers. Economists and political leaders at the helm of affairs are often those trained in Western universities and they may find it difficult to understand the realities of the situation in their own countries. In addition to this there is a kind of intellectual xenophilia for Western ideas and concepts that afflicts the élite of the Third World. It is thus that the American economist, W. Malenbaum, observes in the context of Indian planning that 'there is a much narrower gap between the economic theorists and planners of the world's nations than there is between the general economies of the different nations. India's planners are less well versed in India than they are in the more developed economic systems. It is therefore understandable that India's plans seem to rest so little upon economic characteristics and relationships known to pertain to India.'[12]

Furthermore, the use of procedures and plans formulated with the assistance of economists from the West may be crucially necessary in seeking foreign aid and assistance from the international agencies and developed countries. They are more often than not required to produce development plans cut to the specifications of the donors. Indeed, the performance of developing countries as adjudged by the growth rates they have achieved is accepted at least in principle as a basis for allocating aid. Judith Hart, a former British Minister for Overseas Development, has argued:

> Most donor countries accept the principle that developing country performance, measured bluntly by the rate of growth of per capita GNP, is to be the main factor in allocating aid ... This is endorsed and recommended by the Pearson Commission, with the added refinement that the ability to generate investment from internal savings, and the improvements in the balance of payments position should be the indices by which to measure performance ... At the same time, it is increasingly understood and accepted that growth, whether measured in terms of GNP or per capita GNP, is susceptible to factors which may be unrelated to the general improvements of standard of living; that the figures of growth tell us little about the degree to which the mass of the people in a developing country are escaping from poverty.[13]

When aid allocation and the test of effective utilisation of aid is geared to growth rates the preoccupatio nof developing countries with growth comes as no surprise.

Industry the 'Primum Mobile' of Development

There are a number of persuasive economic arguments for industrialisation. Most of them are grounded in the belief that industry is in some sense the leading sector of development. The subsets of the general theme stem from the thesis of dualism, the economics of externalities and hypotheses concerning the distribution of gains from international trade.

Thesis of Dualism

The term 'dualism' has figured prominently in the discussion of economic development. It has been invoked not only to explain the key phenomenon of underdevelopment but also to suggest possible approaches to development. By dualism is generally meant the existence of two distinct sectors in the economy. A variety of definitions have been offered for the two sectors. Early writers on the subject emphasised the aspect of 'social dualism' based on alleged social and cultural factors that contrast the two sectors.

Writers of later vintage have stressed the aspect of 'technological dualism' based on the differences in resource endowments, methods of production and use of technology between the two sectors. Yet others have concentrated on 'financial dualism', emphasising the nature of the credit facilities that obtains in the two sectors.[14] Generally, however, the distinction is based mainly on the nature of the outputs produced and the modes of production adopted by the two sectors. Thus the two sectors readily identified are the agricultural sector and the manufacturing sector. Traditional modes of production and unorganised money markets are shown to characterise the agricultural sector, whereas the manufacturing sector employs relatively modern methods of production and has access to organised credit facilities.

The arguments for industrialisation stem from the characteristics of the agricultural sector mainly in relation to its resource endowment, modes of production and methods of payment. The agricultural or the subsistence sector is characterised by a heavy endowment of labour relative to capital. The modes of production adopted are traditional, productivity is low and, more importantly, as a consequence of the other characteristics, there is thought to be heavy disguised unemployment in the sector. Institutional forces determine the wage rate in this sector. From the assumption that the sector has a high degree of disguised unemployment it follows that the marginal product of labour is very low, if not zero. Labour gets paid its average product because of institutional factors. The wage rate is institutionally determined in the sense that although labour's marginal product is near zero, it gets paid at least a subsistence wage rate, or to put it in the colourful terminology of Charles Kindleberger, the labourer is at least assured of a seat at the dinner table.[15]

The alleged presence of disguised unemployment in the agricultural sector with labour being paid in excess of its value marginal product leads to two implications. Labour is in plentiful supply and a transference of this labour from agriculture to industry raises national output. The opportunity cost of labour according to this thesis is near zero as its marginal product is near zero. If so, it is only logical to use it in industry, thus effectively the agricultural sector can provide a free supply of labour to industry without suffering any reduction in its own output. Apart from supplying labour there is also a hidden source of savings in the food that the disguised unemployed are consuming while they are not materially contributing to production; this can be transferred to feed them in the new locale of their employment.

The arguments for industrialisation grounded in the dualistic thesis have several strands. First, the traditional sector is a source of supply of labour whose opportunity cost is zero to the industrial sector. Secondly, a logical concomitant of this argument is that industrialisation provides employment for the disguised unemployed. Thirdly, the growing industrial sector, by absorbing the excess labour in the agricultural sector and by providing the requirements for manufactured goods, can provide the momentum and dynamism to transform the traditional sector. In this way the industrial sector plays the role of the leading sector in growth.

The above thesis, however, has not gone unchallenged. The examples of heavy 'disguised unemployment' in the agricultural sector appear to have been drawn mostly from Asia. Whether or not this is the case in most other developing countries is doubtful. Indeed, the very definition of disguised unemployment has been disputed and various possible interpretations given.[16] The symptom of disguised unemployment – the low marginal product of labour in agriculture – may be due to ill-health and poor nutrition among the workers. Improving per capita incomes in agriculture may lead to higher per capita output. There may be a gap between realised and potential output due to inadequate motivation on the part of cultivators to maximise output.

The disguised unemployment may be due to the technical constraints prevailing in agriculture. Land and labour may have to be used in fixed proportions. The deficiency of land leads to work sharing and a reduction of man hours put in by workers. If these be the causes of disguised unemployment the best policies would be to improve nutritional standards, promote institutional change by land reforms and pursue landesque policies like extension of cultivable land, improved fertilisers, and so on. Provision of employment by shifting the workers to the industrial sector would only be a second best policy.

The exact interpretation of the thesis that the marginal product of labour in agriculture is at or near zero is also in dispute. What exactly is the marginal unit of labour – does it refer to an hour, a man or a family? It may be difficult to identify the marginal input when employment is subject to seasonal fluctuations. Even though the average product of labour may be low and labourers may be unemployed for substantial periods, it does not follow that the marginal product of labour is zero in the sense that if labour is withdrawn agricultural output will not fall. Indeed, there are some empirical studies (though seriously challenged) which show that the marginal physical product of labour in agriculture is not in fact zero.[17]

Further, even if the private marginal product of labour in agriculture is zero it does not necessarily follow that the social opportunity cost of employing such labour in industry is zero. One has to reckon with the cost of providing housing, medical facilities and other social infrastructure for the transferred labour in the urban areas. When they are employed in industry their requirements of food may be higher than when they were in agriculture. Even if migration from rural to urban areas leaves agricultural output unchanged, there would be the problem of collecting and transferring the new found surplus of food to the urban areas. The argument that labour is in free supply and could be employed in industry is a debatable proposition.

Although the argument that industrialisation provides employment and can draw on the free supply of agricultural labour has been a popular one, the experience of most developing countries appears to belie the expectations. Whether it is a consequence of conscious policy measures or not, a considerable amount of migration from rural to urban areas has occurred in most developing countries. Both 'pull' factors, like the lure of the bright city lights and the pious hope of finding employment in industry, and the 'push' factor of the pressure of population growth in the rural areas, have resulted in considerable migration. But despite growth in manufacturing output industrial employment has not increased appreciably. Between 1950 and 1960 urban population in developing countries is reported to have increased at an annual average rate of 4·6 per cent, which is nearly one-third faster than the 3·5 per cent annual increase in their industrial employment. In Latin America urban population grew at 5·6 per cent and industrial employment increased only at 2·1 per cent over the same period.[18] The result has been a heavy incidence of 'open' and 'disguised' urban unemployment – disguised in the sense that much of the labour may have been absorbed in services like domestic help and petty trading.

Additional evidence is presented by R. B. Sutcliffe, of the University of Oxford, in his well-documented study of industrialisation in developing countries.[19] Growth in manufacturing output has outpaced the growth of manufacturing employment in most developing countries. In Argentina between 1950 and 1960 manufacturing production rose at an annual average rate of 4·4 per cent while manufacturing employment actually fell at 2·2 per cent. In Egypt between 1952 and 1958 manufacturing employment stayed the same although output increased quite rapidly. As Dr Sutcliffe writes, Egypt is probably one of the very few countries in which assumptions of the unlimited labour supplies model have been fulfilled over a considerable period. Yet as Robert Mabro, of the Oxford Institute of Economics and Statistics, observes, 'the Egyptian situation clearly shows that the expansion of the industrial sector cannot absorb over a relatively long period of time more than a small share of the natural increase in the labour force, even if all [Arthur] Lewis's assumptions with regard to wages, terms of trade and capital intensity are met'.[20]

In fact assumptions regarding wage rates and capital intensity on which the theory is based appear to be rarely met. It is now commonplace to argue that the ruling market wage rates and interest rates in most developing countries do not reflect their true social opportunity costs. Institutional factors like trade union pressure and minimum wage legislation is supposed to have resulted in wage rates being higher than the opportunity cost of labour; the opportunity cost being what labour can earn in an alternative occupation, usually presumed to be agriculture. Similarly government subsidisation of interest rates in the organised capital market coupled with overvalued exchange rates and import licensing is supposed to have driven down the cost of capital equipment below its true opportunity cost. In short, factor prices are distorted. Profit-maximising entrepreneurs in the private sector react to these distorted prices. The consequence is the establishment of relatively capital-intensive industries and adoption of capital-intensive techniques. It may result in higher labour productivity and rapid rates of growth in manufacturing output when valued at domestic prices. It does not, however, provide for increased employment.

Whether or not factor prices are distorted is a moot question. It raises conceptual issues regarding the definition of distortions and the measurement of the opportunity cost of labour. These are discussed in the next chapter. It is, however, true that for various institutional reasons the techniques of production and product patterns are biased towards capital intensity. The available technology may permit little scope for substitution of labour for capital. The pattern of income distribution may favour the production of goods which use capital intensively in their production process. It is also possible that entrepreneurs suffer from a xenophilic preference for imported technology which may be relatively capital-intensive. They may even be simply ignorant of the spectrum of techniques available to them. These and related issues are discussed in Chapter 5. It is sufficient to note here that for a variety of technological and institutional reasons the manufacturing sector has not been able to absorb the increasing labour force. The policy prescriptions deriving from the thesis of dualism appear to collapse in the face of these constraints.

Externalities and Industrialisation

A variety of arguments for industrialisation are grounded in the theory of external economies. The concept, though it has figured prominently in the literature on development, defies proper definition. Alfred Marshall, to whom we owe the concept, defined it as those economies which accrue to a particular firm as a result of the increase in the output of the industry of which it is a member. Thus these economies are external to the firm but internal to the industry.

But, as currently used, it has a wider application. Economies arising out of the interdependence of industries are classed as external economies. A distinction is made also between 'pecuniary' external economies and 'technological' external economies.[21] Pecuniary external economies are those that result in lower prices for inputs or higher prices for outputs in a particular industry as a result of the establishment of other industries. Technological external economies are those arising out of the interdependence of firms or industries in their production process. A technological external economy is best defined by an example that Tibor Scitovsky gives. A particular firm or industry may benefit from the labour market created by the establishment of other firms. Externalities thus primarily arise out of the interdependence of activities. They are labelled 'external economies' as the enterprise that generates them cannot capture the gains. In a broader context, external economies are supposed to arise when the social benefits of an activity exceed its private benefits.

Thus it is the economies arising out of complementarity of activities and those which result in excess of social over private benefits that are classed as 'externalities'. It is argued by proponents of industrialisation that complementarities are relatively higher in industrial activities than in agriculture. In other words, backward and forward linkage effects are more prominent in industry. Although this may be a valid proposition, it can be countered on two grounds. First, agriculture may also have backward and forward linkages with industries supplying inputs to it like fertilisers, agricultural machinery, and construction materials. Secondly, the linkages, although relatively important in industry, may not be prominent in those industries which can be easily set up in developing countries. Industries producing aluminium utensils and tin cans may not have the same degree of linkage effects as, say, steel or automobile industries. This argument may again be an illustration of an erroneous application of the experience of developed countries to developing countries. An enthusiastic proponent of industrialisation may, however, argue that developing countries should go in for steel and automobiles. But such enthusiasm is misplaced if the inputs needed for these industries cannot be produced at home and need to be imported.

Infant Industry Argument

The infant industry argument, which can be traced to Frederick List and John Stuart Mill, stems from the thesis of externalities. In its pristine form the thesis is that certain industries given time can mature and become internationally competitive. They may, however, be unable to withstand international competition in their infant days simply because other countries may have had an early start in establishing the industry. Hence such industries must be protected from international competition by import controls. Such protection admittedly is to be temporary: once the industry has matured and can reap the potential advantages it possesses, the tariffs are to be removed.

The crux of the argument is the emphasis on potential for development or potential comparative cost advantages that certain industries possess in international trade. The advantages are potential because the industry has to become sufficiently large to attain external economies. It is only when the industry is sufficiently large that it can reap external economies of the type discussed earlier. Further, it may require several years to develop the labour skills the industry possesses: learning-by-doing, as it is called.

The central thesis may have a germ of truth, but the argument for protection is weak. How is one to identify an infant? Who is to decide when to remove the tariffs? If the industry does possess potential advantages risk-bearing private entrepreneurs ought to see it, but such animal spirits may be dull among entrepreneurs in developing countries and may have to be awakened by state action.

The real argument is, however, that the industry is capable of conferring social benefits in excess of private benefits. Admittedly profit-maximising private entrepreneurs would pay no heed to gains they themselves cannot capture even if they can visualise them. But even if there is a germ of truth in these arguments, is tariff protection the ideal policy instrument? Tariffs on imports impose a consumption cost on society. Consumers of the good have to pay a higher price for the good while the domestic infant industry is growing. It has been the consensus in recent years that the objective can be better achieved by the payment of a subsidy to the industry rather than by the imposition of a tariff.[22] This would not only avoid unnecessary interference in international trade but would also avoid the consumption costs.

The foregoing illustrates some of the arguments in support of which the thesis of externalities has been invoked. Indeed, a whole array of benefits arising out of industrialisation, such as the impetus to technological change it provides, the opportunities for augmenting labour skills through 'learning by doing', and the educative influence of industrialisation in the sense that it changes the traditional values and attitudes of society towards economic growth, are all listed under the elusive head of 'external economies'. These are all imponderables. Nor is it certain that industrialisation alone and not modernisation of agriculture should result in these benefits. It is difficult to arrive at any definitive judgement on these arguments as they are all very vague. R. B. Sutcliffe's comment on this set of arguments aptly summarises the position: 'Even if it is true,' he says, 'the argument in this form is seldom more than vague. Where it is given economic support this often involves its proponents waving at their critics blank cheques, signed by influential economists and drawn on the bank of external economies.'[23]

From the Infant Industry to the Infant Economy

It needs no giant step to extend the infant industry argument for protection to the economy as a whole. A country at an early stage of development may have a potential comparative advantage in several lines of industrial activity. Present cost ratios may dictate production of primary commodities but the potential advantage may be in industrialisation. Failure to harness these advantages may result in a global loss of welfare. A better distribution of world resources and output may eventually be secured if the developing countries are given a chance to industrialise. Hence the need for protection.

The infant economy case for industrialisation is in terms of future benefits. A case for industrialisation is also made on the basis of the present distribution of gains from international trade between the developed and the developing countries. The intellectual antecedents of this case for import-substituting industrialisation can be traced to the so-called 'Prebisch thesis', propounded in the late 1950s by Raul Prebisch, later Secretary-General of UNCTAD.[24]

It is argued that there has been a long-run deterioration in the prices of primary product exports of developing countries relative to the price of imported manufactures. The relatively low income and price elasticities of demand for primary products and the progressive substitution of synthetic materials for natural raw materials have resulted in a sluggish demand for primary products. Hence to get a given bundle of manufactured goods requires progressively greater exports of primary products.

A further strand of the thesis relates to the unequal distribution of gains from technological progress occurring in the two groups of countries. It is argued that any technological progress that occurs in the export sectors of the developing countries is passed on to the developed countries in the form of lower prices. Pressures of population in the developing countries depress real wage rates and prevent them from rising *pari passu* with technical progress. In the developed countries, on the other hand, due to trade union pressures and scarcity of labour not only do wages rise at the same rate as productivity but often in excess of it. The net impact of all this is to aggravate inequalities in the international distribution of income.

The Prebisch thesis has been comprehensively criticised both on theoretical and empirical grounds. The price indices, time periods and countries chosen for comparison have all been questioned. The concentration on wage incomes to the exclusion of gains accruing to other factors of production from technical progress has been criticised. Alternative statistical evidence has been cited to show that in fact primary products have made gains in prices rather than losses.[25] These issues are discussed in detail in Chapter 7.

It is sufficient to note here that Dr Prebisch was not only one of the early advocates of import-substitution but his thesis also provided a seemingly respectable intellectual case for import-substituting industrialisation.

Costs of Import-substituting Industrialisation

The social costs of the policy have been the subject of a number of studies published in the sixties. In fact, commenting on the Latin American experience, Dr Prebisch himself registered his disenchantment in the following words:

> An industrial structure virtually isolated from the outside world thus grew up in our countries . . . The criterion by which the choice was determined was based not on considerations of economic expediency, but on immediate feasibility, whatever the cost of production . . . Tariffs have been carried to such a pitch that they are undoubtedly on an average . . . the highest in the world. It is not uncommon to find tariff duties of over 500 per cent. The proliferation of industries of every kind in a closed market has deprived Latin American countries of the advantages of specialisation and economies of scale, and owing to the protection afforded by excessive tariff duties and restrictions, a healthy form of internal competition has failed to develop, to the detriment of efficient production.[26]

Dr Prebisch's statement captures the crux of the problem; scant attention to economic cost calculation, proliferation of industries, and excessively high degrees of protection. More recent studies of India, Pakistan and Brazil have come up with similar findings. They are more detailed in their analysis and are novel in their method of approach.

Effective Rates of Protection

The quoted rates of average tariff, such as the 500 per cent duties cited by Dr Prebisch, refer to nominal rates of tariff. Although some of these rates are exceptionally high even they conceal the true degree of protection afforded by the entire tariff structure. An approach employed by recent studies attempts to estimate the true level or the effective rate of protection.

Modern industry involves several stages of fabrication including the purchase and processing of other manufactured inputs. The final value of the product minus the value of all purchased material inputs is the value added of the industry. The effective rate of protection measures the protection afforded by the entire tariff structure to this value added. Clearly the protection afforded to the value added depends not only on the tariffs on the final product but also on the tariffs on any imported inputs. It is conceivable that the true degree of protection afforded by the entire tariff structure could be quite different from that indicated by the nominal tariff rates on the final good only.

An example will clarify the concept. Suppose there is an automobile industry whose imports of parts and components which it assembles amounts to 90 per cent of the value of the final automobile. The industry is adding 10 per cent value to the imported components. This is the value added of the industry. Now suppose a 10 per cent duty is imposed on imports of automobiles, raising the domestic price of automobiles by 10 per cent. Its impact on the value added of the industry is much more dramatic. With the imported components being allowed in duty-free the value added rises from 10 per cent of the original price of the automobile to 20 per cent. The effective rate of protection afforded to the value added of the industry is, therefore, 100 per cent.[27] If the inputs had also been subject to a 10 per cent tariff the effective rate of protection to the industry would also have been 10 per cent, and if the rate of tariff on inputs was higher than on the final product the effective rate of protection would have been negative.

The estimated effective rates of protection have been exceedingly high in most developing countries. The average levels of effective protection for manufacturing industry as a whole is estimated to have been around 200 per cent for India and Pakistan, 100 per cent for Brazil, 215 per cent for Mexico, 50 per cent for the Philippines and 33 per cent for Taiwan.[28] These averages, however, conceal wide variations in the degree of protection enjoyed by individual industries. To cite one example, in Brazil the rates of effective protection ranged from 41 per cent on machinery products to 8,480 per cent on perfumes and soap![29]

Socially Expensive Infants

A major consequence of these high levels of protection is the proliferation of socially inefficient industries. Eminently profitable from the point of view of private entrepreneurs but socially unprofitable. The 'real' contribution of these industries to society is the foreign exchange savings resulting from their establishment. This is because, in most cases, the alternative to producing these goods domestically is to import them (apart from not having them at all, perhaps a desirable solution in some cases). The foreign exchange savings resulting from their establishment can be deduced by estimating their value added at international prices. Recent research shows that in most cases the value added at international prices falls far below that estimated at domestic prices. For example, for a sample of 31 industries in Pakistan it was found that value added fell sharply from Rs 2,293m when valued at tariff inclusive domestic prices to Rs 131m at international prices. In other words, value added measured at tariff-inclusive domestic prices overstates the contribution of these industries by 1,650 per cent. Such examples can be cited in the case of other developing countries.[30]

Even more disconcerting is the finding that in some cases value added when estimated at international prices turns out to be negative. In other words, the value of imported inputs when measured at world prices exceeds the value of the final output measured at the same prices. The phenomenon of 'negative value added' is likely to occur in industries in which material inputs comprise a high proportion of the value of gross output and where inputs are used inefficiently. It can also occur if the tariff structure provides high protection to final processing industries but little or no protection to intermediate and producer goods industries.

This phenomenon is no theoretical curiosity. Value added in fifteen consumer goods industries in Pakistan in 1963–4 was Rs 1,185m as conventionally measured, but turned out to be minus Rs 354m when estimated at international prices.[31] Such cases have been reported for Brazil and India as well.

Clearly most of these industries would not have withstood the chilling winds of international competition but for the high levels of protection. It is also clear from the foregoing that in many cases society as a whole would have been much better off importing the products than producing them domestically.

A Grand Design Gone Wrong

The social costs of the strategy of import-substituting industrialisation can be enumerated *ad nauseum*. The high levels of unutilised capacity experienced by most industries, the adverse shift in terms of trade against agriculture, the bias against exports resulting from such a strategy are all well documented. But this is no reason to disavow the grand design of development through industrialisation. Many of the problems may be due to inattention to prerequisites of industrialisation, disregard of the discipline imposed by the market and general economic mismanagement.

The experience of the so-called 'late industrialising countries of Europe' illustrates the importance of prerequisites. The important characteristics of their development was the stress they laid on industrialisation, with big plants and enterprise, stress upon producer goods as against consumer goods, emphasis on supply of capital and entrepreneurial guidance by the state and the relatively inactive role played by the agricultural sector. Unfortunately most developing countries, with rare exceptions, display none of these characteristics save the last.

Especially significant is their lack of emphasis on capital goods. In most developing countries the sequence of import-substitution runs from the establishment of industries producing light consumer goods to those producing capital goods and eventually to those which produce consumer durables. True many of the developed countries of today also began with light consumer goods. But even when they were in the predominantly light consumer goods stage, they were producing their own capital goods, if only by artisan methods. In the absence of many of these characteristics the developing countries, to paraphrase Albert Hirschman, show little of the inspiring, if convulsive *élan* that was characteristic of the late industrialisers such as Germany, the Soviet Union and Japan.[32]

Admittedly not all developing countries have neglected capital goods production. India and Brazil have laid great stress on producer goods. Both countries achieved substantial import-substitution not only in consumer goods but also in capital goods from the late 1950s up to the mid-1960s.[33] But these two countries, unlike the others, had a history of industrialisation before they embarked upon a strategy of import substitution. They were also at a decided advantage with regard to industrial entrepreneurship, financial institutions and an able civil service.

But the record of even these two star performers is not without its blemishes. The glowing instances of bad planning, disregard of market forces and economic mismanagement mostly came from these countries. The quixotic industrial and import licensing policies of India which militated against the stated objectives of development are lucidly documented by Jagdish Bhagwati and P. J. Desai in the study cited earlier. Similarly in a study of Brazil, Joel Bergsman notes the excessively high levels of protection granted to Brazilian industry, often incommensurate with its needs. Brazil, it is argued, could have achieved all of the import-substitution it achieved with only 30 to 50 per cent of the protection her industries enjoyed.

A New Awakening

Most developing countries have been increasingly turning outward in their economic policies in recent years. Import regimes are being liberalised, exchange controls relaxed and exports promoted. To use a term introduced by Gustav Ranis, of Yale University, an era of Second Post-war Restructuring has begun.

But the years of the First Post-war Restructuring need not be dismissed as a sad episode in the history of development. At best it has laid the base for the outward-looking policies in many developing countries, albeit at a high social cost. The much-heralded 'Brazilian miracle' may owe much to the industrial base created in an earlier era. India may owe her recent strides in exports of manufactures to the capital goods industries established earlier.

Paradoxically enough, the First Post-war Restructuring may have been inevitable and necessary. The politics of industrialisation discussed earlier suggest as much. It may have served to purge most of the developing countries of their economically irrational but politically rational belief that inward-looking policies are the primrose path to development. More to the point it has brought home the importance of rational economic management based on economic cost considerations. The problem of resource allocation is not to be viewed in terms of industry versus agriculture/or, for that matter, any one sector against the other. The challenge is to assess the relative economic costs of various sectors and projects in the light of available resources, institutions and information. This almost platitudinous wisdom may also serve as a warning for the future. Export promotion with an evangelical zeal may also lurk with unforeseen dangers.

NOTES

1. Pearson Report, *op. cit.*, p. 12.
2. *Ibid.*, p. 36.
3. Chenery (ed.), *op. cit.*
4. Principal among these are studies commissioned by the OECD on the industrialisation and trade policies of India, Pakistan, Brazil, Mexico and Taiwan and a companion volume synthesising the findings of these studies, which are cited in the relevant sections of this chapter.
5. Richard Harris, *The Times*, London, 13 April 1975.
6. See Jean-Jacques Servan-Schreiber, *Le défi American* (Paris: Denoel, 1967).
7. H. G. Johnson, 'A Theoretical Model of Economic Nationalism in New and Developed States', in Johnson (ed.), *Economic Nationalism in Old and New States* (London: Allen & Unwin, 1968).
8. *Ibid.*, p. 14.
9. Stephen R. Lewis, Jr., *Economic Policy and Industrial Growth in Pakistan* (London: Allen & Unwin, 1969) p. 68.
10. Joan Robinson, *Economic Philosophy* (New York: Doubleday, 1964) p. 107.
11. Dudley Seers, 'Why Visiting Economists Fail', *Journal of Political Economy*, August 1962.
12. W. Malenbaum, *East and West in India's Development* (Washington: National Planning Association, 1959).

13. Judith Hart, *Aid and Liberation* (London: Victor Gollancz, 1973) p. 45.

14. See Meier, *op. cit.*, Ch. 3, for a discussion of the various interpretations of Dualism.

15. Kindleberger, *op. cit.*, p. 214.

16. Warren G. Robinson, 'Types of Disguised Unemployment and Policy Implications', *Oxford Economic Papers*, No. 3, November 1969.

17. T. W. Schultz, *Transforming Traditional Agriculture* (New Haven: Yale University Press, 1964) pp. 53–63.

18. I. M. D. Little, Tibor Scitovsky and M. F'G. Scott, *Trade and Industrialisation Policies in Some Developing Countries* (London: Oxford University Press, for the OECD Development Centre, 1973) p. 83.

19. Sutcliffe, *op. cit.*, Chs 3 and 4.

20. Robert Mabro, 'Industrial Growth, Agricultural Unemployment and the Lewis Model – the Egyptian Case, 1937–1964', *Journal of Development Studies*, July 1967, p. 346.

21. Scitovsky, 'Two Concepts of External Economics', *Journal of Political Economy*, April 1954.

22. For a lucid discussion of this point see Harvey Johnson, 'Tariffs and Economic Development', *Journal of Development Studies*, October 1964.

23. Sutcliffe, *op. cit.*, p. 85.

24. R. Prebisch, 'Commercial Policy in the Underdeveloped Countries', *American Economic Review*, Papers and Proceedings, May 1959.

25. June Flanders, 'Prebisch on Protectionism: an Evaluation', *Economic Journal*, June 1964.

26. Prebisch, *Towards a Dynamic Development Policy for Latin America* (New York: United Nations, 1963) p. 71.

27. The following tables illustrate the concept:

	Pre-import Tariff	Post-import Tariff	Nominal Tariff	Effect of Tariff
Automobile selling price	£1,000	£1,100	10%	
Cost of imported inputs	£ 900	£ 900		
Local value added	£ 100	£ 200		100%

Although the import duty only enables the domestic producers to raise their selling price by £100 or 10 per cent of the free trade price, the effect on local value added is to double it.

28. Little, Scitovsky and Scott, *op. cit.*

29. Joel Bergsman, *Brazil: Industrialisation and Trade Policies* (London: Oxford University Press, 1970) p. 15.

30. Scott, 'Effective Protection and the Measurement of Output', Nuffield College, Oxford, mimeographed.

31. *Ibid.*

32. A. O. Hirschman, 'The Political Economy of Import-substituting Industrialisation in Latin America', *Quarterly Journal of Economics*, February 1968.

33. See Bhagwati and Desai, *op. cit.*, and Bergsman, *op. cit.*

CHAPTER FIVE

Challenge of Technology

Fashions wax and wane in development economics. The so-called 'neo-classical' model with its emphasis on savings rates and capital accumulation is now an old shibboleth. The 'vicious circle' breakers and 'big push'-ers have had their moments of glory. The strategy of import-substituting industrialisation has not resulted in the hoped-for El Dorado. Technology is the new deity to which policy makers and economists are making obeisance these days.

The talk now is in terms of technology transfer models of development.[1] The search is for employment-augmenting labour-intensive technologies. Empiricists are busy accumulating evidence to show that output growth and employment creation are not necessarily conflicting objectives. Theoreticians are rediscovering the fact that the choice of technology itself contains a distributional formula; certainly not new wisdom, but a reawakening, considering the long-cherished belief that distribution comes after production.

It is easy to be euphoric about the benefits the new god can shower. But the subject bristles with complex issues. Should the developing countries follow the Japanese model and borrow from the existing shelf of technologies in the West? Should they follow the Chinese example of utilising the scientific skills they possess to innovate labour-intensive technologies? Would setting the relative factor prices right result in the adoption of labour-intensive technologies and a change in the product mix towards more labour-intensive products, as is supposed to have happened in Taiwan and Korea? What are the implications of adopting labour-intensive technologies for income distribution and growth? Finally what are the administrative and managerial problems posed by the adoption of labour-intensive technologies? These and other issues too numerous to catalogue are the focus of recent debate. We review some of the major issues in the knowledge that justice cannot be done even to these in the confines of a brief chapter.

Technological Dependence

The availability of a pool of scientific and technical know-how, tested, tried, and perfected in the advanced countries, is often seen as a distinct advantage that the less developed countries of today enjoy over those of the past. Edward Mason, writing in the 1950s, contended that 'if this technological heritage were not available, economic growth in the underdeveloped world would be even slower than it promises to be'.[2] That the developing countries can make great strides in development by borrowing from the pool of knowledge used to be an often propounded thesis. Japan's success story with imported technology was often cited in its support.

The thesis, however, has met with a spate of criticism in recent years. The most common and almost conventional criticism is that the technologies perfected in the advanced countries are inappropriate to the factor endowments and production conditions of the developing countries. The technologies of the West are capital-intensive whereas the developing countries are endowed with relatively more labour than capital. If the objective of full employment is to be achieved they require labour-intensive technologies. Moreover techniques perfected for large scale production may be ill suited to production on a smaller scale in the developing countries.

This criticism of inappropriateness in fact strongly refutes the thesis of development through technological borrowing. The thesis implicitly assumes the availability of a range of efficient techniques for manufacturing particular products. The inappropriate factor-intensity criticism is further reinforced by the inappropriate products argument. The products manufactured in the developed countries embody characteristics which are often excessively sophisticated in relation to the income levels of the developing countries.[3] It could be argued that these are complex high-quality products embodying capital-intensive techniques of production.

The importation of such inappropriate technologies results in technological dependence. The adverse consequences of such dependence is a widely discussed phenomenon. Prominent among these adverse effects are the alienation of local scientific effort from production and the bolstering of private as opposed to social profits. Local scientific talent and innovative effort are likely to be swamped because in the presence of foreign technologies there would be no demand for them. Entrepreneurs respond to market prices in their choice of techniques of production. If factor prices are distorted, overstating the price of labour relative to the price of capital, they not only choose capital-intensive methods of production but also choose to produce goods which are naturally capital-intensive. This may be privately profitable but result in reduced employment and increased foreign exchange costs to pay for imported technology. Further technological dependence may result in foreign firms charging 'monopoly' prices for technology. Beyond that it may result in growing control over the economy by foreign firms.[4]

These arguments shed cold water on the initial enthusiasm about development through borrowed technology. But they do not prove conclusively that technological borrowing has no role to play in the development process. They serve more to emphasise the need for more careful policy selection and choice. Beyond that they point to the need to view technological borrowing as an integral part of development policy.

The Japanese success story underscores these points. True, in certain respects Japan is a special case. As is often noted, she possessed human skills, producer capabilities and institutional backing in the form of state support to restructure and innovate borrowed technology, skills that most developing countries lack. What is usually missed out is the Japanese philosophy towards technical development. The objective of technical borrowing was to use it as a basis for developing local technical skills rather than as a substitute for it. It is the dovetailing of foreign technology and indigeous know-how that is the essence of her success.

Japanese experience has valuable lessons. It has implications for the type of research-and-development activity and investment in education that developing countries should concentrate on. Furthermore, not all developing countries are devoid of local scientific talent and human skills. India may be a good example of a country which possesses such talents. Indeed India, after the fashion of Japan, has encouraged technological borrowing through licensing agreements. But it has not been an unqualified success.[5] This is mainly because of a lack of absorptive capacity, or, more specifically, a lack of institutional support for developing such capacity.

Rejecting *in toto* what is at hand may be short-sighted. The challenge is to utilise what is at hand as judiciously as possible. A. K. Sen's comment is apt in this context: 'The view that the past menu is basically "inappropriate" and we must make our own technology by looking for it, while full of healthy vigour is not always a very useful approach. To recognise that a whole lot of techniques already exist no matter what we do would seem to be not entirely a negligible thought'.[6]

Self-reliance

The advocacy of self-reliance does not often go beyond waxing eloquent about the inappropriateness of Western technologies and the need to develop labour-intensive techniques. There is a good deal of talk about developing 'intermediate' technologies – intermediate in the sense that it involves upgrading traditional methods of production and downgrading Western methods. It is a combination of those parts of modern technology which are of value and developments oriented in a labour-intensive, yet modern, direction.[7] Examples of such successful innovation are few and far between.

The basic problem is one of generating such technologies. Who is to do it and by what methods? Setting up a few government-financed research institutions packed with eager young scientists may not be the solution. Technological change is a complex phenomenon. Research-and-development activity cannot be divorced from the actual production process. Moreover technological development responds to market forces. Successful innovations mostly depend on the enterprise of the businessman and occur in the factory rather than in an isolated laboratory.

This is not to say that technological development is not science-dependent. But more often than not science-based innovations are for producing capital-intensive high-income goods. Moreover the scientist, pure or applied, is less likely to be concerned with factor proportions. His preoccupation is with the grand simple design that overwhelms or eludes a host of irritating obstructions. To the economist the problem of factor proportions may be important but to the scientist it may be an irksome obstruction. As it has been succinctly put, 'anyone who thought an invention less meritorious because of capital intensity was like the fisherman's wife who, when turned into a queen by the weird heilbut complained of not being empress. When you are pushing out a production function, you do not worry about its shape until you are through.'[8]

The foregoing is not an indictment of scientific research in general. We are not opposed to pushing out the frontiers of knowledge. We are only sceptical of the ability of uncoordinated scientific research to further the development of labour-intensive technologies.[9] If scientific research is to succeed in doing so it needs to be coordinated with production. Beyond that it needs a basic change in the attitudes and objectives of science policy: a realisation that technological change cannot be superimposed but needs to be integrated with general development policy. The engineer and the scientist need to be brought together. The Chinese experience, although limited in terms of evidence of results achieved, is illustrative. The increase in technical capability experienced by this country has been mainly due to the development of a local innovative capability, involving worker-innovation and the engineers, and organically linked to the scientific system and to production.[10]

The Chinese example appears to be a far cry for most of the developing countries. Differences in political philosophy and organisation apart, their current efforts at research and development exhibit little of the Chinese vigour and orientation. Whether or not it is a consequence of low levels of income, investment in research and development is minuscule. It ranges from 0·2 to 0·5 per cent of GNP for most developing countries in contrast to the reported 1·5 per cent figure for China. More disconcerting than the quantitative dimensions are the pattern and nature of these activities. Even these low levels of expenditure, as Hans Singer has observed, are directed at marginally contributing to 'pushing the frontiers of knowledge' in ways and directions automatically determined by the conditions and factor proportions of the richer countries;[11] a phenomenon labelled by the Sussex Institute economists as the 'internal brain drain' as opposed to the 'external brain drain' or visual movement of qualified personnel to the developed countries.

Demonstration effects appear not to be confined only to imitating the consumption patterns of the rich countries. They also extend to intellectual and scientific pursuits. Furthermore, the lack of a concrete science policy oriented towards development may also be due to political factors. The political élite may favour prestigious projects and showpieces. They may make declarations about science policy to create a façade of progressiveness without actually implementing them. They may fail to implement the necessary social and economic reforms required to create a real relationship between science and production lest it undermine their economic and political power.[12]

The current research and development scene is characterised by an emphasis on basic as opposed to applied research, by a lack of interconnections between various research projects and an absence of coordination between science and production. Hardly a happy hunting ground for labour-intensive technologies.

Using the Resources at Hand More Effectively

A science and research based policy of generating labour-intensive technologies is clearly a long-run solution. But short-term solutions centring on utilising what is available more effectively exist. Restructuring and innovating imported technologies discussed earlier is one such. Perhaps this may fit the bill of 'intermediate technology' more than any other.

Labour absorption can also be increased by using the existing capital equipment more intensively. It needs to be noted in this context that there is a distinction between capital-intensity and mechanisation. The case for lower capital-intensity does not imply a lower degree of mechanisation. The degree of mechanisation refers to the value of the stock of machinery and to the number of labourers who can be employed *at a point of time* when the machinery is in operation. By contrast, capital-intensity is concerned with the ratio of capital stock to the total amount of labour time *over a given period* (a week, a month or a year) taking into account the points of time when the machinery is in operation as well as those when it is not.[13] It is clear that a highly mechanised technique can none the less be relatively less capital-intensive if it is utilised more intensively by working round the clock. Thus multiple-shift operations and increased number of work days can result in more employment.

Admittedly there are snags. Multiple-shift operations result in a need for increased supervisory personnel. Non-availability of such personnel may be a reason for most firms in developing countries operating on single shifts. Productivity may sag and costs increase if second and third shift workers are to be paid more and work under less expert supervision. These problems, though, are not intractable. Training supervisory personnel may be less expensive than investing in additional machinery.

Another important avenue for increasing employment is the use of second-hand machinery. It is conceivable that second-hand machinery uses relatively more labour than the latest designs. More importantly, gains in employment arise because of the demands such machinery makes, in terms of repairs and maintenance. It provides employment for maintenance personnel and repair workers. True, breakdowns may be frequent. There is loss of output when this happens but when output is down costs are down too. Material costs are not incurred and there is less wear in some parts of the plant. The only cost incurred is wages paid to idle operators, but wage costs are low in developing countries. Moreover, frequent breakdowns and repair work give an excellent opportunity for learning by doing. Second-hand equipment may be ideally suited for low-wage and high capital cost countries. Obviously the sources of supply for such second-hand equipment are the developed countries. There is, however, a need for policies directed at improving channels of communication and international trade in second-hand equipment.[14]

Market Forces and Choice of Technology

A theme which has been frequently and monotonously stressed in the literature is the influence of factor-price distortions on the choice of techniques. As stated in an earlier section it is argued that factor prices in developing countries do not reflect their relative factor endowments. The price of labour, the relatively abundant factor, is higher in relation to that of capital, the scarce factor. Such distortions from the true social opportunity costs of these factors of production result from institutional factors. Trade union power and minimum wage legislation serve to raise the price of labour above its opportunity cost. Usually the opportunity cost of labour is regarded as what labour can earn in agriculture. In the extreme it can be very low if not zero compared with what it earns in industry. Further, for various sociological and cultural reasons migrant labour from agriculture has to be paid a relatively higher wage in industry. Capital costs are relatively low because of subsidised interest rates in the organised capital markets. And overvalued exchange rates and import quotas result in artificially low prices for imported capital equipment. A result of all this is that profit-maximising entrepreneurs prefer capital-intensive methods of production.

It is but one further step to argue from this thesis that the objective should be to get relative factor prices right. Once this is done there will be a move towards relatively labour-intensive techniques and production of labour-intensive products.

This assertion that getting the relative factor prices right will do the trick may be too naïve a view. It implicitly assumes the existence of a shelf of technologies to manufacture a particular product from which to choose – a highly debatable proposition. Moreover the thesis that factor prices are distorted may have been over-emphasised. The idealised state when there is a high degree of labour mobility and there are no institutional obstacles may not exist in the best of circumstances. It is frequently argued that the wage gap between the agricultural and urban sector is due to institutional factors. If it is trade union pressure and minimum wage legislation that is causing the gap then there must be a number of people looking for jobs ready to work below the ruling wage rates. This should result in a weak bargaining position for the trade unions resulting in lower wages. It is also argued that the wage gap is caused by other sociological factors such as labourers' job preferences, indivisibilities in labour supply and the desire to be compensated for the loss of a share in the family income when the labourer moves from the family-owned farm to the urban sector. If this were the case there would not be a mass of people hanging around looking for jobs at lower wages.[15]

It is easily seen that neither of the two arguments substantiate the factor price distortion thesis. The arguments are inconsistent and unconvincing. True there may be deviations from the ideal situation where all institutional obstacles are absent and markets work perfectly. Such an ideal situation hardly obtains even in developed countries let alone in developing countries. The ruling market wage rate may indeed more or less approximate to the opportunity cost of labour. Similar arguments can be cited to explain the supposedly low cost of capital. Low interest rates may prevail only in the organised capital markets. It is, however, a well-known phenomenon that in the unorganised capital markets the interest rates are exorbitant. Not all entrepreneurs have access to the organised market. It is also not infrequently heard that those who can obtain cheap imported inputs by virtue of having access to import licences often sell them at inflated prices to those who do not possess import licences.

If the foregoing analysis is correct why then are capital-intensive techniques chosen? The simple answer may be that labour-intensive techniques are non-existent. Even if they are available and factor prices dictate their adoption they may not be chosen. The administrative skills and managerial expertise needed to operate labour-intensive techniques may be very high. Problems of absenteeism, lack of industrial discipline and the absence of a work ethos on the part of the available labour force is a frequently mentioned reason for the non-adoption of labour-intensive techniques.

Income Distribution and Employment

Employment and income distribution are closely intertwined. Providing more employment may be one method of redistributing income. It could be argued that if redistribution is the aim why not just grant subsidies without actually providing jobs. But doles and earnings for work performed are not the same. Having a job and being paid for it can be a source of satisfaction. Moreover the payment of subsidies unrelated to employment may be administratively unfeasible.

The other side of the coin is also important. Redistributing income in favour of the poor may generate demand for labour-intensive products. This thesis of course smacks of Keynesianism. The underlying assumption is that effective demand is the constraint on employment creation. It could be easily argued that in the face of structural rigidities such demand creation will only result in inflation. The main bottleneck would be the inability of the system to produce the sort of wage-goods demanded by labour. But the argument is not without its merits. Such redistribution and generation of effective demand for labour-intensive products may be an important incentive for innovating labour-intensive goods. The scope for varying the product mix in favour of labour-intensive products may be much higher than is usually thought. A number of seemingly disparate goods may satisfy the same need. It is, for instance, reported that sugar and kerosene oil are close substitutes in the Indian peasant's consumption basket. They are substitutes in the sense that the psychic need for consumption is satisfied by either of the two goods. Wage-goods may thus be composed of an extended range of products.

The empirical evidence of the impact of redistribution of income on employment generation is inconclusive. In general the empirical estimates show that even significant redistribution of income results only in marginal increases in employment, usually by less than 5 per cent. But these empirical studies suffer from conceptual problems and data deficiencies.[16] Moreover, the impact may be higher in the longer run than in the short run. In the short run the poor consume little of the output of the 'services sector' which is labour-intensive in operations. It is also noted in the study cited that the consumption pattern of the poor in many countries is skewed towards labour-intensive goods. It should, however, be noted that income redistribution policies encompassing fiscal devices may have an adverse impact on employer incentives. Moreover, advocacy of redistribution either as an objective in itself or as a means to create more employment presupposes the existence of an efficient fiscal system; an implausible supposition in most developing countries.

A Challenge to Economic Management

The foregoing illustrates the complex issues in the field of technological development. The problem of technical development is an integral part of the development problem. True, the scope for generating labour-intensive techniques and promoting employment are considerable. But the interdependences involved need to be recognised. Research directed at devising labour-intensive technologies must take this into consideration. A particular project may be capital-intensive in itself, but its institution may result in employment generation elsewhere. The setting up of a capital-intensive steel mill may generate demand for housing and transportation services which are labour-intensive.

It is for this reason that all capital-intensive techniques should not be rejected out of hand. Examples of capital-intensive operations generating demand for more labour also come from agriculture. Although the evidence is by no means conclusive, case studies on the introduction of tractors into Indian agriculture shows that it can often lead to an increase in employment rather than a decrease. It has been found to increase the demand for permanent servants and replace casual labour. Tractors may also expand employment because of the complementarity between tractorisation and irrigation and the use of high-yielding varieties.[17] To reiterate, the evidence is by no means conclusive, yet it points to the need for recognising the employment-generating aspects of some capital-intensive projects.

The choice between capital-intensive and labour-intensive projects may also depend on the objective evaluation placed on employment now versus more employment in the future. This problem has to do with the age-old controversy regarding the conflict between employment maximisation and output growth. Simply put, the argument states that capital-intensive projects generate a higher level of output and yield a larger surplus over wage costs for reinvestment. Labour-intensive projects may maximise employment and consumption in the short run but for the same reason result in a lower surplus for reinvestment. Recent studies have argued that this conflict between employment and output growth are not all that serious. Labour-intensive techniques can result in higher output and provide for reinvestment.[18] To the extent though that the conflict does exist, it again poses a challenge to policy makers. It is a problem of inter-temporal choice and the weights attached to current as against future employment. It must be added, however, that the problem of maximising the available surplus for reinvestment depends not only on the level of output but also on who gets it and how it is spent. Again this poses a challenge to fiscal management of the economy.

It is also to be noted that labour-intensive development also calls for considerable managerial and administrative talents. It is an organisational problem as much as a technical one. The demands made by labour-intensive development on administrative skills are lucidly discussed in a recent article by two political scientists[19] – an indication that the problem of technology extends beyond the purview of economics alone.

Finally, successfuly technological development depends crucially on institutional reform. This point has been made earlier while discussing science policy. An excellent example of the need for institutional reform in the form of land reforms is provided by the well-documented adverse effects of the Green Revolution. Although the new varieties of wheat may have resulted in spectacular increases in yields, they also exacerbated income inequalities. The gains of the revolution appear to have accrued to the big landlords rather than the small-scale peasants.

Conclusion

Technology, or the bag of tools as Arnold Toynbee put it, can open up new vistas for development. The scope for augmenting employment through the adoption of labour-intensive techniques may be considerable. But harnessing technology to the needs of development is a major challenge facing the developing countries. It is a challenge in the sense that its myriad dimensions must be understood and the need for treating technological change as an integral part of the development problem must be recognised.

NOTES

1. R. R. Nelson, 'Less Developed Countries, Technological Transfers and Adoption and the Role of the National Science Community', Yale Centre, 1971, mimeographed.

2. Edward Mason as quoted by Myrdal, *Asian Drama, op. cit.*, Vol. I, p. 691.

3. Frances Stewart, 'Choice of Techniques in Developing Countries', in C. Cooper (ed.), *Science, Technology and Development* (London: Frank Cass, 1973).

4. These issues are discussed in detail in Chapter 8 on Foreign Private Investment.

5. For a detailed discussion see V. N. Balasubramanyam, *International Transfer of Technology to India* (New York: Praeger, 1973).

6. A. K. Sen, *Employment, Technology and Development* (London: Oxford University Press, 1971) p. 12.

7. Hans W. Singer, 'Employment Problems in Developing Countries', in Singer (ed.), *The Strategy of International Development* (London: Macmillan, 1973) p. 38.

8. Paul W. Strassman, *Technological Change and Economic Development* (New York: Cornell University Press, 1968) p. 236.

9. The story of the development of the Pilkington float glass process is one of the triumphs of the entrepreneurs and production engineers over the scepticism of the research scientists. See the talk given by T. C. Baxter, 'Development of the Pilkington float glass process', to staff at the Graduate Students Seminar at the University of Lancaster Department of Economics.

10. Genevieve Dean, 'A Note on the Sources of Technological Innovation in the People's Republic of China', in Cooper (ed.), *op. cit.*, p. 198.

11. Singer, *op. cit.*, p. 154.

12. See Amilcar Herrera, 'Social Determinants of Science in Latin America: Explicit Science Policy and Implicit Science Policy', in Cooper, *op. cit.*

13. Sen, *op. cit.*, p. 47.

14. For an extended discussion of the use of second-hand equipment and its employment implications, see Strassman, *op. cit.*, pp. 195–220.

15. Sen, *op. cit.*, p. 56.

16. D. Morawetz, 'Employment Implications of Industrialisation in Developing Countries', *Economic Journal*, September 1974.

17. Case studies cited in Sen, *op. cit.*, p. 156.

18. Streeten and Stewart, 'Conflicts between employment and output objectives', *Pakistan Economic Journal*, Vol. xxi, No. 1, 1970/1.

19. Warren F. Ilchman and Norman T. Uphoff, 'Beyond the Economics of Labour-intensive Development', *Public Policy*, Vol. 22, 1974.

CHAPTER SIX

Official Aid to Developing Countries

The Development Assistance Committee (DAC) of the OECD very properly uses the term 'flow of financial resources' to describe what is loosely called aid. Much of these flows are closer to normal commercial transactions than to the gift without strings which common sense would recognise as true aid. Clearly this applies to private capital flows, commercial transactions in which the investor expects directly or indirectly to make a profit. They are more akin to international trade, from which all hope to benefit, than to assistance, in which one side may be expected to make some financial sacrifice in order to benefit another.

Definition of Aid

As a first step, aid may be defined as flows of finance at concessional rates of interest and repayment terms which are not explicitly for commercial gain or for military purposes. On this basis, grants and loans at concessional terms from governments, multilateral organisations and private voluntary agencies all count as aid. This definition may be considered too narrow on the one hand and too broad on the other. For example, it excludes measures such as the payment of prices which exceed free market prices for commodity exports from developing countries and preferential entry into rich country markets for manufactured exports of developing countries. Both of these measures do transfer resources from rich countries to poor, but we prefer to treat these in the following chapter on trade relationships. The exclusion of military assistance may also be questioned on the grounds that it may aid political stability and so provide a good environment for development and also that it may release local resources for developmental purposes. It is excluded from this exercise partly because that is the normal convention and partly because in our judgement the provision of modern weaponry has often simply increased the amount of damage which armed conflict has brought in developing countries and on balance has harmed economic and social progress.

The definition may be considered too broad because it appears to take too complacent a view of what is genuine assistance. This is a well-founded criticism. As was argued in Chapter 1, the greater part of 'aid' takes place under the incentive of commercial or political gain, usually of a fairly short-run nature. Most bilateral aid is tied to both projects and donor exports, which has the general effect of reducing the real value of the aid by raising the price which the host country pays for the developmental imports above the freely competitive world price for the goods and services provided under an aid contract. Attempts to estimate this suggest a reduction of 10 to 20 per cent in the total value of aid resulting from aid-tying.[1]

Also the official figures give the financial flows net of amortisation, but, if the capital repayments are subtracted, why not also the interest charges? Indeed, if a grant is regarded as the ideal form of aid it follows that the correct estimate of the real transfer from rich to poor countries should involve estimating the grant equivalent of the loans made to developing countries. This can be done by comparing the present value of the disbursements on a loan with the present value of the stream of repayments of interest and capital repaid over the lifetime of the loan. To estimate the true cost to the donor one should discount the actual payments and receipts by the domestic opportunity cost of capital; that is, the return obtainable within the donor's economy or on the international market for commercial loans with a similar risk element. The actual rate of interest which is appropriate to this calculation is subject to dispute between economists, but not to such an extent as to alter the general effect of such calculations on the total aid flows. They reduce the nominal amount of aid by between 20 and 35 per cent.[2]

Donor Burden

Clearly the cost of aid to the donor nations and its value to the recipients is greatly exaggerated in most national and international statistics. Even at its face value the flow of official resources from the DAC members to developing countries and multilateral aid organisations has been small in relation to their total national product and has grown rather slowly even in nominal terms over the decade from the mid-1960s to the mid-1970s. When account is taken of the general rise in the price level of aid goods the real value of official development assistance (ODA) has been rather stagnant. After adjustment by the DAC deflator, the 1973 aid total was $6,270m at 1970 prices, compared with 1970's $6,832m (see Table 6.1).

The main reason for the poor aid performance has been the decline in the United States contribution from a peak of $3,592m in 1964 to $2,968m in 1973. With the major exception of the United Kingdom, almost all other members of DAC have increased their contributions. In relation to the national incomes of the rich countries, official aid is very small, about 0·3 per cent in 1973 (0·33 per cent in 1974 according to provisional DAC figures). The Pearson Commission proposed a target of 0·7 per cent of GNP by 1975 or 1980 at the latest, but many donors, including the United Kingdom, have not agreed to accept the target. The total figure of $6,832m for aid in 1970 compares with the world's expenditure on armaments of at least $200,000m in roughly the same period.[3]

Table 6.1

Net Flow[a] of Financial Resources from DAC Countries, 1960–73 (net disbursements in $m)

	1960	1965	1970	1973
Percentage of total Official Development Assistance to GNP of all DAC Donors		0·42	0·32	0·28
Official Development Assistance, of which:	4,664	5,895	6,832	9,408
1. Bilateral grants, etc.	3,692	3,714	3,323	4,481
2. Bilateral loans	439	1,833	2,384	2,674
3. Contributions to Multilateral Institutions	534	348	1,124	2,253
Deflator 1970 = 100		88	100	150

Source: *Development Assistance, 1971* (Paris: OECD, 1971) and the companion volume for 1974.

[a] Gross disbursements minus amortisation receipts on earlier lending.

In relation to other economic magnitudes in the poor countries, aid flows look rather small. Even when the private investment flows are included the total annual resource flow is less than $5 per head when spread over the population of the Third World. The countries which have received most 'aid' in total are India, Pakistan and South Vietnam. When reduced to a per capita per annum basis these sums amounted in recent years to only $2.3 for India, $4.00 for Pakistan and a substantial $27.50 for South Vietnam. Israel and Jordan have each received relatively high per capita figures of $30.70 and $25.90. These figures illustrate some of the hard facts about aid distribution in the past when it has been a great advantage to a country to be small, friendly to a large donor nation with trading links to the donor, and under some external threat. Several analyses of aid distribution show that in general it has had little connection either with need, in terms of poverty, or with any demonstrable ability to make highly productive use of the resources.[4]

Aid Benefit

When regarded in terms of aid per capita or as a proportion of the total GNP of the developing nations it is clear that international aid is not very significant. Still, it may be argued that aid was never intended to make a major direct contribution to raising current living standards in developing countries. Its purpose was rather more of a 'pump-priming' nature, intended to supplement domestic savings and foreign exchange earnings so as to promote increased formation of both social overhead and directly productive capital which would raise output in the longer run. How well has it succeeded in doing this?

In crude statistical terms 'aid' has amounted to a sum equivalent to about 10 per cent of total domestic capital formation in developing countries and about 20 per cent of total imports. On that basis it looks quite substantial, but can it be assumed that this was a net addition to domestic savings and investment or is it possible that some aid merely replaced domestic savings and that the influence of aid programmes may have distorted the domestic allocation of resources so as to lower the productivity of all investment? Critics of international aid programmes from both the right and the left of the political spectrum have argued that this is largely what has happened. They allege that aid has not assisted economic development and that it may even have been counterproductive. In the discussion which follows the writings of three writers whose work seems to exemplify three schools of criticism of the effects of international aid flows on economic development in the Third World will be drawn on. The first is Peter Bauer, of the London School of Economics, whose standpoint may be characterised as that of an economist with great faith in the allocative efficiency of free market forces and grave suspicion of governmental interference with these. The second is Keith Griffin, of the University of Oxford, a left-wing critic, and the third is Teresa Hayter, a writer sympathetic to the views of the radical 'new left'.

Case Against Aid

'Foreign aid is plainly not indispensable to economic progress, and is indeed likely to obstruct it.'[5]

The present developed countries all began as poor countries and achieved their current relative affluence without benefit of foreign economic aid. Many of the less developed countries in the Far East, South-east Asia, East and West Africa and Latin America have advanced rapidly over the last century or so without foreign aid. Countries which Professor Bauer has in mind in this statement include Japan, Hong Kong, Singapore, Malaysia, Thailand, Kenya, Ghana, Ivory Coast, Nigeria and Mexico. These all made rapid progress between the last quarter of the nineteenth century and the middle of the twentieth century without either much foreign aid or austerity in consumption.

'Nor is foreign aid a sufficient condition.'[6] Many countries and backward social groups within nations have received substantial aid without apparent benefit. This is because other factors such as the general level of skills, managerial capacity, capacity for administration, law and order and social attitudes conducive to progress are more important than capital. If they are absent capital will simply be wasted. If these other factors are present aid will not normally be required since finance can then be obtained by credit-worthy nations. The debt will easily be serviced because the productivity of the capital in raising income will be high. One exception to this general rule which Professor Bauer notes is where political risks such as an external threat to the nation may make private investors shy off. In these circumstances official aid and a commitment to help militarily as in the case of Taiwan can, by restoring confidence, yield great benefits. Once the confidence is present the official development aid can be terminated, as has happened in that case.

Professor Bauer usually cites India as an outstanding example of a country which has received massive aid but whose economy continues to display symptoms of clear economic distress with recurrent famine conditions, balance of payment crises, heavy unemployment and evidence of wasteful industrial investment. Ceylon and Indonesia are also included in some of these charges, nor is there any reason to believe that Pakistan's record has been much better; Burma's may be rather worse. The general finding of the Pearson Commission that 'the correlation between the amounts of aid received [by individual countries] in the past decades and the growth performance is very weak',[7] is quoted as some additional evidence for the ineffectiveness of aid. But on the whole Professor Bauer regards statistical evidence as of little value because weaknesses in the data and the complexity of the forces at work on development make it implausible that existing statistical methods can sort out the effects of this one variable of aid. In this he is in accord with the Pearson Report (p. 52).

Having dismissed statistical evidence, Professor Bauer turns to *a priori* reasoning. He accepts that the provision of additional resources makes a higher level of investment and/or consumption possible but insists that this need not increase the rate of development. On the contrary, the repercussions of aid may be so adverse as to outweigh these benefits. Funds may be misallocated and badly administered so that the cost of domestic resources used up in production may exceed the real value of the output. The indirect effects of aid may be adverse; by encouraging the belief that development can be had without any personal sacrifice; by encouraging the prevalent Asian fatalism and disbelief in the effectiveness of self-help. Also aid is often provided to nations whose governments pursue policies which are inimical to economic progress, such as expelling the most productive groups in their population: Asians in Africa or Chinese in Asia. Aid may actually encourage or make possible the pursuit of such policies. Aid enables rich countries to pursue policies of protection of agriculture, and certain industries, in the interests of particular sections of their communities, the aid being a sop to the conscience of the rich society and a bribe to the poor countries to accept this otherwise intolerable inefficiency in resource allocation and inequity in income distribution.

Other defects in aid are that it denies to countries the beneficent side effects of struggling to raise the resources themselves: the development of personal initiative, the creation of social institutions and economic opportunities conducive to economic progress. 'Capital is much more likely to be productive when deployed by these groups and persons who accumulated it, because accumulation and effective deployment require much the same abilities, motivations and institutions.'[8]

Aid also leads to the imitation of western methods of production and of institutions which are inappropriate to the factor endowments and general state of progress in the economies of most developing countries. Excessively capital-intensive production methods and expensive universities and hospitals are much-criticised examples.

A major charge, in the eyes of Professor Bauer, is that aid encourages an excessive concentration of power in the hands of central governments partly through increasing the flow of resources directly under their control and partly through encouraging comprehensive development plans as a precondition for aid. Most aid funds do go directly to governments and the anxiety of donor agencies to show that aid funds have been properly allocated and controlled does tend to favour central economic planning. The meetings of the World Bank-sponsored consortia of donors to India and Pakistan lend support to Professor Bauer's thesis, though not necessarily to his conclusion that this is bad for economic development.

Financial irresponsibility is encouraged by aid since the generation of a budget deficit and a foreign exchange gap are regarded as preconditions for much aid. This enables governments in developing countries to follow policies which deter both foreign private investment and domestic savings and investment. Such private capital may be socially more productive than aid. As the Pearson Commission puts it: 'There can be no doubt about the contribution which private capital can render to economic development. Indeed, dollar for dollar, it may be more effective than official aid both because it is more closely linked to the management and technology which industrial ventures require, and because those who risk their own money may be expected to be particularly interested in its efficient use.'[9]

A final argument put by Professor Bauer attacks the claim that aid is necessary for social infrastructure (railways, roads, bridges and harbours) required before much private economic activity such as commercial agriculture and manufacturing can take place. He challenges this on two grounds: (*a*) such infrastructure does not precede but accompanies the growth of the private sector and has in the past often been in the private sector; and (*b*) even when it is decided to make these public-sector activities, a well-run economy can borrow commercially to finance them. This was what was done in the past and the only reason that poor countries find it difficult in the mid-1970s is because of faulty policies which have involved inflation, balance-of-payments crises, controls on payments of interest and capital to foreign lenders, and other measures likely to deter portfolio investment in their countries.[10]

Criticism of the Bauer Case against Aid

Some of the arguments summarised above are common to those of Dr Griffin and Miss Hayter. It may be convenient to leave these for consideration after their views have been outlined and to concentrate here on those which are peculiarly Professor Bauer's, which will be taken in the same order as they have been set out in the foregoing pages.

The fact that the rich countries of the mid-twentieth century developed without official aid is hardly relevant if conditions are currently very different from those of the nineteenth century. In a number of ways they are crucially different. The current rates of population expansion in developing countries exceed 2·5 per cent per annum. Few countries in the nineteenth century exceeded one per cent growth rates in population. It has already been shown in Chapter 2 what a severe obstacle to economic progress this is in terms of the extra load on social overheads, the effects on the dependency ratio through the age structure which it produces, and the pressure on the land resources of the crowded areas of Asia. Many of the rich countries did in fact benefit from large flows of resources of capital and skilled labour. This is particularly true of North America and Australasia. The circumstances of these movements were peculiar to that age and unlikely to be repeated.

While the economic effects of the colonial period were complex and do not lend themselves to a crude Marxist evaluation, the colonial powers did benefit from cheap raw materials and wider markets for industrial goods as a result of the colonial relationship. The enormous gap in technology between present-day rich and poor countries, and the rate at which technology advances in the modern world probably make it much more difficult for newcomers to break into the markets for manufactured goods. The advantages which they possess in the form of cheap unskilled labour are often outweighed by the much higher productivity of labour in the same industries in the rich countries, due to their use of capital and technologically intensive methods of production. The difficulties which the developing countries face in attempting to increase their exports are of course exacerbated by the protectionist policies of rich countries, rightly criticised by Professor Bauer. But once again this represents a very different situation from that faced by most of today's rich countries in the course of their development.

It is true that a number of developing countries have made rapid progress with little or no official aid, but when the record is examined there are often special reasons for this. They have mostly been relatively small areas: Hong Kong (4m people), Singapore (2m), Ivory Coast (5m), Kenya (11m). Thailand (36m) and Mexico (51m) are of course much bigger, but they have received quite a lot of aid and Mexico's possession of oil and proximity to the United States for tourism has benefited her enormously. Hong Kong, Singapore and Thailand have all gained from heavy military expenditures. The citation of a few countries on either side of this argument is really a vain endeavour. It can only be used to knock down the absolutist position of a few eccentrics who argue either that no developing country can make progress without foreign aid or that no developing country can make progress if it does receive foreign aid. Whether, on balance, aid has promoted or retarded development cannot be answered with such crude arguments.

Most scholars in the field of economic development would completely accept the position that social and institutional factors are crucial to economic progress. The importance of capital was overstressed in some of the literature of the 1950s and 1960s and crude economic models sometimes swept all the other factors into effects on the productivity of capital or appeared to ignore them altogether. Since then education and technological change have been stressed in most writing on the subject and even the purest economists have at least acknowledged the importance of social and institutional factors. This is true of all the textbooks in the field. Where many would part company with Professor Bauer is in considering the relevance of aid to this situation. He appears to be saying that if an economy lacks entrepreneurial types, has a poorly educated labour force and is ill-equipped with roads and ports, aid resources will simply be wasted.[11] These are the characteristics of the poorest countries and his suggestion implies that little or nothing can be done for them until somehow they change themselves. But official aid can have a direct impact on these factors. It is quite true that they limit the absorptive capacity of a nation – its ability to make productive use of aid – but they do not prevent some aid being used properly. Teachers can be trained and put to work in simple schools and supplied with relevant books and other tools of their trade. Agricultural assistants can be trained to help by example and advice to raise the standards of farming. Road engineers can be lent to direct road construction and train others in the work. These sorts of aid will involve technical assistance and some capital. They may not give rise to a rapid increase in GNP but they should help to lay the foundations for future progress of those for whom, on humanitarian grounds, development is most urgent.

Is it true that even those paragons among developing countries who exhibit the high achievement-oriented standards laid down by Professor Bauer could borrow on the international capital markets at reasonable terms? This seems doubtful today. The pre-1914 world seemed one of order and stability. It is true that there were large-scale bankruptcies but the rights of creditors were well recognised and in the last resort could be defended against government appropriation by gunboat diplomacy. In any case, most of the portfolio investment was in the areas of white settlement which remained closely tied to the 'mother country' or accepted the codes of behaviour of Europe. Colonial governments had privileged access to the London capital market and their financial stability was guaranteed by the currency boards or sterling exchange system which prevailed. The world of the mid-1970s is very different. Governments change via the ballot box or revolution. Often they do not regard themselves as bound by obligations taken on by their predecessors.

Straightforward default on debt or uncompensated confiscation of foreign property have in fact been surprisingly rare occurrences, perhaps too rare, but when they happen the attendant publicity is likely to damage borrowers' prospects even when they are guiltless.

New and well-intentioned governments in developing countries often find themselves saddled with the financial results of the follies of their predecessors (Indonesia, Ghana and Sri Lanka are examples of this). Faced with a foreign exchange crisis, heavy debts and a badly maladjusted economy, they are neither in a position to seek private capital nor able to meet commercial loan terms. The case for public grants or loans at concessional rates in these situations is much stronger than the critics concede.

A cornerstone of Professor Bauer's critique is that aid either encourages or makes possible policies which adversely affect economic progress. To establish this point, it is not enough to demonstrate that many developing countries have received aid and have adopted such policies as neglect of agriculture, expulsion of productive people, excessive protection of heavy industry and the like. It is necessary to establish a causal connection. In a few cases a plausible connection does exist. Many commentators have argued that the supply of surplus commodities such as wheat, rice and oilseeds under the United States PL 480 Program of surplus disposal has adversely affected agricultural development. On the one hand it has depressed both local and international prices for these goods, so reducing incentives for the development of food production for local consumption and export. On the other, it has taken the pressure off governments, especially the Government of India, to devote sufficient energy and resources to the development of agriculture. This has allowed them to forge ahead with investment in manufacturing industries which are capital-intensive in their use of resources, so heavily protected as encourage inefficiency and even where they will eventually become viable the pay-off comes much too late to have a significant present value.

On the face of it both India and Pakistan fit this thesis. Up to 1966, and on occasion since then, both countries have been dependent on PL 480 food. Both did for years neglect agriculture and foster industrial development – much of which is inefficient.[12] However, to claim that this was the result of PL 480 aid is excessive. The governments of both these countries were firmly committed to industrial development for several reasons: the prevailing climate of economic advice in the 1950s was in favour of this and the example of Soviet industrial development was in the minds of many leaders of new countries as an inspiration to similar policies; the risk of war between India and Pakistan and the threat from China made the war potential of industry a factor in the argument; the prospects for rapid growth based on agriculture seemed poor at that time. It could well be claimed that they were so 'hell bent' on industrialisation that the absence of aid would have resulted in even more autarkic policies to conserve foreign exchange, and greater austerity for their populations. The aid agencies did put pressure on both of these countries to liberalise their import policies and with some success. The actual use of PL 480 counterpart funds in rural public works programmes probably in fact helped to commercialise agriculture by improving transport, provided employment to landless labourers and small farmers in the off-season and by supplementing their incomes raised the demand for food so that the increased supply from imports may have had little or no effect in depressing the prices of agricultural products below what they would have been in the absence of the programmes. United States Agency for International Development (USAID) often made self-help in agriculture a condition of PL 480 assistance.

Such leverage over economic policy as aid has given to the donor agencies has generally been used in favour of sound fiscal and monetary policies, exchange rates at equilibrium levels and freer international trade,[13] all policies with which Professor Bauer would be in sympathy. Throughout the 1960s, with the major exception of Vietnam, requests for aid have been scrutinised by the donor agencies, both multilateral and bilateral, with great care. Their analyses have included not only project appraisal but consideration of the general economic policies of the recipients. Aid requests for extravagant or inappropriate projects have been turned down, but this does not always stop the projects.[14] The country may finance them from its own resources or borrow privately at very high cost. Even poor countries seem obliged to have their Concordes, aerospace extravaganzas, and Ronan Points, albeit on a rather smaller scale.

Would discrimination against Asians in East Africa or Chinese in Asia have been less in the absence of aid? This is very dubious. History is full of examples where religion, nationalism and racialism have led people to actions which are against their own economic interest. Aid gives some influence to donors and they have used it to try to check racial abuse.

The aid agencies have a reasonable record on education. It is they, rather than the host countries, which have pressed for reforms in this field, for replacement of outmoded, over-academic and irrelevant curricula with modern curricula designed for the local environment and with the local manpower requirements in mind. The prestige university in Ghana[15] is a hangover from colonial days, as are a number of other such institutions in Africa. The colonial heritage and the attitudes and culture which it passed on have probably been the major cause of the misallocation of resources in education, not aid.

It may well be possible to sustain Professor Bauer's contention that aid is neither a necessary nor a sufficient condition for economic progress, but nothing in his argument can sustain the proposition that aid either has been or necessarily will be counterproductive. Are the other attacks more convincing?

The Griffin Case[16]

The views of the Oxford economist Keith Griffin are summed up in this quotation: 'Foreign assistance has neither accelerated growth nor helped to foster democratic political regimes. If anything, aid may have retarded development by leading to lower domestic savings, by distorting the composition of investment and thereby raising the capital-output ratio, by frustrating the emergence of an indigenous entreprenurial class, and by inhibiting institutional re-forms.'[17]

A good deal of the earlier literature on aid and development assumed that the paramount objective of the leadership in the developing countries was rapid growth. This led to the implicit assumption, in many discussions and models of growth, that any increase in resources made available to them would be invested rather than consumed. This is clearly a questionable assumption and it is indeed likely that at least some part of foreign finance would be used to support consumption. Without the foreign resources they might well have imposed greater austerity and squeezed more savings out of their subjects. It is inherently plausible that any addi-tional foreign resources should lead to some more consumption as well as some more investment. Humanitarian considerations would surely applaud a situation where aid made growth possible with less hardship, but it is also true that the basic purpose of aid was to accelerate development and there would be disappointment if most aid simply raised current consumption through the switching of domestic resources.

One situation, of which much has been made in the literature, would result in aid raising domestic savings. This is the so-called 'foreign exchange gap' situation. Here it is argued that immobility of domestic resources makes it possible that a country has the poten-tial to raise the level of domestic savings but is unable to increase its level of investment because the investment requires imported capital goods for which it cannot earn enough foreign exchange. Inability to obtain these investment goods thus frustrates the domestic savings. If foreign resources are provided and the capital goods become available, domestic savings can then rise. The foreign resources complement, instead of substituting for, domestic savings.[18]

In the long run this is not a very plausible case. Even in poor countries with relatively immobile resources savings can be translated into reduced imports or increased exports, so providing the needed foreign exchange.[19] However, in the short run for certain countries which have got themselves into severe balance-of-payments difficulties it is possible to see how supplying a modest amount of foreign resources can allow a much higher volume of domestic savings. For example, India and Pakistan have both experienced periods when they could not afford to buy raw materials and spare parts for their existing factories so that capacity utilisation fell to under 50 per cent. Aid for these goods then allows existing capital to be used productively, raises national income and at given savings rates would increase domestic savings.

It is also possible to envisage circumstances in which foreign resources would be almost entirely complementary to domestic savings and investment. If aid is used to provide energy resources and transport systems this may induce private farmers and businessmen to undertake investments which otherwise would not have been profitable. Some aid goes into joint ventures with local industrial development corporations where without the foreign finance and technical assistance the venture could not have been undertaken by locals without a delay of several years.

In general one can agree with Dr Griffin *et al.* that the flow of financial resources from overseas is likely to replace some domestic savings and allow higher consumption, but (*a*) this may be acceptable on humanitarian grounds and (*b*) permitting higher levels of consumption may in fact stimulate faster development through raising the ability to work with better nourishment and through allowing the production or importation of incentive goods. Secondly, there will be cases where foreign resources will permit a higher level of output and increased savings through allowing underemployed resources to be more fully utilised. Thirdly, there are situations where complementary activities and joint ventures will stimulate local entrepreneurs.

Dr Griffin also uses the neo-classical argument that the inflow of foreign capital will lower the marginal productivity of capital and hence the interest rate. This in turn will lower domestic savings and investment. It is a static argument which depends on the assumption of equilibrium in all markets, and that all other factors remain as they were. This is unlikely in many developing countries where price controls, rationing and licensing are common. But a major effect of both official aid and private foreign investment is to reduce the need for controls and to bring in new ideas and new technology. These are likely to shift the marginal productivity of capital upwards and so stimulate investment.

To sum up, theoretical reasoning does not establish a strong *prima facie* case that aid is likely to have much adverse effect on domestic savings.

Empirical Evidence on Effects of Aid on Savings and Investment

There now exist a considerable number of studies seeking to analyse statistically the relationship between inflows of foreign capital and key domestic variables such as savings, investment and the rate of growth of GNP. They conclude generally that 'aid' has reduced domestic savings and that 'all of the critical analyses agree that the average impact has been to increase investment by only $0.11 to $0.77 for every dollar inflow'.[20] However, as Gustav Papanek, of Harvard University, points out, these conclusions have to be taken with more than the usual pinch of salt: (i) the definitions of savings and of aid used by them are unsound; (ii) the basic data are of poor quality and inappropriately aggregated; and (iii) the correlations found do not demonstrate causality.[21]

The statistical proxy for 'aid' used in these studies is the deficit on current account in the balance of payments. This actually reflects all capital movements including official bilateral and multilateral aid, long- and short-term private capital flows, changes in the country's foreign reserves and 'errors and omissions' in the overall balance of payments account. Over a longish period, say ten years or more, it might be reasonable to assume that reserve movements and short-term capital movements would balance out so that net official and private long-term capital inflow would equal the deficit in the current account; but over the actual periods used in the cross-sectional analyses which form most of the studies, it is not reasonable. In fact, long-term capital inflow and the current account deficit have a very variable relationship – much too great to allow the latter to stand proxy for the former.[22]

Inflows of foreign resources are sometimes quite explicitly for consumption, as for example food relief for famine situations or government grants to support host country government services such as education and health. Conventional accounting includes such activities in consumption though they may actually promote development more than some capital investment. These actions raise domestic consumption, but they do not reduce domestic savings now, or in the future, for as grants they represent no claim on future savings in the way that a loan would do. Nevertheless conventional accounting would show such inflows of foreign resources apparently reducing domestic savings. This follows from the usual definitional relationships summarised in the following equations:[23]

$$\text{domestic investment} = \text{total investment} - \text{foreign investment}$$
$$\text{foreign investment} = \text{current account deficit}$$
$$\text{domestic savings} = \text{domestic investment}$$
$$\text{therefore domestic savings} = \text{total investment} - \text{current deficit}$$

Since the current deficit arises as a result of the imports financed by the grant, local savings would appear to fall.

There are many problems associated with the calculation of both investment and foreign resource inflows in the context of developing countries. Much investment in the poorest countries escapes the market nexus and tends to be under-estimated. Distortions in the prices of capital goods due to import restrictions also reduce the accuracy of investment data in countries like Argentina, tending to inflate the figures. These two errors may produce a spurious negative correlation between aid and home investment if the poorer countries receive more aid.

Times of crises are likely to lead to both low domestic savings and inflows of aid or IMF credits, but in these cases both are caused by the crisis, not low savings caused by the influx of foreign resources as the critics' analyses imply.[24]

In practice, 'there are no good answers to the question "What would have happened with less or more foreign resource inflows?" In some circumstances, foreign inflows undoubtedly stimulated savings, so that each dollar of inflows led to more than a dollar of investment, while in other cases they discouraged savings and a dollar of inflows may have led to much less than a dollar of investment. However, as long as both savings and inflows are substantially affected by third factors, the negative correlation between the two found in many studies sheds little or no light on their causal relationship.'[25]

Other work by Dr Papanek, in which statistical analyses separate out the influence of aid from the other resource inflows, concludes that aid has been significantly and positively related to growth. However, this result, although based on a larger sample of countries and finer breakdown of resource inflows, is still subject to the weaknesses of data, of cross-sectional analyses, and risks of omission of significant explanatory variables.[26]

Kathryn Morton, of the Overseas Development Institute in London, has carried out a careful and critical analysis of the effects of aid on development in Malawi. Her overall conclusion is that, far from inhibiting economic development, aid was crucial to Malawi's economic progress. In particular, Malawi's savings and tax receipts as well as investment rose steadily and these efforts at self-help were encouraged by the aid policies of the main donor, Britain.[27]

The Attack on 'Aid as Imperialism'

Teresa Hayter's thesis in her book *Aid as Imperialism* is that aid, whether from government agencies such as USAID or multilateral agencies such as the World Bank, is based on ideology.[28] Governments consciously, and aid staff either consciously or subconsciously, are bound by the basic ideological framework of Western capitalism in all their analyses and actions with respect to aid to developing countries. Their influence, their economic and political leverage will inevitably be used in ways which will prop up capitalism. This will include backing up foreign private investment in dealings with governments of developing countries, trying to preserve freedom of entry to markets of developing countries for exports of the rich countries, supporting orthodox monetary and fiscal policies and opposing radical change in the social structures of developing countries. She illustrates such aid relationships mainly from the workings of USAID and the World Bank in their dealings with Latin American countries.

It seems acceptable to say that the education and environment of most Western academics and aid officials necessarily leads to their having a presumption in favour of private enterprise as likely to lead to the most efficient use of a nation's resources in terms of output per unit of input. Politically a high proportion of such people tend to be social democrats of one variety or another with a considerable degree of concern for a fair distribution of income within their own countries and a much higher than average concern for the welfare of the poor in the less developed countries. To some extent their choice of occupation in an aid agency implies such concern. From our personal knowledge of staff members of the World Bank, of the British Ministry of Overseas Development and of the USAID, it would be a travesty of the truth to say that they consciously support any form of economic exploitation of Third World countries or are in favour of the exploitation by Third World governments of their own citizens.

If the analyses and actions of such people appear to Miss Hayter to be inimical to the development of the less developed countries, then it is because she thinks Western capitalism cannot promote economic development in terms of raising the standards of living of the vast majority of the citizens of developing countries. That is a fairly difficult position to maintain in the face of the enormous improvement in living standards which capitalism has produced in the Western world. Not only are per capita incomes much higher than a century ago, but the distribution of income after tax and social security transfers is much more equal than it was in the past.[29] It would be very hard to maintain that the average standard of living in countries like Taiwan, Singapore, Israel, Greece, Turkey, Iran, Zambia, Ghana, Ivory Coast, Brazil and Mexico, has not risen very fast in the postwar era and that this growth has not benefited workers as well as capitalists in these countries. Aid may or may not have helped them, but it does not appear that their dependence on capitalist methods of organising production, distribution and exchange has prevented development; nor has their close involvement through trade and private foreign investment with the Western economies.

Aid officials may therefore have more than ideological bias leading them to support market-oriented policies in developing countries. They also have a certain amount of empirical support for the view that capitalism works. There exists no comparable body of empirical evidence in support of alternative systems working in a wide range of differing societies.

The same point can be made for the relationship between the IBRD (or World Bank) and its clients. The Bank has used its influence in favour of relatively free trade, avoidance of artificially inflated exchange rates, stable prices, and reduced budget deficits, but has also tried to stimulate and support policies making for social justice, particularly in recent years. The Bank's attitude is pragmatic, not ideological. A Colombian official has said, 'On this whole question of income redistribution, the politicians are more conservative than the aid agencies. The resistance of the ruling class is an important limiting factor for us'.[30] In truth, as Judith Hart aptly puts it, the real image of the Bank is not that of a ruthless agent of imperialism, but rather that of 'a well-meaning English nanny, nagging and fussing her children into sensible behaviour and good manners'.[31]

Under Mr McNamara's leadership the three goals stressed by the World Bank have been rapid growth, jobs at proper pay and progress in increasing the share going to the poorest two-fifths of the population. Admittedly not a great deal of progress has been made so far in achieving the latter two goals, not even in making the Bank's lending pattern and influence reveal these intentions clearly. In fact, in the fiscal year ending in June 1972, over half of the total Bank lending went to Brazil ($437m), Mexico, Iran and Turkey (between them $539m), and these are hardly the poorest of the developing countries. Nor in fact have many Bank loans gone to activities with a high intensity of labour use such as small-scale industry or small-scale rural development works over the last five years. However, there has been some improvement in the years from 1973 to 1975.[32] The delay is partly due to the time it takes to switch long-term economic aid, partly to the real difficulties of assessing the feasibility of smaller projects in industry and agriculture, and very importantly to Mr McNamara's desire to expand Bank lending rapidly in total. To do this requires finding good projects capable of absorbing large foreign exchange amounts and these are more easily found in the better-off developing countries. Since loans to them are on terms fairly close to commercial this may not be particularly at the expense of the poorer countries as profits from IBRD activities are transferred to the International Development Association (IDA), a branch of the Bank for lending at very soft rates to really poor countries.

The Bank stands accused of using the leverage of its lending power to influence governments to favour market solutions and relatively free enterprise; yet its staff is international, drawn from socialist as well as mixed capitalist economies, and its actual loans have mainly gone to public-sector projects. Only a very small proportion of Bank loans have gone directly into private-sector activities. For the most part this is also true of bilateral aid. Between 1947 and 1974 by far the greater part has gone into transport, power, irrigation, communication, education and health.[33] These are all public-sector activities. Moreover, the sale of Public Law 480 food products has provided many governments in developing countries with substantial revenues which have enabled them to increase significantly the economic role of government. Given the difficulties in raising tax revenues which face most governments in the poorer countries, these PL480 counterpart funds have had a particularly important role in government finance. In several countries they have made rural development programmes possible which have put at least some resources into the hands of the generally neglected poor farmers. In practice, aid has gone quite a long way towards socialising investment in developing countries which is why it has earned the hostility of Miss Hayter's opposites on the extreme right.

Bilateral aid is much more open to criticism as serving the interests of the donor nations rather than the recipients. The Americans have been very frank about the political objectives of their aid and the statistics on United States aid flows show clearly that it fits neither of these criteria for aid – the need for it, or the ability to use it effectively. As we have pointed out in Chapter 1 and earlier in this chapter, all the large donor nations have used their aid to promote their own political and commercial interests. The smaller nations of Scandinavia and a few others may have been more idealistic, but their small size would, in any case, limit the leverage which their aid could exert. They would seldom be the dominant aid donor anywhere.

Evidently the approach of the Western aid agencies is one of gradualism. This is inevitable in such a touchy area of international relationships but may also be justified by the weakness of the analytical tools at their disposal for analysing and forecasting economic behaviour. Those developing countries which have experienced revolution and the adoption of extreme socialist or fascist policies are not good advertisements for these radical solutions in the Third World. Revolutionary coups in developing countries have not, on the whole, been followed by any more rapid improvements in the general standard of living than in those countries which have avoided revolution. From 1960 to 1970 Cuba's growth rate of per capita income was minus 0·6 per cent in spite of massive Russian aid, and that of Egypt and Algeria 1·7 per cent, the latter despite the discovery of petroleum. Over the same period the figure for Burma was 0·6 per cent, Guinea 2·7 per cent and the People's Democratic Republic of the Yemen minus 5 per cent. These compare with average growth rates of per capita income of about 3 per cent for developing countries.[34] Perhaps in the long run the revolutionary approach will pay off, but it should be noted that it demands very heavy initial sacrifices in terms of blood as well as economic progress and often seems to end by merely replacing one oligarchy by another.

The Future of Aid

Up until the 1970s the main problems which have confronted aid donors have been how to allocate aid between countries and how to allocate it within countries between various projects and sectors of the economy. In fact there is little sign that criteria such as need or ability to make effective use of aid had a significant influence in allocating aid, despite the long discussions on these two criteria which took place inside many aid agencies. In the event politics, historical accident and commercial interests dominated. How can this be changed? The obvious answer is to channel more of the aid resources through the multilateral agencies. This has the additional merit of removing the obnoxious procurement tying of aid which reduces its real value to recipients. On the whole, the multilateralisation of aid appeals to recipient nations as reducing their dependence on particular donors and yielding them greater freedom of political manoeuvre. It also apparently appeals to a significant group of United States legislators, led by Senator Fulbright, who have pressed strongly and persistently for the United States to switch a large part of its aid to the World Bank and regional development banks.

The main objections to the increased multilateralisation of aid are: (i) it will lower the volume of aid by reducing the rich countries' motivation and direct involvement; (ii) the disbursement of aid will be slower and more bureaucratic because of the elaborate analysis required by the IBRD and other United Nations agencies; (iii) the staffs of these agencies are not adequate in number or quality to handle the huge resources which would have to flow through their agencies; (iv) the World Bank is too dominated by the rich nations and especially the United States, while the other United Nations agencies are too dominated by the votes of tiny developing countries to ensure satisfactory control; and (v) compared with France, Belgium, the Netherlands and Britain the international agencies lack the intimate knowledge of particular ex-colonial areas necessary for the efficient and sympathetic administration of aid programmes in these large areas of the developing world.

The first of these objections carries some weight. The motivation for aid clearly includes the hope of some political benefits, some commercial benefits, and, in the case of the ex-colonial powers, an element of conscience money for past oppression. Aid-tying has also been partly fostered by the balance of payments problems of the United States and Britain and these problems appear to be persistent. There is a risk that more multilateral aid would mean less aid from these nations. On the other side of the coin is the example of several smaller donor nations, who already channel most of their aid through United Nations agencies, such as Denmark, Norway and Sweden, and whose aid has been increasing rapidly over the last ten years as shown in Table 6.2.

It is also significant that their aid terms are particularly generous. The grant element in their programmes is over 95 per cent in each case (for Norway 99·6 per cent) as compared with the average for countries associated with the Developments Assistance Committee of the OECD (DAC) of 85 per cent. The Scandinavian countries have each promised to achieve the official aid target of 0·75 per cent of GNP by around 1975. These examples, as also those of Australia and Canada, suggest that a programme which involved a much larger proportion of aid being channelled through the International Development Association affiliate of the World Bank and other multilateral agencies need not mean a smaller overall programme. For the Scandinavian nations the basis for aid seems largely moral; and where they have led, others may follow.

The second objection regarding the delays in obtaining aid from United Nations agencies also has some validity. They tend to require more detailed scrutiny of projects and take longer to recruit technical assistance staff and place them in posts. But USAID has been subject to similar charges in the past and the enormous delays between commitment of aid funds from East European countries and their eventual disbursement shows that bilateral aid is often no better. If careful analysis is required to ensure proper use of scarce aid resources then the delays imposed by the IBRD are justified. Initial project aid applications are often badly drawn up and considerable assistance from Bank staff or international consultants is often needed before well-designed projects can be put forward for finance. The charge of bureaucratic delays is often misplaced.

Table 6.2

Official Development Assistance as a Percentage of GNP

Country	1962	1966	1972	1973
Australia	0·43	0·53	0·59	0·44
Austria	0·03	0·12	0·09	0·14
Belgium	0·54	0·42	0·55	0·51
Canada	0·09	0·33	0·47	0·43
Denmark	0·10	0·19	0·45	0·47
France	1·27	0·69	0·67	0·58
Germany	0·45	0·34	0·31	0·32
Italy	0·18	0·12	0·09	0·14
Japan	0·14	0·28	0·21	0·25
Netherlands	0·49	0·45	0·67	0·54
Norway	0·14	0·18	0·43	0·46
Portugal	1·26	0·54	1·79	0·59
Sweden	0·12	0·25	0·48	0·56
Switzerland	0·05	0·09	0·21	0·16
UK	0·52	0·45	0·39	0·35
USA	0·56	0·44	0·29	0·23
Total DAC	0·52	0·41	0·34	0·30

Source: OECD Press Release, 'Development Assistance 1972 and Recent Trends' (Paris, 28 June 1973), and 'Annual Review of Development Cooperation', 1974.

The charge of inadequate staff in terms of quality is probably unjustified as far as the World Bank is concerned. The Bank and the IMF are not bound by national quotas on recruitment and can look for the most able recruits over a wide market. Their salaries and working conditions are attractive and their staff seem to compare very well at a professional level with the aid staff of national governments. If there were a substantial switch of aid funds from bilateral programmes to the IDA affiliate of the Bank at least some staff would probably move from the national agencies to the Bank. The regional organisations such as the Asian Development Bank, the African Development Bank and the Inter-American Development Bank have the merit of more intimate contact with the regions they serve, but may be more open to the charge, in at least the African case, of insufficiently well-qualified staff.[35] However, they could be strengthened and they do represent an alternative route for capital aid. The United Nations agencies such as UNIDO, FAO, WHO, ILO and UNESCO suffer from the problems of the national quotas on staff and their salaries are no longer as competitive as they once were. In any case the United Nations as such does not have the confidence of the developed nations in administering aid. Several attempts to set up a special United Nations Fund for Economic Development have foundered on this. The developed nations appear to be quite unwilling to trust their funds to an organisation dominated by the votes of the poorer nations.

On the other hand the World Bank is felt by developing countries to be too subservient to the wills of the developed nations and especially to the wishes of the United States government. Escott Reid, a former member of the Bank's staff, suggests that population size should be a major factor in determining voting power in the IBRD. He suggests a formula which would leave 54 per cent of the votes in the hands of the rich nations, but would clearly share power with developing countries a great deal more than at present. He suggests also that staff from developing countries should be brought into the Bank on five-year contract appointments to increase their influence and also their knowledge. Since Mr McNamara's appointment to the presidency of the World Bank, it has greatly increased the number of its staff members from developing countries. This, together with more involvement of the professional staff in policy-making, constitute reforms designed to make the Bank more of a powerhouse for economic and social progress in the Third World than it has been hitherto.[36] Reforms such as Professor Reid suggests would have the effect of increasing the acceptability of the Bank to developing countries while stopping short of reducing developed countries' confidence in the government and policies of the Bank.

The final objection considered here is the view that the ex-colonial powers have the experience, knowledge and expertise which multilateral agencies lack in dealing with developing countries. If true it is a wasting asset. Most of the ex-colonial civil servants are now retired or on the point of retirement. Men and women with twenty years' experience in Africa or Asia are now very hard to find, and of those that remain not a few are already in the employ of the World Bank and other United Nations agencies. It is a standard joke in some parts of Africa that they might as well ask the British for certain types of technical assistance because if they ask the United Nations they will simply provide the same British experts only with a greater delay and at a higher cost. The objection may have a grain of truth, but it may be outweighed by suspicion of the ex-colonial power and by the risk that ex-colonial civil servants may be unable to shed old attitudes to local staff and to recognise their own purely advisory role in the new situation.

Most of these objections to multilateral aid seem to have little weight. Compared with the advantage of freeing the aid relationship from politics and commerce they seem unimportant. Despite Teresa Hayter's charges, the IBRD probably remains the most progressive and enlightened as well as efficient administrator of aid programmes. If some or all of Professor Reid's suggestions for reform can be implemented we should see great advantage in most nations gradually moving closer to the Scandinavian proportions as between bilateral and multilateral aid channelled mainly through IDA.

There is no doubt that the aid relationship in the past has often proved unproductive in terms of economic development. In the light of its motivation this is hardly surprising. Nevertheless, that financial and technical assistance can have a useful role to play in improving development prospects is equally undeniable. It has worked in some countries already. Taiwan, Malaysia, Kenya, Malawi and Brazil have been successes. Many mistakes have been made, but donor agencies and recipients alike have gained experience in the relatively new business of handling international resources so as to assist the economic and social development efforts of the Third World.

NOTES

1. Mahbub ul Haq, 'Tied Credits: a Quantitative Analysis', in J. Adler and Kuznets (eds), *Capital Movements and Economic Development* (New York: St Martin's Press, 1967) and Baghwati, 'The Tying of Aid', *UNCTAD (New Delhi) Conference Proceedings*, Vol. IV (New York: United Nations, 1968).

2. See, for example, calculations by John A. Pincus, *UNCTAD (New Delhi) Conference Proceedings*, Vol. IV, *op. cit.*, pp. 133–7. Quoted in Baghwati, *Amount and Sharing of Aid* (Washington: Overseas Development Council, 1970) p. 16.

3. Aid figures from *Development Assistance Review 1974; Resources for Developing Countries 1974;* and *Recent Trends* (all Paris: OECD, 1975).

4. Keith Griffith and J. Enos, 'Foreign Assistance: Objectives and Consequences', *Economic Development and Cultural Change*, April 1970; *Development Assistance Review 1968* (Paris: OECD Secretariat, 1969), p. 145. For a detailed statistical analysis of various factors which might

influence aid flows see Alan Strout and P. Clark, 'Aid Performance, Self-help and Need' (USAID, 1968, mimeographed). Recent research by R. D. McKinley and A. S. Cohen of the University of Lancaster (1975, mimeographed) tests a 'humanitarian' model. It fails to explain aid from the major OECD donors – the United States, France, Germany and the United Kingdom. In all cases, donor preferences rather than recipient needs governed aid distribution.

5. Bauer, *Dissent on Development*, *op. cit.*, p. 95. The summary of the views of Bauer presented here is based on this book, pp. 95–135, and on a review article by Bauer and B. S. Yamey, 'The Economics of the Pearson Report', *Journal of Development Studies*, January 1972.

6. *Ibid.*, p. 97.

7. Pearson Report, *op. cit.*, p. 49.

8. *Ibid.*, p. 103.

9. *Ibid.*, p. 122.

10. Bauer, *op. cit.*, pp. 10–11.

11. *Ibid.*, pp. 97–8.

12. See Bhagwati and Desai, India: *Planning for Industrialisation* (London: Oxford University Press, 1971); and Lewis, Jr., *Economic Policy and Industrial Growth in Pakistan* (London: Allen & Unwin, 1969).

13. See Hayter, *op. cit.*, ch. 2, for an elaborate discussion of leverage by USAID and the IBRD. Pressure from the Aid India Consortium was instrumental in causing India to devalue in 1966 and in leading Pakistan to a significant liberalising of her import policy in the early 1960s.

14. Malawi, for example, sought aid for setting up a second capital city from various Western donors in vain, but eventually got the finance from South Africa.

15. Criticised just as much by Lord Balogh as by Peter Bauer.

16. Griffith, 'Foreign Capital, Domestic Savings and Economic Development', *Bulletin*, Oxford University Institute of Economics and Statistics, May 1970; and Griffith and Enos, *op. cit.* Many authors writing in the learned journals between 1967 and 1970 have made similar quantitative analyses of capital flows.

17. Griffith and Enos, *ibid.* It is also possible that a government may use aid to release resources for consumption programmes which cannot subsequently be cut back. See D. C. Dacy, 'Foreign Aid, Saving and Growth', *Economic Journal*, September 1975.

18. See Chenery and A. Strout, 'Foreign Assistance and Economic Development ', *American Economic Review*, September 1966, and Staffan B. Linder, *Trade and Trade Policy* (London: Pall Mall, 1967).

19. For a more detailed critique of the Foreign Exchange Gap model, see MacBean, 'Foreign Trade Aspects of Development Planning', in I. G. Stewart (ed.), *Economic Development and Structural Change* (Edinburgh: Edinburgh University Press, 1969).

20. Gustav F. Papanek, 'The Effect of Aid and Other Resource Transfers on Savings and Growth in Less Developed Countries', *Economic Journal*, September 1972, p. 938.

21. *Ibid.*, pp. 938 *et seq.*; and Papanek, 'Aid, Foreign Private Investment,

Savings and Growth in Less Developed Countries', *Journal of Political Economy*, January/February 1973; and Frances Stewart, 'Comment on Griffin', *Bulletin*, Oxford University Institute of Economics and Statistics, May 1971.

22. *Ibid.*

23. See Papanek, 'The Effect of Aid and Other Resource Transfers on Savings and Growth in Less Developed Countries', *op. cit.*, p. 939, for a fuller account of this.

24. *Ibid.*, pp. 941–3, gives numerous examples.

25. *Ibid.*, p. 950.

26. Papanek, 'Aid, Foreign Private Investment, Savings and Growth in Less Developed Countries', *op. cit.*, Table 1 and pp. 129–30.

27. Kathryn Morton, *Aid and Dependence* (London: Croom Helm, for the Overseas Development Institute, 1975).

28. Hayter, *op. cit.*

29. Using various different measures for income distribution, Professor Jan Tinbergen finds that 'the developed market economies have experienced a considerable reduction in inequality per user'. See 'Tendencies and Determinants of Income Distribution in Western Countries', in Bhagwati and R. S. Eckaus (eds), *Development and Planning: essays in honour of Paul Rosenstein Rodan* (London: Allen & Unwin, 1972) pp. 178–82.

30. Quoted in Hart, *op. cit.*, p. 214.

31. *Ibid.*, p. 218.

32. These points are summarized from Escott Reid, 'McNamara's World Bank', *Foreign Affairs*, July 1973, pp. 794–8. The same group of countries – Brazil, Mexico, Iran and Turkey – shared over 32 per cent of World Bank loans in fiscal 1973/4 according to figures in the *Europa Year Book, 1975* (Washington: World Bank, 1975).

33. *Europa Year Book, 1975, op. cit.*, gives the sectoral distribution of World Bank loans.

34. *World Bank Atlas* (Washington: World Bank, 1972).

35. John White, *Regional Development Banks* (London: Overseas Development Institute, 1970).

36. Reid, *op. cit.*

CHAPTER SEVEN

Challenge of Trade and a New International Economic Order

The demands for a New International Economic Order, expressed at the Sixth Special Assembly of the General Assembly of the United Nations in May 1974, represent the culmination of years of attack on the international trading system. That system, embodied in the principles and rules of the General Agreement on Tariffs and Trade (GATT) and the IMF, aims at progress towards free international trade. Since its inception at Bretton Woods in 1944, this system has seen enormous progress towards liberalisation of trade and finance, but progress has been concentrated on manufactured products mainly produced in the industrialised nations. No comparable progress has been made in either agricultural trade or trade in manufactures of special interest to developing countries.

Agricultural protectionism, the main offender in Western Europe, largely affects the producers of temperate zone food products. These are overwhelmingly the rich countries of North America and Australasia. It also, however, severely damages the export prospects of some developing countries, especially the sugar producers. The various sugar agreements inadequately compensate them for the gains they would have made were the industrial countries to end their protection of domestic beet sugar production.[1] The remaining tariff and non-tariff barriers in the developed countries discriminate against products which developing countries have the best prospects of exporting. This remains true despite the extension of the Generalised System of Preferences (GSP) adopted by most of the developed nations. Exclusions and market disruption clauses have so limited the range of eligible goods and made sustained exports so uncertain that the benefits of the GSP have been rather small and concentrated on relatively few developing countries. These realities of the existing trading relationships are contrary to the basic philosophy of the postwar economic order. The main objectives of the GATT are free trade and non-discrimination, but in agriculture the industrialised nations remain steadfastly protectionist, and in the field of labour-intensive manufactures and processed raw materials they discriminate severely against the interests of developing countries.

These are entirely legitimate grievances for developing countries. Strangely, they have laid more emphasis on the much more questionable issue of the terms of trade for primary commodities. It has been their constant complaint that they have an unfair deal in terms of the prices of their exported food and raw materials as against the prices of their imports. Their demands for 'just and equitable prices' have rung through meeting after meeting of UNCTAD, the GATT and other United Nations bodies. It heads the list of their trade demands in the resolutions on the New International Economic Order. The action they want here is support for producers' associations, an integrated programme of commodity arrangements, with quota controls, buffer stocks and long-term trading agreements to stabilise prices of commodity exports and to support them above the levels they would attain in the absence of intervention.

In fact most emphasis in all of the developing countries' (Group of 77) proposals is on policies which run counter to free trade. In commodities they seem to prefer state trading arrangements and cartels between developing country exporters. In manufactures, they appear to prefer extensions of the GSP to the general lowering of tariffs on a most favoured nation basis. There seems to be a fundamental lack of belief in the faith held by most economists in the Western world that free international trade confers great benefits on all participants with very few, and rather unlikely, exceptions. For example, in the Declaration on the Establishment of a New International Economic Order, it is stated that: 'It has proved impossible to achieve an even and balanced development of the international community under the existing international economic order. The gap between the developed and the developing countries continues to widen in a system which was established at a time when most of the developing countries did not even exist as independent States and *which perpetuates inequality*'.[2]

Of course the system involves more than trade. Aid and foreign investment are also charged with responsibility, but it is clear from previous UNCTAD literature and from the proposals in the 'Action Programme' that trade is the main target for condemnation.

Raul Prebisch and Hans Singer, in their United Nations capacities, have attacked orthodox trade theory and lent academic respectability to the view that trade between the rich and poor nations has been damaging to the latter. Gunnar Myrdal has also argued that 'market forces will tend cumulatively to accentuate international inequalities', and that 'a quite normal result of unhampered trade between two countries, of which one is industrial and the other underdeveloped, is the initiation of a cumulative process towards the impoverishment and stagnation of the latter'.[3]

Trade and Development

Before considering these radical criticisms of international trade it may be worth while reminding ourselves of the rationale which underpins the GATT system. At base it is the orthodox economist's case for free international trade. That case is founded on the proposition that trade, with very few exceptions, will raise the potential economic welfare of all participating nations. The word 'potential' is included because welfare is a function of the distribution of benefits within countries as well as of an increase in output. But distribution is to a considerable extent under the control of national governments.

Gains from Trade

First of all there is an exchange gain from trade. If two individuals with similar tastes but different collections of goods meet, they can trade to mutual advantage. Suppose one has eight bottles of wine and two loaves of bread and the other has two bottles of wine and eight loaves, each can gain by exchanging wine for loaves. If their taste pattern is such that they rate a loaf equal to one bottle, then both would be happiest with five loaves and five bottles of wine. Similarly, even when production patterns are fixed because of resource immobility, countries can gain through trade provided that their domestic cost ratios differ from the relative prices at which goods exchange in the rest of the world.

Secondly, a nation can alter its pattern of production to increase the output of those goods which it can produce at relatively lower cost and exchange these for goods which it can only produce for itself at relatively high cost. In this way the nation can consume more than it can produce directly for itself with the same effort. This does not depend on the rest of the world following optimal policies. As long as the relative costs of goods in international markets differ from their relative costs within the country, that country can gain from international trade.

Thirdly, if an economy which is brought into contact with the rest of the world, or one in which discovery of a new resource is made is being considered, trade opens up the possibility of a 'vent for surplus'.[4] Goods which could not be consumed at home can be exported and exchanged for goods for which it has an unsatisfied demand. The export of petroleum from the Middle East, rubber and palm oil from East Asia, cocoa from Ghana or coffee from Uganda are examples of cases where unused or under-utilised resources were brought into use by trade. In these cases, there would be little or no resources transferred from producing other goods in order to produce these exports.

These three types of gains from trade are all classed as static. They involve a long-run adaptation of the economy to a new pattern of production and consumption with a higher level of national income than would normally result from autarky. But the resulting improvement is once only, not continuous, once the move towards free trade is complete.

Classical economists and many modern economists would, however, claim that the benefits which flow from free trade are dynamic as well as static.

The attainment of a higher national income through trade makes possible a higher level of savings. More resources can be devoted to creating capital which can raise the productivity of the economy in the future. This is clearly a cumulative dynamic process.

Specialisation brings possibilities of an improvement in skill, raising the productivity of the work force. It permits the realisation of economies of scale in the export industries. Trade brings contacts between local producers and foreigners allowing the interchange of ideas useful in commerce, finance and production. These ideas may spread through the export sector to other areas of the economy stimulating improvements in efficiency in these activities. Foreign investment and transfers of technology tend to follow close upon the heels of trade and may also confer dynamic benefits, but the arguments for and against foreign private investment are treated in the next chapter.

Competition from foreign suppliers keeps local management on their toes, forcing them to re-examine their methods and to keep searching for ways to raise efficiency.

To summarise, classical economists and perhaps most modern economists, while noting certain exceptions, and noting the issue of income distribution for further consideration, would expect free trade to be decidedly better than no trade and in general to be preferred to even limited protection.[5]

Case for Protection in Developing Countries

Free trade means specialisation in the export of those products in which a nation has a comparative advantage. For most developing countries this has meant in the past, and may continue to mean, specialisation in the export of primary products – this results from the nature of their resource endowment. Most developing countries lack the educated and trained work force, management, cheap energy and other requisites of large-scale manufacturing industry. Instead they have tropical climates which give an enormous advantage in products like cane sugar, coffee, cocoa, tea and exotic fruits. Many have valuable minerals like petroleum, phosphates, copper, tin and bauxite which have little or no domestic use at present (though local processing may well be a future option).

A popular argument against their continued specialisation in primaries is that the terms of trade between primary goods and manufactures has moved against them and will inevitably continue to do so. This argument, associated mainly with the influential Dr Prebisch, was based on some dubious empirical evidence and rather imprecise theorising.

The statistical evidence was on the favourable movement of the commodity terms of trade of Britain between the 1870s and 1938. The prices of Britain's exports divided by the price of her imports improved from 100 to 163. This was taken as evidence of a tendency to deterioration in the terms of trade between primary commodities exported by developing (periphery) countries and exports of manufactures by developed 'centre' countries. This evidence has been challenged frequently. Since Britain's trade statistics used c.i.f. (including cost of insurance and freight) prices for imports and f.o.b. (free on board) prices for exports, any improvement in productivity in transport would show up as a fall in the price of imports. The period studied did indeed show a substantial fall in freight rates. Statistics of the commodity terms of trade make no allowance for changes in the composition, or improvements in the quality of manufactures; yet over time both of these take place. If the price of a bulldozer doubles, but it moves four times the quantity of earth that the old model did, the cost of earth moving has fallen. A given quantity of exports of cotton or copper buys more bulldozer services now than ten years ago, even though the price of a bulldozer has risen more than cotton or copper prices.

Other attempts to measure trends in the relative prices of the exports of developing countries are much more cautious in their findings.[6] A report by a group of experts for the Secretary General of UNCTAD finds no evidence of any long-term deterioration in the terms of trade of the developing countries (even when oil is excluded).[7]

In any case, movements in the commodity terms of trade, of themselves, have no particular implications for welfare or resource allocation. The price of rubber might fall because productivity in the production of rubber rose, for example, through the replacement of old trees by new and better varieties. The fall in the price of natural rubber could then be consistent with a rise in the total value of rubber exports because of the increase in volume which caused the fall in price.

The *a priori* reasoning used to support the thesis of a tendency for a secular decline in the terms of trade of developing countries has also been effectively undermined by subsequent analyses. The main strands of the argument were that primary products suffered from low income and price elasticities of demand, that the exogenous technological change in the industries of the rich countries economised on the use of raw materials and developed synthetic substitutes for several of them, and that differences in factor and product structures as between developing countries and rich countries ensured that the former passed productivity gains on in the form of lower commodity prices, while the latter captured their productivity gains in the form of higher factor rewards, so that the prices of manufactures moved only upwards.

It has been shown that demand for most primary products has not been as price-inelastic or income-inelastic as had been suggested.[8] Export proceeds from primary products (excluding oil) have grown at a rapid and sustained rate with a sharp acceleration in the 1972-4 commodity boom. Interestingly, exports of primary commodities from the rich countries have done rather better than from the poor countries. This may be a reflection of the greater adaptability of the economies of developed countries so that producers respond more rapidly to changing market situations by shifting among products toward the more profitable ones or by exhibiting greater supply elasticity in response to changes in demand.[9]

For many primary commodities it is unlikely that the price elasticity of demand facing the developing countries even as a group is low because they face competition from production in the industrialised nations of the same commodities or synthetic substitutes for them. This is the case for natural fibres such as cotton, wool, jute and sisal; natural and synthetic rubber are nearly perfect substitutes; oil seeds and their products compete with fats and oils produced in developed countries. It is also the case that many primaries face relatively high income elasticities, non-ferrous metals and rubber, for example. The demand for meat is highly income-elastic, as evidenced by Japan's dramatically increased consumption of beef. Derived demands for coarse grains to feed cattle and poultry, and cattlecake, also rise rapidly. Beef is a significant export for some developing countries and many of them do, or could, grow feed grains. The applicability of Engels' law is really limited to staple foods, not primary products in general.

It is true that technological change in the rich countries has eroded the markets of a number of exports. Natural rubber, cotton, wool, jute and sisal are examples. However, their often forecast demise has proved to be excessively pessimistic. Moreover, the petrochemical industry and the acetate industries which have produced the substitutes boost demand for the petroleum and wood-based cellulose products of developing countries. High prices for these raw materials will certainly check and may even reverse the trend away from natural fibres and rubber.

The last argument, based on market structures and the distribution of productivity gains, has been tackled at length by an American economist, June Flanders, who has shown its logical weakness.[10] The basic argument was set out by Dr Prebisch in his report, *Towards a New Trade Policy for Development*, for the first UNCTAD in 1964. In outline, his argument appears to be that a highly elastic supply of labour in developing countries keeps wages at a conventional subsistence level while a high level of competition in the market for their produce ensures that product prices are held down to average costs. Consequently any technological progress which raises productivity will generally be passed on to the buyers of primary products in the form of lower prices. In the industrialised countries, however, strong labour unions together with monopoly in product markets lead to the result that improvements in technology simply raise wages and profits with stable or even rising product prices.[11] This leads to his conclusion that the prices of manufactured goods will rise faster than the prices of the primary products exported by the developing countries.

In the real world it appears that his characterisation of export markets in developing countries is wide of the mark. The dominant export from developing countries is petroleum, and this is a highly organised market with the Organisation of Petroleum Exporting Countries (OPEC) pushing oil prices up to over ten dollars a barrel when the marginal cost of producing a barrel of oil is under twenty cents.

Marketing boards exist for a number of tropical products. Large expatriate companies are involved in most of the metal ore exports and often have strongly unionised labour forces to deal with. Other exports from developing countries like wool, wheat, tobacco, beef, maize, hides and skins are in markets where their share varies from 10 to 30 per cent with the rest being met by suppliers located in rich countries. In these markets the price elasticity of demand facing developing countries should be very high. Trade restrictions, quotas on imports and other barriers to trade such as the Common Agricultural Policy of the European Community reduce the elasticity of demand somewhat, but these are market interventions open to attack in the GATT. The situation facing exports from developing countries is really much more diverse than is implied in the Prebisch model.

On the other side, most manufactured exports from industrial nations generally sell in very competitive conditions. Often there are accusations of dumping – selling below average cost – in export markets. While many large firms have some degree of monopoly power within their own national markets because of protection by tariff and non-tariff barriers, all the evidence suggests that fierce competition on price, quality and service in international markets is the norm. But even if the assumptions of the Prebisch model really held, would this necessarily mean that the dollar price of primary exports from developing countries could tend to fall in relation to the dollar price of their manufactured imports? In terms of logical relationships this could only occur if the Marshall-Lerner rules for balance-of-payments adjustment were not fulfilled, that is, if the sum of the price elasticities of demand for the exports of the two areas was less than one. Otherwise the effect of a fall in the export prices of the developing countries relative to the prices of exports of the developed countries would bring about a balance-of-payments surplus in the former and a deficit in the latter which would have to be corrected by devaluation of the exchange rate or deflation which would lower the dollar price of the exports of the developed countries. It may be, of course, that various controls on imports and exports in both developing and developed countries drastically reduce the response of demand and supply to price changes, preventing balance-of-payments adjustment, but then the blame for the difficulties of the developing countries lies there, not in the basic supply and demand characteristics of primary and manufactured goods.

From the viewpoint of practical policy the whole terms of trade debate is really rather irrelevant. No sensible government or private investor would base investment decisions on such broad generalisations about trends in prices for a group of products which on examination are really very dissimilar. Even if it were true for a particular primary product that its price would decline over time, this would on its own be an insufficient reason for diverting resources from it. If it were an annual crop, the relevant question is whether a better return for the resources used in its production is obtainable in that year elsewhere. If not, it is sensible to carry on and reconsider the position after each crop has been sold and the question of replanting reoccurs. If it is a matter of whether to plant new trees which will not come into full production for four to ten years, then information on price trends becomes more important, but even then it is only one piece of information to be put into the investment analysis. Questions about what is happening to productivity are equally important. At the level of actual decisions nothing can take the place of detailed cost-benefit appraisal.

Export Instability

Another argument for market intervention is the instability experienced by exports from developing countries. The effects on developing countries of this instability are held to justify market intervention in the form of international commodity agreements, compensatory financing arrangements and protectionist policies to encourage diversification away from primary exports.

It can be readily accepted that the instability of both prices and earnings from exports of developing countries is greater than for exports from developed countries. Analysis of the effects of this instability on welfare and growth in developing countries is, however, fraught with difficulty. Clearly a drop in exports below trend must be damaging, but equally a rise above trend is likely to be beneficial. What has to be established is either that the benefits from upswings are less than the harm done by downswings and or that instability itself is damaging.

Price instability is unpopular with producers and consumers alike. It creates uncertainty which involves some cost and there is a risk that the greater instability of natural raw materials may enhance the attraction of synthetics. Substitution of synthetics for natural materials may be irreversible. For example, high jute prices may encourage investment in bulk handling equipment which will not be abandoned in favour of jute sacks even if jute prices subsequently fall substantially. However, in the past neither producers nor consumers have shown much willingness to pay even a quite small premium to moderate price fluctuations. Forward markets and private stocks exist to reduce risks. Large buyers of raw materials such as Dunlop Rubber may simply average over the long run, reckoning to come out even over a number of years.

Some commodities in some countries may be subject to excessive, and often lagged, reactions to prices; coffee in Brazil is an often-quoted example. This characteristic can be damaging, but it should be noted that the likely cause of price fluctuations in the case of Brazilian coffee would be changes in supply interacting with a stable and rather inelastic demand. In these circumstances earnings fluctuations will be much smaller than price instability.

In many products exported from developing countries the prices paid to producers are not determined by export markets. Government marketing boards or *caisses de stabilisation* break this connection. In many others expatriate companies absorb much of the shock of unstable prices and earnings. Certainly, barring administrative or political weakness, it is within the competence of national governments to operate sliding-scale export duties or subsidies, or marketing boards, to even out swings in export prices or earnings.

The effects of instability of export proceeds upon growth have been the subject of several studies, but as it is intrinsically difficult to specify precisely the determinants of economic growth it is not surprising that the results are rather inconclusive. Most studies have found very weak or non-significant relationships between economic growth and export instability. This should not be too startling when it is recognised that for a number of the largest developing countries trade is a very small proportion of total national income. Moreover, reserves, the use of IMF quotas, international credit and the special compensatory financing facility of the IMF all exist for the purpose of tiding nations over temporary balance of payments difficulties of the kind likely to arise from short-term, reversible fluctuations in exports. For some countries large foreign companies have absorbed some of the impact of fluctuations in export proceeds. Their payments in the developing country in hiring workers, buying local raw materials and paying taxes to the government are the relevant expenditures affecting the local economy. In countries such as Zambia and Chile, the foreign copper companies have tended to keep these expenditures much more stable than export proceeds from copper sales. Similar behaviour is likely in other mineral and plantation sectors of developing countries.

On the basis of available evidence and theorising it seems probable that short-term export instability is a very much smaller obstacle to growth than is lack of sufficient growth in export proceeds.[12] Moreover, many of the alleged effects can be dealt with by national governments. The impact on producers can be ameliorated by national stabilisation measures such as crop insurance, marketing boards or funds, and sliding scale export duties.

In the light of that judgement (if accepted) elaborate international schemes to moderate fluctuations in exports from developing countries seem likely to show low or negative benefit to cost ratios. However, the main driving force behind the demands for international control schemes for primary goods lies less in the instability issue than in the possibility of using such schemes to transfer resources to developing countries through higher prices or compensatory financing schemes.[13]

Commodity Schemes an Economic Aid

The success of OPEC in raising oil export revenues has greatly stimulated interest in emulation by producers of other primary products. However, the conditions for a successful cartel are very stringent. Oil meets most of them:

(*a*) Oil is essential to most modern industries, transport and heating in OECD nations. In the short run, there are few possibilities of finding substitutes. This gives oil the vital characteristic of highly inelastic demand.

(*b*) OPEC nations control over 90 per cent of oil exports. Oil can be simply left in the ground without deterioration and without causing significant unemployment in the OPEC countries. There is no need for costly stockpiling and no need to deal with the problem of unemployed miners or plantation workers likely to arise from restrictions on output in other primary industries.

(*c*) There is one dominant producer, Saudi Arabia, who can afford to carry the major burden of cutting back production because her export revenues so enormously exceed current import requirements. Several other oil exporters, Kuwait, Abu Dhabi, Qatar and Libya, are in a similar happy position (Libya, because of a quarrel with Occidental, less so than the others).

(*d*) A significant group among the oil exporters, the Organisation of Arab Petroleum Exporting Countries (OAPEC), share a common political objective and have cultural and religious affinities which enhance their cohesion.

Despite all these advantages some oil is still sold below OPEC prices, and occasional cracks appear in the cartel. By the early 1980s most commentators expect the supply of oil from non-OPEC sources and the development of technology in economising in the use of oil and developing other energy sources to have severely dented the power of OPEC.

No other commodity of any quantitative importance in world trade displays these advantages. Copper, tin and bauxite are sometimes mentioned as possible subjects of cartel agreements. Compared with oil their share in the value of world exports is small; copper 1·29 per cent, aluminium (bauxite) 0·67 per cent, and tin 0·21 per cent in 1970. All of them face competition from mineral production and reclamation of scrap in the rich nations as well as competition in many cases with plastics and other metals. Reductions in exports to enforce higher prices would result in many miners losing their jobs and since many of the mineral-exporting nations are hungry for foreign exchange there would be strong temptations for members to smuggle exports out if the controlled price were high. Existing but presently uneconomic sources of the materials could be opened up, including exploitation of sea-bed nodules known to be rich in minerals.

Recognition of the difficulties involved in cartels has led some commentators and UNCTAD to advocate international commodity agreements (ICAs) with full consumer participation as a means to the same end of transferring resources to developing countries. In the short compass of this book it is not possible to go into the many forms of international commodity agreements which can in theory effect transfers.[14]

Two approaches will be discussed here: quota agreements and international long-term compensatory financing arrangements.

International commodity agreements relying on quotas are open to most of the same objections as cartels. Their main advantage over the cartel is that consumer participation eases the problem of non-member exporters, and of discipline among member exporters. The importers agree to buy only from the parties to the agreement and to buy from them only those amounts permitted and certified by the authority. The International Coffee Agreement approximated to this type of international commodity agreement and met both of the problems described. It took several years to persuade the importing nations to police imports of coffee reasonably effectively and even then some so-called 'tourist coffee' probably slipped by. Clearly the need to obtain consumer nations' participation limits the extent to which prices can be raised above free market levels.

Quota agreements are disliked by most economists because they tend to freeze the pattern of production and export, preventing efficient suppliers from expanding and protecting inefficient ones from the forces of competition. The International Coffee Agreement did just that, discriminating against the rapidly growing East African producers in favour of the large Latin American ones. This caused severe strains on the agreement and contributed to its demise.

The commodities which are, in principle, suitable for international commodity agreements of this type are relatively few. The major academic study on the subject, by John Pincus, of the Rand Corporation, puts it at five: coffee, cocoa, tea, sugar and bananas. Even if successful, the total sums that could be transferred by means of these agreements would be fairly small. The benefits would be distributed in ways which would have no relation to need or ability to make use of funds. On the basis of the figures given in this study nearly 70 per cent would go to Latin America (40 per cent to Brazil alone), 20 per cent to Africa, and 10 per cent to Asia. Unless offset by domestic policies in the rich nations, the system would act like a regressive tax, hitting poorer people more severely than rich.[15]

International Compensatory Finance

International compensatory finance schemes could be much broader in scope. Since they do not interfere directly with supply and demand they have no need of elaborate controls and enforcement systems. They simply involve the definition of a target price or export revenue and a transfer to the exporters when actual prices or revenues fall below target. The payments involved would be direct government-to-government transfers. A rather limited version of this type of arrangement formed part of the Lomé Convention (February 1975). Under the STABEX system members of the European Community will make loans to associate members from developing countries so as to partially offset falls in their export revenues from a specified list of commodities.

From the viewpoints of efficiency and equity international compensatory finance schemes are almost certainly better than international commodity agreements of the control type. Their main drawback is that the resource transfer requires an explicit budgetary transaction on the part of the importing nations. As such, the OECD nations might regard it as meeting part of their general financial aid target. It would displace rather than supplement other aid. The same is of course also possible with commodity agreements or cartels. The net resource transfer to developing countries is a result of a combination of activities including official aid, foreign private investment into, and capital flows out of, developing countries, and transfers through commodity arrangements.

The United Nations demands for action in the field of primary commodities amount to an attempt to increase the real transfer of resources through some combination of international commodity arrangements and producer cartels. It is quite possible that in the words of Hugh Corbet, of the Trade Policy Research Centre, London, 'the efforts to obtain additional resources through combinations to increase commodity prices would be likely to diminish the inflows of private investment and official assistance and, to the extent that the incipient confrontation breeds insecurity on the weaker side, might even increase the outflow of domestic capital from developing countries'.[16]

To avoid risks of the breakdown of dialogue between rich nations and the developing countries, the former may be prepared to make some concessions to the latter. The industrial importing nations may support further investigations on commodity agreements and agree to join some; but whether they do or not, it is unlikely that international commodity agreements, whether 'integrated' or not, will significantly increase resource transfers to developing countries. There are other approaches to commodity trade which could yield much greater benefits. It might be better to concentrate on them rather than expend much effort on schemes which involve misallocation of resources and highly questionable distributional effects.

Trade Policies for Primary Exporters

There are at least two areas of trade policy which could bring real gains to developing countries and would also raise world output. The first is agricultural protection in industrial nations, and the second is in the processing of food and raw material exports so as to increase the value added in the exporting nation.

The policies of agricultural protection in Western Europe, although they bear directly in the main on temperate zone agriculture, do also affect current and prospective exports from developing countries. Sugar is the main product of export interest to developing countries which is at present adversely affected by European Community, American, Japanese and East European commercial policies. As has been argued earlier, a shift to the more rational deficiency payment system of support to farmers in Western Europe and the United States, or better still a move to free trade, would substantially improve earnings for sugar exporters.[17]

Tropical fruits and citrus fruits produced in developing countries are good substitutes for fruits produced behind protective barriers in Western Europe. Removal of these barriers would assist an increase in fruit production in these areas. This could earn quite high returns in many developing countries.

Several huge land masses in Africa are suitable for meat production and have little or no alternative use. Given access to growing markets in the rich countries they could develop valuable exports of beef and mutton. Protection and subsidies given in Western Europe to butter production also affect the demand for fats and oils used in margarine and which are significant exports from many developing countries.

Campaigning to abolish restrictions on trade in agricultural products could produce an alliance of interests between the United States, Canada, Australia, New Zealand and the developing countries. They could also look for support from Britain with her long-standing preference for cheap food imports and dislike of the common agricultural policy of the European Community. Even Germany might be favourably disposed. Consumers in all the industrial nations would benefit from increased competition in food supply, and their views have now gained a little more influence through consumer organisations than they had in the past.

It is very difficult to estimate the potential gains to developing countries of genuine free access to the markets for agricultural products in the industrial nations, but it must be very large; for sugar alone an estimate of $500m to $750m was made some years ago.[18] In other products it would take some years to expand production, but the stimulus to agricultural development could be very valuable in increasing job opportunities in the rural areas and creating demand for locally produced consumer goods.

Processing

The structure of tariffs in the industrial nations in the mid-1970s discriminates powerfully against the processing of raw materials in developing countries. This is the result of tariff escalation so that the effective protection given to processing industries in the developed countries is much higher than implied by the nominal tariffs on the processed import. In the European Community, for example, oilseeds enter duty-free, but in the form of oils they pay a duty of 15 per cent. Since the value added in processing is a small proportion of the cost of the refined oil this gives an effective protection rate of 150 per cent for the refining process within the European Community. Similarly the effective rate of protection on plywood entering the United States is about two and a half times the nominal rate.

The reduction or abolition of tariff escalation would encourage the establishment of more processing in developing countries. There are other advantages attached to locating the processing stages in developing countries. For some products processing near the source of the raw material can significantly reduce transport costs. Unfortunately this is not always the case. Bulk handling methods sometimes favour transportation of the cruder product; alumina rather than aluminium, petroleum rather than the variety of products made from it. There are, however, two other arguments which have recently become more powerful for locating refining processes in developing countries. These are the difficulties which industries now find in locating plants which cause any environmental pollution in the rich industrial countries, with high concentrations of industry already polluting water and air in many regions, and the further problem of attracting labour to work in some of these industries at the going wage. Western Europe has used emigrant 'guest workers' for some of these tasks, but social and political problems have affected their willingness to depend on this solution. Both of these factors increase the attraction of locating industrial plant such as copper refining or chemical processing in developing countries, where labour costs are lower and environmental consciousness less of a problem. Obviously locational decisions for specific industries are based on a great many considerations, but transport costs, labour costs and pollution costs will generally favour developing countries. In pressing for an end to tariff escalation, developing countries could attract support from some transnational companies, consumers and environmental pressure groups, but could meet with opposition from trade unions worried about the export of jobs.

Exports of Manufactures from Developing Countries

One result of denying the benefits of trade was to stimulate attempts to industrialise via import substitution. However, many of these alleged infant industries failed to grow up. The initial enthusiasm for this route after World War II has waned in the light of the evident high costs and inefficiency of many of the industries created, and the increasing difficulty in finding industries which could be successful in the home market alone. In the earlier phases of the policy the more obvious import replacing industries such as textiles, shoes and beverages were set up. Often they used indigenous raw materials and were relatively labour-intensive. Many developing countries possessed or would soon acquire a comparative advantage in such industries. Subsequent phases such as intermediate and capital goods industries faced the difficulties of the small size of the domestic market and the increased sophistication of their technology. Moreover, the extension of import substitution to more complex industries usually involves increased imports of raw materials, intermediate goods and capital goods and payments to foreign companies for technology and management. This, together with their inefficiency, often exacerbates the balance of payments problem it was intended to alleviate.

Now, in the mid-1970s, many developing countries are swinging away from the inward-looking policies of the past towards policies designed to stimulate exports of manufactures. For several these policies have borne fruit. The rate of growth of exports of manufactures from developing countries to developed countries was about 14 per cent per annum during the 1960s.[19] In 1953 exports of manufactured products were a mere 7 per cent of total exports from developing countries; by 1969 they had risen to over 20 per cent.[20] This is still concentrated for the main part on a relatively few countries. However, some thirty developing countries have become significant exporters of manufactured goods and several of them including India, Pakistan, Brazil, Mexico, Egypt, Korea and Argentina are populous.

The countries most benefited, however, are not among the least developed. They tend rather to be at the upper end of the per capita income scale or, as in the case of large poor countries like India and Pakistan, to have substantial urbanised communities with relatively high incomes and Westernised consumption habits. Nevertheless continued rapid growth of manufactured exports could make a large contribution to growth and welfare in a number of developing countries affecting the lives of many millions of people.

Export markets increase the feasible size of industries enabling greater economies of scale, lowering costs and thus spreading benefits to domestic markets through lower prices. Expanding exports help to improve the balance of payments, provide jobs in industry and may raise the general level of efficiency in the economy through the training of labour and management and other external economies.

Meeting competition in export markets stimulates efficiency in the home economy. Survival in an export market requires the firm to meet world market prices. Trade also encourages the acquisition of new ideas, attitudes and skills. These factors emphasise the potential gains to many developing countries from exporting manufactures. This in no way conflicts with comparative cost theory. Many of these countries have very large labour forces combined with a scarcity of good agricultural land. For them it makes sound economic sense to produce labour-intensive manufactures and exchange them for capital-intensive and land-intensive food products from rich countries such as the United States, Canada and Australia, as well as for capital- and technology-intensive goods such as machinery and electronic equipment. As education and experience in manufacturing build up, some developing countries will gain a comparative advantage in skill-and-technology-intensive products. With the aid of transferred technology, through the overseas subsidiaries of American and Japanese companies, Taiwan, North Korea, Hong Kong, and Singapore are already blazing this trail.

Obstacles to Manufactured Exports

Several barriers to developing countries' manufactured exports exist as a result of the policies of the importing nations. In their most direct forms these are tariffs and quotas on manufactured imports; but they take more subtle forms such as 'voluntary' quotas, government health regulations and safety standards which may arbitrarily discriminate against developing countries' exports, and discriminating trading systems such as the European Community, the European Free Trade Association (EFTA) and arrangements between the United States and Canada. Regional economic policies within the industrial countries also have the effect of subsidising the operations of some of their less efficient industries, often ones which are in competition with manufactured exports from developing countries.

Tariffs

Over the twenty years from the mid-1950s, culminating in the full implementation of the Kennedy Round, tariffs on industrial goods have declined to fairly low average levels. In the United States, for example, the average tariff is less than 10 per cent. Unfortunately averages can be misleading; the variation between products is very large and bears most heavily on the types of manufactures which developing countries can export. On textiles the United States tariff remains at over 20 per cent in 1975 and tariffs on footwear, leather products, stone, ceramic and glass products are all above average. This pattern is repeated in Japan, the United Kingdom and other member countries of the European Community. Manufactures imported from developing countries all bear higher tariffs than do goods imported from other developed countries. The discrimination is even more apparent when the protective effect of these nominal tariffs is estimated by calculating the implied effective tariff rates.[21]

In the face of these barriers the achievements of some exporters in developing countries appear remarkable. In fact several have been assisted by preferential arrangements with developed countries, for example, Commonwealth Preference, association with the European Community or special arrangements with the United States, such as items 806.30 and 807.00 of the United States Tariff Act which allow duties on imports to be levied only on the value added abroad when these inputs originated in America. Also, the last few years up until 1975 have seen most developed countries adopt generalised preference systems towards manufactured exports from developing countries as well as the extension of Associate status through the Lomé Convention of the European Community. The 1964 UNCTAD had urged the adoption by all developed countries of a general preference system for exports of manufactures from developing countries. In the event, no agreement upon a general system could be achieved, but many of the industrialised countries have, since 1970, adopted some system of preferences for these exports. In most cases, however, the goods which at present form the main component of manufactured exports from developing countries, textiles, leather, rubber and wood products, are excluded.

Japan, for example, still has a large sector of light manufacturing industries which are small-scale and labour-intensive. These are finding themselves squeezed between rising labour costs at home and very competitive imports from countries like Taiwan and Korea. This makes it politically difficult for the Japanese government to grant preferences in the very goods which are the most suitable exports for many less developed countries. As a result raw silk, silk fabrics, plywood, glue-gelatin, rubber and plastic footwear, footwear parts and leather garments are excluded and some 57 other items are classed as 'sensitive', receiving only 50 per cent tariff cuts. Extremely low ceilings were set on the amounts which could be admitted under the preference system – only 10 per cent more than the 1968 levels of imports. Because of this and the exceptions, the gains to developing countries are very small.[22] While Japan's case may be extreme, the same general tendency has been present in the preference systems adopted by most of the rich countries. Wherever there has been any threat to domestic industries the goods have been made exceptions or quotas have been invoked to bar significant entry by developing country exports. Up to the present, the scheme has brought only rather slight gains to developing countries. The apparent advantage of the GSP is reduced by uncertainty. The initial investment in plant and marketing effort could only be justified by a relatively large and growing market, but if rich countries react to successful market penetration by imposing quotas all these initial costs would be lost.

It is quite probable that a general reduction of tariffs on a most favoured nation (MFN) basis could, in practice, bring greater benefits than the GSP. Under the rules of the GATT, MFN duty-free access is a right which cannot be arbitrarily withdrawn. This gives security as against the precarious nature of GSP access.

Quotas

Physical import restrictions are particularly iniquitous and widely used. A highly efficient producer can succeed with exports even against high tariff barriers, but with physical restrictions the most efficient and the least efficient are equally barred from increasing their sales. A most important measure of this kind was the Long-term International Cotton Textiles Arrangement, now absorbed into the Multi-fibre Agreement of 1973. It was intended to rationalise the chaos of quotas and other restrictions in this field of great importance to developing countries (between 30 and 40 per cent of total Third World manufactured exports have been textiles over the ten years to 1975). Originally negotiated in 1962 but with subsequent amendments, it obliges each importing nation to admit at least a stipulated annual minimum increase in cotton textiles imported from developing countries, unless this causes 'market disruption'. The definition of this term is left to the importing country. When it claims that market disruption is occurring it is entitled to impose quotas restricting imports to their previous level. In effect the 'minimum' increase has also been the maximum for many importers. The Arrangement also permits the continued use of 'voluntary' export quotas which are often agreed to by developing countries under threat of worse measures being unilaterally imposed by the importing rich nations.[23] The all-pervading nature of quantitative restrictions is noted in a study in which the statement is made that 'there is almost no export, apart from a few non-ferrous minerals, of any less developed country which is not subject to quantitative restrictions in some developed countries'.[24] A particularly vicious form of restriction is discretionary licensing of imports. *Ad hoc* decisions are made by administrators. This creates uncertainty and deters sustained export efforts. There is also evidence which suggests that, like tariffs, non-tariff barriers discriminate against the exports of developing countries.[25]

Effects on Manufactured Exports of Developing Countries' Own Policies

Another major obstacle to successful exporting of manufactures from developing countries is their own current and past commercial policies. This subject has been studied intensively and is discussed more fully in Chapter 4.[26] In brief, the attempts to industrialise through import substitution have in many cases created inefficient industries which cannot themselves compete in export markets and whose activities raise the costs of other industries which might otherwise have been successful. The degree of protection in most developing countries also has the effect of supporting a highly overvalued exchange rate which raises the cost of export goods to foreigners. Government licensing of foreign exchange has led to corruption, diversion of management resources in search of windfall profits derived from possession of a licence, and misallocation of resources. These effects have been well documented in the series of studies mentioned in note 26.

Economic Size

A point which has been stressed several times in this study is that the vast majority of developing countries are small; most have less than 10 million people. Including Mainland China there are only eight with populations of more than 40 million.[27] Even in these countries large sections of the population have insignificant purchasing power, thus the domestic market for industrial goods is very small in most nations of the Third World.

As most modern industry requires large markets to operate efficiently this can be a serious handicap. Certainly it is likely to limit the kinds of industry which make economic sense. Because they lack large internal markets, developing countries need to export to achieve economies of scale, but it is often argued that success in exporting is usually based upon prior development of the industry in a large home market. Clearly this places small countries at a disadvantage. A study by the World Bank's Bela Balassa gives an empirical confirmation of this theory. He found that both the share of manufactured goods in total exports and the share of finished as opposed to semi-finished goods in total manufactured exports were significantly correlated with country size.[28] Exceptions to this are, however, not uncommon. Hong Kong and Singapore have respectively 3·96 and 2·1 million people and are very successful exporters of manufactures, but their cases may be rather special. For many African nations, to small size are added the additional handicaps of low general levels of education, lack of technical and administrative skills and little experience of even simple manufacturing or commerce.

*Policies to Assist Developing Countries to
Export Manufactures Successfully*

A distinction has to be made between those obstacles which are man-made, those which are the result of factors which are amenable to change in the medium term and factors which appear to be fixed and unlikely to change. Examples of these three categories are: (i) protection in both rich and poor countries; (ii) lack of skills or knowledge of how to market exports; and (iii) possession of a large comparative advantage in agriculture or mining based on the natural resource endowment of the nation. The attributes of the third category do not bar a nation from the development of some industries but they make it unlikely that it would be socially profitable for it to export manufactures – apart, possibly from some processing of raw materials.

The major man-made obstacles to increased exports of manufactures from developing countries are the barriers erected by the rich nations. Not only do these hinder the development of the developing countries, but they operate against a sensible international division of labour. Both the poor and the rich countries could benefit in the long run from their removal. In the short run some of the industrialised nations would have to face adjustment costs in moving factors of production out of labour-intensive industries which compete with exports from developing nations into industries better suited to their factor endowments. At least one study suggests that the adjustment costs – compensation for loss of employment and retraining costs – would not be excessively high.[29] Further, more detailed studies of the likely costs and of policies to minimise the economic and social costs of adjustment ought to be made as soon as possible so that governments can be made aware of the likely high benefit to cost ratio of moving fairly rapidly towards adoption of general preferences or genuine free trade in manufactures of special significance to developing country exporters. Removal of both tariff and non-tariff barriers to all developing countries' exports to the rich countries would probably be the single most important step which the developed countries could take to assist the growth of many countries in the Third World.

A number of other questionable practices discriminate against developing countries. The rich countries, because of their large domestic markets, are often able to adopt marginal cost pricing for exports, which makes it very difficult for developing countries to compete in third markets. The provision of export credits – financed on easy terms, sometimes with government subsidy – is also unfair to poor countries which cannot make similar offers. The GATT ought to take a greater interest in these matters since they violate the principle of non-discrimination implicit in the GATT Charter.

Some Hopeful Trends

One major obstacle to manufactured exports from developing countries has been the difficulties of penetrating unfamiliar markets in competition with organisations which are already established there.[30] However, there are trends in international trade which are helping to overcome this difficulty. Japanese and American firms are taking labour-intensive parts of their production processes and locating them in less developed countries. Mexico, Hong Kong, Taiwan, South Korea and Singapore have been major beneficiaries from this development. No marketing problem exists as the parent company simply takes the intermediate goods produced overseas into its home factories for final assembly. As long as the transfer prices are honest the system benefits all. A similar effect is achieved when some of the huge American retail organisations, such as Sears Roebuck and K Mart, supply manufacturers in developing countries with precise production specifications and market all their produce through their stores in the United States. The growth of large retail stores and discount houses in Japan has stimulated similar links with developing countries in Asia.[31] A Swiss organisation has a market garden and landing strip in Kenya from which flowers are flown direct to Switzerland for marketing there.[32]

Plentiful supplies of unskilled and low wage labour has been, in the past, the main motive for the migration of industry to developing countries, but some such as Singapore and Hong Kong are now also attracting industries which require skilled labour. As already suggested, other motives for migration have come to the fore. Densely populated and highly industrialised areas are discovering increasing difficulty in locating polluting industries within their own borders. Government regulations and environmental pressure groups are making it worthwhile to seek overseas locations in areas where waste disposal problems are less acute or governments more pliant.[33] Dependence on guest workers for unskilled or unattractive jobs in countries of the European Community has created social problems and political strains. The practice is likely to be curtailed, making location of plants in developing countries more attractive as labour becomes a major cost.

This migration of industry through subsidiaries, joint ventures and technology-sharing arrangements is a very important trend. It has played a significant role in the dramatic rise of manufactured exports from less developed countries in South-east Asia. Because of excessive tax inducements and perhaps unfair transfer pricing the social return to the developing countries may have been less than the apparent gains. Nevertheless the gains appear to have been great in terms of employment, exports and GNP. It would seem sensible to encourage the continuance of the trend. Developing countries ought also to learn from the mistakes of the industrialised nations and legislate so as to minimise damage to their environments from steel plants and chemical industries. They ought also to avoid too much inter-country competition in giving tax concessions to foreign firms to induce them to locate in their country.

It has been argued by the Canadian economist, Gerald Helleiner, that the main growth in manufactured exports from developing countries will derive from the activities of the multinational firms in locating in developing countries labour-intensive segments of production processes within vertically integrated international industries.³⁴ This is a continuation of the trend already noted above for American and Japanese firms to locate the manufacture of some components such as semi-conductors, television tubes, valves and tuners in Hong Kong, Singapore, South Korea, Taiwan and Mexico. Manufacturing processes, from making piston rings to punching data on computer cards, are being carried out by multinationals in various developing countries.³⁵

Production abroad of components is, in Professor Helleiner's view, less likely to attract hostile reactions from groups in the developed countries and has a powerful lobby in favour of it in the multinationals. It is clearly in the interests of the multinationals to relocate the labour-intensive parts of their production process in areas where labour is plentiful and cheap, as long as these locations also offer some security. The capital commitment may be relatively low because the processes are labour-intensive and the technology is so tied up with the integrated operations of the firm that it is unlikely to lose control of it. It is also in the interests of the developing countries, because it provides them with jobs and a contribution to national income from the amount by which the local retained value added exceeds that possible from feasible alternative uses of the labour. Since the latter will often be low in these countries there is a significant direct gain to the host economy. Some tariff concessions for such products already exist in legislation in the United States. Japan has also negotiated similar arrangements with South Korea whereby only the value added abroad and not the full value of the import is subject to tariff. The multinationals may well have sufficient influence to gain similar concessions in other industrialised nations. The increasing internationalisation of young business managers bodes well for the dispersal of labour-intensive component manufacture around developing countries which can offer a reasonably secure environment and plentiful supplies of cheap labour.

Professor Helleiner is almost certainly correct in picking out this trend in dispersing component manufacture as a highly significant development for the export prospects of developing countries, but he may underestimate the opposition from trade unions and from sub-contractors in developed countries. American auto workers are already complaining about both imported cars and imported components and are appealing to the government for protection, at least while the American auto industry adjusts to the shift in demand towards smaller cars. Unions are bound to see any switch of labour-intensive processes out of their country to overseas branches as a threat to their relative standard of living. Japanese labour unions may have been complacent during the period of exceptionally high employment and rapid growth which Japan has enjoyed during the

1960s and 1970s, but their attitudes could soon change in different circumstances.

The gains to the developing countries, as he notes, may be rather less than from foreign investment in subsidiaries or joint ventures which involve production of finished articles. The major gain from foreign private investment in developing countries is usually considered to be the transfer of technology and some spread effects of this on the rest of the economy. Such gains are likely to be much smaller in the case of a process which is totally linked to the parent company's integrated production process.

The current general hostility of the multinationals in both rich and poor countries ought not to obscure the very real benefits which their activities can bring to the developing nations. As long as governments are well-informed and tough-minded in their dealings with foreign companies they should be able to ensure that their economy and their citizens gain from the activities of the multinationals. The access to capital, control of technology and marketing expertise of these companies make them a very useful means of expanding developing countries' exports.

However, the major issue on the supply side of exporting manufactures lies in the commercial policies of developing countries discussed above. Quantitative restrictions on imports or the use of foreign exchange through licensing appear to have seriously damaged the efficiency of many developing countries. The wide-ranging and complex nature of these controls have required a vast bureaucracy to administer them. Delays, inefficiency and corruption have been characteristic. The morass of controls and the side-effects they produced have made it impossible for economic planners or businessmen to tell which industries were efficient.

Professor Balassa's summary conclusion on the effects of protection is that 'it appears that in countries with high protection a considerable burden has been imposed on the economy in the form of static (allocative) inefficiencies. Protection has further limited the scope of introduction of large-scale production methods and provided few inducements for improvements in productivity.'[36] His estimates of the costs, admittedly crude, do show them to be very high: 9·5 per cent of GNP for Brazil and 6·2 per cent for both Chile and Pakistan. He adds that, 'high protection has also contributed to a slowdown in the production and exports of manufactured goods'.[37]

In so far as restriction of particular imports is required a tariff presents a much more sensible method than quantitative controls. Tariffs provide revenue to government instead of monopoly profits to smart operators; they remove a lot of the stimulus to corruption; they are measurable and easily manipulated for policy purposes;

and they demand much less time and effort from administrators and businessmen.

If the main reason for restricting imports is the balance of payments it will generally be more efficient to deal with this by lowering the exchange rate, thus stimulating exporters as well as import substitution. This method has the advantage of simplicity, avoiding the battery of controls on imports and subsidies for some exports which many developing countries apply.

Of course it is not that easy. Structural rigidities, difficulties of moving resources from one activity to another, political commitments to sectional interests and other factors make it no easy matter to switch quickly from a tightly controlled economy to a more liberal trade regime. In this context one conclusion of a study by Jagdish Bhagwati and Anne Kreuger may point the way to a less drastic reform. They find that the developing countries which have had export-oriented development policies have had just as many and just as chaotic a set of controls and incentives as have those who aimed at import substituting development. But, 'the economic cost of incentives distorted toward export promotion appears to have been less than the cost of those distorted toward import substitution, and the growth performance of the countries oriented toward export promotion appears to have been more satisfactory than that of the import-substitution oriented countries'.[38]

Subsidies and other incentives to exporters may be more justified than would appear from the static allocation rule of equating the marginal cost of earning and of saving foreign exchange. They give inherently plausible explanations for the superiority of export subsidies which may be summarised as: (i) their visibility, hence there is less likelihood of their becoming exaggeratedly high; (ii) they are more indirect than the detailed intervention characteristic of import substitution; (iii) the products are subject to the test of the international market for quality and price; (iv) under this system exporters are more able to realise any economies of scale than would firms in a typically limited domestic market.

At least in the area of manufactures the major policy recommendation for both rich and poor nations is 'liberalise'.

Prospects for Developing Countries' Exports[39]

The most important factor in the trade prospects of the Third World is the rise in the price of oil. As it is the most important single export from developing countries this has had profound effects. On the one hand, the foreign exchange earnings of all the oil exporters have been dramatically increased and are likely to stay at these levels at least until the 1980s. On the other hand, the net importers, many of whom, like India, Bangladesh and Pakistan, are very poor and whose industry, transport and power are all heavy consumers of petroleum, have suffered severely and will continue to be handicapped if no special relief is provided for them. The scarcity and high cost of fertilisers, partly due to the oil crisis, may cause famine and is likely to reduce supplies of agricultural raw materials. The increased costs of the petrochemical industries will raise the prices of most of the synthetics which compete with the natural raw materials exported by developing countries. This will shift demand towards the natural products, but sluggish growth of national product in the United States, Japan and Western Europe has depressed demand for industrial inputs in 1974–6. If, as is probable, this 'recession' is only temporary, solutions are found for the problems of inflation and the balance of payments difficulties of the industrial nations and growth is renewed, the prospects for exports of primary products are good. High petroleum prices, environmental factors and inflation are all working to raise the costs of synthetics. Unless productivity in the production of synthetics can rise fast enough to compensate for these cost increases, synthetic prices must rise and so enhance the export prospects of developing countries. An exception to this will be exports in which transport costs form a large part of delivered prices. High costs of fuel may weaken their competitiveness.

Industrial exports from the Third World should also continue to grow rapidly. They are mainly labour-intensive and so less affected by high fuel costs. The trend towards assembly of components in developing countries seems likely to continue to grow and helps solve the severe marketing problem which constrains Third World exporters. Bulk purchases, accompanied by technical advice by the large retail organisations such as Sears Roebuck or Marks and Spencer bring similar benefits.

The principal challenge to the rich nations is to adopt more rational trade policies. Acting in their own long-term interests by removing restrictions on trade in the primary product, the processing, and the manufacturing fields which discriminate against the exports of developing countries, they would bestow huge benefits on the Third World. It is a challenge to researchers in the social sciences to investigate the social costs involved in transition to freer trade and to evaluate policies to prevent hardship to workers in the industrial nations whose jobs would be eliminated.[40]

The same recommendation to liberalise also applies to the developing countries. Given the severe distortions already built into their economies and the balance of payments difficulties which many of them face, however, most of them could only move gradually towards this goal. An easing of international liquidity and provision of a long-term programme of loans to aid structural change may be necessary and would certainly ease the hardships involved.

Economic integration among groups of developing countries is, in principle, another way in which their trade prospects could be improved. The creation of a larger internal 'common market' may make possible the achievement of economies of scale which could justify the setting up of industries which would otherwise be uneconomic. There might be some improvement in the terms of trade and increased attraction for foreign investment. However, most of the static theoretical gains of 'trade creation' familiar in the literature on customs unions are unlikely to be significant, and the past experiences of developing countries in setting up customs unions or free trade areas have not proved very successful. Economic integration between groups of developing countries is probably worth pursuing, but experience in negotiating their creation, in bringing down barriers to trade among the members, and in ensuring a fair distribution of the benefits, points to immense difficulties to be solved. None of the twenty or so arrangements of this kind set up so far can be demonstrated to have brought great benefits to the member nations.

NOTES

1. See H. G. Johnson, *Economic Policies Toward Less Developed Countries, op. cit.*, Appendix D.

2. UN Press Release, May 1974, para 1 of 'Declaration of a N.I.E.O.' (italics added).

3. Myrdal, *An International Economy* (New York: Harper & Row, 1956), pp. 55 and 95; Singer, 'The Distribution of Gains Between Investing and Borrowing Countries', *American Economic Review* (Papers and Proceedings, May 1950; Prebisch, 'The Role of Commercial Policies in Underdeveloped Countries', *American Economic Review* (Papers and Proceedings), May 1959.

4. Myint, *Economic Theory and the Underdeveloped Countries* (London: Oxford University Press, 1971) p. 180.

5. Paul Samuelson, 'The Gains From International Trade', *Canadian Journal of Economic and Political Science*, 1939, and 'The Gains From International Trade Once Again', *Economic Journal*, 1962. Reprinted in Bhagwati (ed.), *International Trade* (Harmondsworth: Penguin, 1969).

6. See, for example, Kindleberger, *The Terms of Trade: a European Case Study* (New York: John Wiley, 1956); and R. E. Lipsey, *Price and Quantity Trends in the Foreign Trade of the United States* (Princeton: Princeton University Press, 1963).

7. See *New York Times*, 26 May 1975, and *Guardian*, London, 2 June 1975.

8. B. de Vries, *The Export Experience of Developing Countries* (Washington: International Bank for Reconstruction and Development, 1967): Richard Porter, 'Some Implications of Post-War Primary Product Trends', *Journal of Political Economy*, May–June 1970; Angus Hone, 'Export Earnings and the 1973 Commodities Boom: the Extent of its Impact on Developing Capitalist Economies', *New Left Review*, No. 81, 1973. See also Thomas Wilson, R. P. Sinha and J. R. Castreet. 'The Income Terms of Trade of Developed and Developing Countries', *Economic Journal* December 1969; and Irving B. Kravis, 'Trade as a Handmaiden of Growth', *Economic Journal*, 1970.

9. The index of prices of primary commodities exported by developed countries rose from 100 in 1963 to 134 in 1972 and 175 in the second quarter of 1973. For developing countries the same index rose to 125 in 1972 and 155 in the second quarter of 1973 (UN *Monthly Bulletin of Statistics*, September 1973, Special Table B).

10. Flanders, 'Prebisch on Protectionism: an Evaluation', *Economic Journal*, June 1964. See also H. G. Johnson, *Economic Policies Towards Less Developed Countries, op. cit.*, Appendix A.

11. Prebisch, *Towards a New Trade Policy for Development, op. cit.*, p. 15.

12. MacBean, *Export Instability and Economic Development* (London: Allen & Unwin, 1966); International Bank of Reconstruction and Development staff papers on 'Export Instability and Economic Growth' (Washington, 1972) quoted in *Terms of Trade Policy for Primary Commodities*, Commonwealth Economic Papers No. 4 (London: Commonwealth Secretariat, 1975) pp. 15–6; Peter B. Kenen aand C. S. Voivodas, 'Export Instability and Economic Growth', *Kyklos*, 1972, Fasc. 4.

13. MacBean, *Export Instability and Economic Development, op. cit.*: ch. 12 considers the main arguments for and against international commodity arrangements to combat export fluctuations. See also M. Radetzki, *International Commodity Market Arrangements* (London: Hurst, 1970).

14. See 'An Integrated Programme for Commodities', TD/B/C.1/166 and various supplements plus TD/B/C.1/184 (Geneva: UNCTAD 1974/75) for exhaustive coverage of possibilities.

15. Pincus, *Economic Aid and International Cost Sharing* (Baltimore: Johns Hopkins, 1965) ch. 6.

16. Hugh Corbet, *Raw Materials: Beyond the Rhetoric of Commodity Power*, International Issues No. 1 (London: Trade Policy Research Centre, 1975) p. 25.

17. See above and reference to H. G. Johnson, *Economic Policies Towards Less Developed Countries, op. cit.*, Appendix D.

18. *Ibid.*, Appendix D.

19. *Trade in Manufactures of Developing Countries: 1969 Review* (Geneva: UNCTAD, 1969) Table 12.

20. G. K. Helleiner, *International Trade and Economic Development* (Harmondsworth: Penguin, 1972) p. 66. See also Chenery and Helen Hughes, 'Industrialisation and Trade Trends: Some Issues for the 1970's', in Hughes

(ed.), *Prospects for Partnership* (Baltimore: Johns Hopkins Press, for the International Bank for Reconstruction and Development, 1973).

21. The effective tariff rate attempts to measure the protection given to processing. Suppose that a textile fabric at import pays 20 per cent tariff, but the yarn required to make it pays 10 per cent. Further suppose that £100 worth of yarn is needed to produce £200 worth of fabric. At tariff-ridden prices the local value added is £240−£110=£130. If there were no protection the local value added would be £200−£100=£100. The increase in value added resulting from the tariff structure is £30, a 30 per cent increase in the return to processing in the importing country resulting from the tariffs.

22. Terutomo Ozawa, 'Labor Resource Oriented Migration of Japanese Industries to Taiwan, Singapore and South Korea' (IBRD Working Paper, mimeographed, August 1972) pp. 30–2.

23. See Helleiner, *op. cit.*, pp. 70–2. The Arrangement has since been absorbed into the 'Multi-Fibre Textile Agreement', Geneva, General Agreement on Tariffs and Trade, December 1973. This also covers synthetics, wool and clothing.

24. David Wall, 'Opportunities for Developing Countries', in H. G. Johnson (ed.), *Trade Strategy for Rich and Poor Nations* (London: Allen & Unwin, for the Trade Policy Research Centre, 1971) p. 36.

25. Ingo Walter, 'Non-tariff barriers and the export performance of developing countries', *American Economic Review* (Papers and Proceedings), May 1971.

26. See Little, Scitovsky and Scott, *op. cit.*, and the various studies in the series edited by them. See also Bhagwati and Anne Krueger, 'Exchange Control, Liberalisation and Economic Development', *American Economic Review* (Papers and Proceedings), May 1973; and Bela Balassa *et al.*, *The Structure of Protection in Developing Countries* (Baltimore: Johns Hopkins Press, 1971).

27. China, India, Indonesia, Brazil, Bangladesh, Pakistan, Nigeria and Mexico.

28. Balassa, 'Country Size and Trade Patterns: Comment', *American Economic Review*, Vol. 59, No. 1, 1969.

29. Little, Scitovsky and Scott, *op. cit.*, pp. 285–9.

30. Staffan B. Linder, *Trade and Trade Policy for Development* (New York: Praeger, 1967) p. 27.

31. Ozawa, *op. cit.*, p. 85.

32. We owe this example to Professor Richard Porter, University of Michigan, Ann Arbor.

33. Ozawa, *op. cit.*, p. 4.

34. Helleiner, 'Manufactured Exports from Less Developed Countries and Multinational Firms', *Economic Journal*, March 1973.

35. *Ibid.*, p. 29.

36. Balassa *et al.*, *op. cit.*, p. 88.

37. *Ibid.*

38. Bhagwati and Kreuger, *op. cit.*, p. 420.

39. A much fuller account of export prospects is given in MacBean 'Trade Prospects for Developing Countries after the Rise in Oil Prices', in T. M.

Rybczynski (ed.), *The Economics of the Oil Crisis* (London: Macmillan, for the Trade Policy Research Centre, 1976).

40. *1973 Review, Development Co-operation* (Paris: OECD Secretariat, 1973) pp. 83–94, discusses technical assistance and other measures undertaken by member countries of the Development Assistance Committee of the OECD to assist LDC exports.

CHAPTER EIGHT

Challenge of Foreign Private Investment

The role of foreign private investment in the development process is an area rich in controversy. Advocacy and opposition to such investment ranges to extremes. The supporters believe that it can not only confer all the benefits of official aid on the recipients but also impart certain additional benefits. The foreign capital that it provides can bridge both the foreign exchange and savings gaps; and the technology that it imparts can bridge the technology gap. It can redress regional disparities and confer a host of other benefits in the form of linkage effects which it creates, and employment opportunities which it provides, all congealed in the catch-all phrase, 'externalities'. The advent of the multinational corporation in recent years has even produced prophetic visions of a new integrated world order. It is argued that, under the aegis of these giant international corporations, managerial and financial resources would flow to sources of raw materials, and cheap labour and the fruits of technology would be widely disseminated. The trend would be towards the development of an integrated world economy dominated by the international corporations with wide access to financial and technical resources, and not towards the development of national economies.

At the other extreme are the opponents to whom foreign investment is no more than an instrument of neo-colonialism; the substitution of economic for political domination. In their eyes 'foreign private investment is seen as no more than a mere twentieth-century refinement or economic outcome of the gunboat diplomacy of the imperialist powers of the last century'.[1] Most developing countries still in the shadows of yester-year's colonialism and jealous of their political independence are wary of widespread foreign domination. It is not only a fear of imperialist exploitation but also economic nationalism, crystallised in the desire for ownership and control of the economy by domestic nationals, that feeds this antagonism to foreign investment.

The case against foreign private investment does not rest on political factors and economic nationalism alone. It is often buttressed by economic arguments which cannot be lightly dismissed. It is argued that foreign private investment may have an adverse effect on the balance of payments of the host countries, destroy instead of creating employment opportunities, thwart national economic objectives, and aggravate income disparities. Some antagonists would not only advocate expropriation of existing investment but also bar future flows of foreign capital.

In between the ardent advocates of foreign private investment and its trenchant critics, there is a third school of thought which can be called the 'strategic pragmatists'. They would advise the governments of developing countries to devise policies directed at harnessing the benefits of foreign private investment and curtailing its damaging effects. They would also encourage them to seek out alternative channels of foreign enterprise participation, such as joint business ventures, technical collaboration agreements and management contracts. An attractive feature of these alternative arrangements is the apparent absence of the most objectionable features of foreign direct investment: ownership of capital and control over operations.

Although theoretical argument for and against foreign private investment abound, there is very little empirical evidence available to arrive at settled conclusions on the subject. Indeed, economic analysis itself is inconclusive about the costs and benefits of foreign private investment. It should, therefore, come as no surprise that most developing countries have adopted an ambivalent attitude towards foreign private investment. On the one hand most of them have been wooing foreign private capital by offering tax incentives, high levels of tariff protection and guarantees against expropriation, and on the other they have imposed various controls and regulations on the operations of the foreign firms. Most developing countries have also been increasingly favouring alternative arrangements such as joint ventures and technical collaboration agreements.

Nature and Pattern of Foreign Private Capital and Enterprise

Portfolio capital flows and foreign private investment constitute the two main forms of foreign private capital flows. The former refers to the acquisition of securities by individuals or institutions issued by foreign institutions, without any associated control over, or participation in, their management. Much of the international capital flows of the last century – between two-thirds and three-quarters – was in the form of portfolio capital flows or bonds. The present-day officials aid flows can be regarded as a replacement for these.

Although foreign private investment is of comparatively recent origin, it has been expanding rapidly. The main distinguishing feature of foreign private investment, which sets it apart from port-folio capital flows, is the exercise of control over the decision-making process of the investor entity by the investing entity. This power of control over decision making, exercised by the foreign entity, varies with the extent of its equity participation, particularly in relation to other investors. John H. Dunning, of the University of Reading, points out, 'a 30 per cent ownership of equity by the foreign entity, with no other single shareholder holding more than 10 per cent of total equity, is likely to afford a more significant element of control than a 49 per cent shareholding, where the remaining shares are held by one enterprise'.[2] It is thus the ownership of capital in a major way and the power to exercise control over the operations that flow from it that distinguish private investment from portfolio capital flows.

The power to exercise control over operations immediately suggests that something more than mere flows of financial capital is involved in the case of private investment. This relates to the transference of technical and managerial skills or more generally knowledge and ideas. The ownership of capital by the foreign firms, the degree of control exercised by them and the extent to which technology is transmitted may all be closely interrelated. It is the ownership of capital that buys the foreign firms the power to exercise control over operations. In turn, the extent to which they are prepared to transfer technology and skills may depend largely on the degree of control over operations which they can exercise. Indeed, it is argued that a major factor motivating a firm to undertake private investment abroad is the monopoly over technology and skills it possesses.[3]

The foreign firm must find production abroad preferable to any other means of operating in the markets abroad, such as servicing the foreign markets by exports or by selling the technology it possesses. But given the fact that there are imperfections in the markets for goods and factors, foreign direct investment may be the preferred alternative. The fact that the foreign firm possesses a monopoly over technology renders the market for such technology imperfect. The best means of exploiting such a monopoly would be by setting up a production facility abroad. Further, the monopolistic advantage it possesses may be one which cannot be marketed in the international markets. It may not be possible to divest the knowledge of production from the production process itself. Even if such marketing of knowledge were possible, it may result in the eventual loss of the monopolistic advantage and patents may not afford enough protection against such losses. Thus, it is the need to exploit a monopolistic advantage, principally monopoly over technology, that motivates firms to engage in private investment abroad. Exploitation of these advantages necessitates control over operations and such control can be had only by majority ownership of capital.

Even the severest of critics of foreign private investment concede the potential it has for transmitting technology and skills to the host countries. Yet the widespread aversion to ownership of capital and control over operations that goes with it has led to a search for alternative avenues of foreign enterprise participation. Joint business ventures, technical collaboration agreements (licensing agreements) and management contracts are the suggested alternatives. A joint business venture is defined as one in which there is the commitment, for more than a short duration, of funds, facilities and services by two or more legally separate interests, to an enterprise for their mutual benefit.[4] The emphasis in this form of organisation is on the commitment of resources by both entities. The resources committed by the foreign firm need not entirely be financial resources. Its contribution in terms of managerial and technical skills may be more important than its financial contribution. Even if the financial contribution of the foreign firm is less than that of the local firm, its contribution in terms of organisational and technical resources would give it an equal status in the venture. The important point to note, however, is that neither of the two partners exercise exclusive control over operations.

A technical collaboration agreement is broadly defined as an agreement between a foreigner and an entity created under local law and owned by local public or private interests, in which the foreigner provides management services, technical information or both, and receives payment in money.[5] The significant features of a technical collaboration agreement are that it precludes ownership of capital by the foreigners, and payment received by the foreigners are in return for technical services rendered and not for equity contributions. In so far as the foreign firm has no equity interests in the venture, it follows that a technical collaboration agreement also precludes the exercise of formal control over operations by the foreign firm.

Although the absence of capital ownership and exercise of formal control over operations renders these arrangements attractive to the developing countries, their effectiveness as vehicles for technical transfers is subject to qualifications. Such arrangements, however, are gaining in popularity in the developing countries.

Size and Growth of Foreign
Private Capital Flows

Data on different types of capital flows to the developing countries and the percentage share of each in the total capital flows are shown in Table 8.1.

Three main points emerge from the table. First, official aid accounts for more than half of the total capital flows to the developing countries. Secondly, foreign direct investment accounts for nearly half of all private capital flows. Indeed, in 1971 it accounted for about a quarter of all capital flows. Thirdly, although portfolio capital and export credits account for a relatively low proportion of total capital flows they have grown at a faster rate than other forms of capital flows. Over the period 1956–71 official flows increased two-and-a-half times, export credits increased six times and portfolio flows grew eightfold.

The main concern of this chapter is with foreign direct investment both because of its magnitude and its controversial nature. A few salient points, however, about other forms of private capital flows need to be noted. The figures for portfolio capital flows cited in Table 8.1 include borrowings by multilateral agencies. Indeed, their relatively fast growth may be accounted for by that category. Direct borrowing on the international capital markets by the developing countries themselves remains relatively small and is confined to a few countries. Over the five-year period 1964–68 only three developing countries outside Europe, namely Israel, Mexico and Argentina, were able to float bonds totalling more than \$100m on world capital markets.[6] The main obstacles to raising a greater volume of funds on the international capital markets stems from the absence of an established record of creditworthiness on the part of the developing countries. Added to this are the restrictions on portfolio lending imposed by the developed countries for balance of payments reasons.

The prospects for increased flows of portfolio capital clearly depends on the removal of these two obstacles. In the foreseeable future only the middle-income countries of the Third World may hope to borrow increasingly on the world markets. Even they may have to contend with the restrictions on portfolio flows placed by the developed countries, particularly in view of their additional balance of payments problems posed by the oil crisis.

Assuming that the developing countries could have easy access to the world capital markets, is such borrowing superior to foreign direct investment? Although the rates of profit earned on direct investment may be higher than the interest rates to be paid on portfolio capital, it does not follow that the latter is a less expensive

Table 8.1

Capital Flows from DAC Countries, 1956–71

$m

| | Private Capital Flows (net) | | | | | | Official Flows | | Total |
| | 1 | | 2 | | 3 | | 4 | | 5 | | 6 |
	Total private capital flows	Per-centage to total	Direct invest-ment	Per-centage to total	Portfolio and bank lending	Per-centage to total	Export credits	Per-centage to total	Grants and net loans	Per-centage to total	
1956	2,998	47·9	2,350	37·6	190	3·0	458	7·3	3,260	52·1	6,258
1957	3,779	49·5	2,724	35·7	601	7·9	454	5·9	3,856	50·5	7,635
1958	2,917	39·9	1,970	27·0	733	10·0	214	2·9	4,387	60·0	7,304
1959	2,820	39·5	1,782	25·0	691	9·7	347	4·9	4,311	60·4	7,131
1960	3,150	38·8	1,767	21·8	837	10·3	546	6·7	4,965	61·2	8,115
1961	3,106	33·6	1,829	19·8	704	7·6	573	6·2	6,143	66·4	9,249
1962	2,453	29·1	1,495	17·7	386	4·6	572	6·8	5,984	70·9	8,437
1963	2,557	29·8	1,603	18·7	296	3·5	660	7·7	6,015	70·2	8,572
1964	3,729	38·7	1,572	16·3	1,298	13·5	859	8·9	5,916	61·4	9,645
1965	4,121	39·9	2,468	23·9	902	8·7	751	7·3	6,199	60·0	10,320
1966	3,959	38·1	2,179	21·0	655	6·3	1,124	10·8	6,431	61·9	10,390
1967	4,381	38·3	2,105	18·4	1,269	11·1	1,007	8·8	7,060	61·7	11,441
1968	6,377	47·5	3,043	22·7	1,738	12·9	1,596	11·9	7,047	52·5	13,425
1969	6,587	47·7	2,910	21·2	1,630	11·8	2,047	14·9	7,192	52·2	13,779
1970	7,019	46·8	3,557	23·7	1,251	8·3	2,211	14·7	7,984	53·2	15,003
1971	8,399	48·3	4,087	23·5	1,510	8·7	2,802	16·1	8,997	51·7	17,395
Total	68,352	42·0	37,441	23·0	14,691	9·0	16,221	10·0	95,747	58·0	164,099

Source: Grant L. Reuber et al., *Private Foreign Investment in Development* (London: Oxford University Press, 1973) p. 5.

method of raising capital. In comparing the relative costs of the two forms of capital, the costs of importing know-how and training managers need to be taken into account. Such costs may be lower in the case of direct investment, which is a package of equity capital and know-how, than in the case of portfolio funds where such assets may have to be separately bought under licensing agreements or management contracts. Furthermore, foreign private investment allows for a greater degree of flexibility in servicing capital flows than portfolio borrowing. In the case of the former, profits have to be remitted only when the project is successful. Profit remittances are therefore a direct function of the increase in profitable domestic output. In the case of portfolio capital flows, however, interest and amortization charges have to be met regardless of the success of the project financed by such flows.

Such considerations have prompted the World Bank to warn the developing countries about their heavy reliance on the Euro-currency market since 1971. Euro-currency borrowing of the developing countries, estimated to have been around $2,500 to $3,500m in 1971, is reported to have reached a figure of $10,000m at the end of 1973. More than 40 per cent of all the Euro-currency loans publicly announced in 1972 are reported to have gone to the developing countries, compared with only 10 per cent in 1970. Such Euro-currency loans admittedly have many attractions for the developing countries. First, they represent a truly international form of finance in that the borrowing countries are less subject to supervision and regulation by the lender. Secondly, the interest rates on Euro-dollars at 4 to 6 per cent have been comparatively low and they run for ten to twelve years.

These facts do not, however, suggest that the Euro-currency market has opened up new vistas of international lending to the Third World. It may represent only a temporary phenomenon fraught with unforeseen dangers to the borrowers. The explosive growth of this source of funds to the developing countries is partly a reflection of the continuing expansion of available funds in this market and the relative shortage of first-rate borrowers in the industrialised world. The United States balance-of-payments deficits, the increased oil revenues of the Arab countries and the diversion of funds to the Euro-market from domestic national capital markets in which foreign participation was restricted, are the principal reasons to which the increased availability of Euro-currencies is attributed. Such a situation may not last. Indeed, it is speculated that the Arab countries may not place their funds in this market, mainly because it has catered for developing countries with low creditworthiness.

Perhaps of greater concern is the possibility that a less propitious international climate may result in a sharp jump in interest rates. If, as in the case of normal flotations, the interest rates were fixed, such a rise in interest rates should pose no problems. But in the case of a Euro-currency loan the developing country may have no idea of the future interest costs. Many of the Euro-currency loans are of the so-called 'roll-over' type. Under this arrangement the loan is calculated on the basis of the prevailing interest rates. In fact, the Euro-currency loans are effectively floating and the borrower may not be able to foresee the future interest cost. If the Euro-currency market slows down, the consequent interest rate increases can impose a heavy repayment burden on the developing countries. Those countries which are using the loans for financing infrastructure and long-term development projects would be especially hard hit. It is also noteworthy that the principal beneficiaries of the Euro-currency loans have been mineral-producing countries. Those which lack an attractive mineral resource, like Bangladesh, have had no access to this market and India has been able to raise only $10m, that being for its shipping lines which can earn hard currency.

This discussion of the recent role of the Euro-currency market illustrates the problems inherent in relying on portfolio capital flows for financing long-term development. These are, however, problems that need to be tackled by international action and an easing of restrictions in the developed countries on the purchase by institutional investors of bonds backed by developing countries.

Extent and Pattern of Foreign
Private Investment

As noted earlier, foreign direct investment accounts for nearly half of the private capital flows to the developing countries. Yet, in comparison with the other forms of capital flows, in recent years it has been the least dynamic element. This sluggishness is in part due to political factors. In addition, economic factors like the high risks associated with such flows, restrictions on outflows of capital from industrialised countries, administrative inefficiencies and the limited markets for manufactured goods in the developing countries, may also have contributed to the relatively slow growth of private investment.

It is also evident from the available data that since the mid-1950s private investment flows among the developed countries have been substantially higher than such flows to developing countries. In 1956–7 private investment flows to the developing countries averaged $2,500m. In 1970–1 these flows averaged $3,800m. Over the same period such flows among the developed countries are estimated to have trebled. At the end of 1968 the total book value of foreign private investment in the developing countries stood at $33,000m. This represents around a third of the total stock of foreign private investment in the world.

The developing countries in the Western Hemisphere accounted for around 56 per cent of the total stock of foreign private investment in the developing world at the end of 1967. Within this region, the South American countries accounted for 36 per cent of the total and the Central American countries for 19 per cent. The African countries had around a 20 per cent share in the total while the share of Middle East and Asian countries were 9·4 and 15·1 per cent respectively.

The sectoral distribution of foreign private investment shows that it is heavily concentrated in the petroleum industry and in the manufacturing sector. Nearly 33 per cent of the total investment in developing countries was in petroleum, whereas only 28 per cent of total investment in the developed countries was in this sector. Manufacturing accounted for around 29 per cent, followed by mining with an 11 per cent share and agriculture with a 6·2 per cent share. Public utilities and the services sector accounted for the rest. In general, the relative importance of private investment in petroleum and manufacturing has been increasing and the share of primary sectors, the traditional stronghold of private investment, has been declining. This change in the pattern of foreign private investment in the developing countries is partly a reflection of the reduced profitability of investment in primary products. Perhaps more important may be the xenophobic attitude of developing countries towards foreign private investment in industries based on natural resources. The reduced attraction of such industries for the foreign investor may in large part explain the sluggish growth of private investment in the developing countries.

This broad pattern, however, conceals the variation in private investment between different sectors in the major regions of the developing world. Table 8.2 shows the sectoral distribution of direct investment in the different regions.

Petroleum accounts for 90 per cent of the total foreign private investment in the Middle East and for 39 per cent in Africa. Investment in manufacturing predominates in Asia and the Western Hemisphere. The relatively high share of investment in agriculture in Asia is accounted for by foreign investment in rubber plantations in Malaysia and tea plantations in India.

Another significant characteristic of foreign private investment in the developing regions is its concentration in a few countries in each of the major regions. Only a few countries have a stock of direct

Table 8.2

Sectoral Distribution of Stock of Private Investment in the Developing Regions, 1967

	Africa		Western Hemisphere		Asia		Middle East	
	$m	%	$m	%	$m	%	$m	%
Petroleum	2,597·6	39·4	4,485·5	24·3	1,102·3	22·1	2,776·4	89·5
Manufacturing	1,236·4	18·8	6,652·7	36·1	1,547·7	31·0	190·3	6·1
Mining	1,279·8	19·4	2,016·1	10·9	252·5	5·1	6·0	0·2
Trade	398·2	6·0	1,668·3	9·0	504·4	10·1	30·0	1·0
Agriculture	496·8	7·5	607·4	3.3	939·1	18·8	2·5	0·1
Public Utilities	66·3	1·0	1,370·7	7·4	123·0	2·4	10·5	0·3
Others	516·1	8·9	1,648·6	9·0	522·5	10·5	87·0	2·8
Total	6,591·1	100·0	18,449·3	100·0	4,991·5	100·0	3,102·7	100·0

Source: *Multinational Corporations in World Development* (New York: United Nations, 1973) p. 177.

investment in excess of $1,000m. Principal host countries in the Western Hemisphere are Argentina, Brazil, Mexico and Venezuela. In Asia it is Malaysia, the Philippines and India that have attracted substantial amounts of foreign private investment.

The facts and figures show the broad pattern and distribution of foreign private investment in the developing countries. In absolute terms the stock of private investment in the developing countries is not very high. However, the developing countries in 1967 accounted for only one-sixth of world gross domestic product and one-fifth of world exports. Relative to these figures a one-third share in the world stock of private investment is of great significance to these countries. Further, it is estimated that the contribution of foreign enterprises to the total product of the developing countries was around 6 per cent in 1970, compared with a figure of 4 per cent for the developed countries. Its contribution to net domestic capital formation in the developing countries is estimated to have been around 8 per cent.[7]

While the foregoing provides a general perspective on foreign private investment in the developing countries it does not provide an adequate basis for assessing the economic impact. For one thing the subject is clouded by political considerations which evoke strong emotional reactions. For another, much of its impact is in the nature of imponderables not amenable to quantification. It could, for instance, be argued that the fact that foreign enterprises contributed 6 per cent to the total output of developing countries is a gross underestimate. It leaves out of the reckoning a major characteristic of direct investment – its contribution in terms of technology and skills. It could, however, be argued with equal vehemence that the costs of foreign private investment in terms of the control it exercises, the balance of payments burden it imposes and the distortions it introduces outweigh its benefits. It would, indeed, be difficult to counter the view that these countries could have done as well or even much better in the absence of such investment.

How is one to assess what these countries would have done in the absence of foreign private investment? Maybe local capital and enterprise would have entered the fields in which foreign enterprises are active. Maybe they would have imported the required technology under licensing agreements. As is often readily asked, did not Japan do so? Maybe it would have been better for these countries to do without, at least for the time being, many of the projects in which foreign private investment has occurred. These are all clearly presumptions – but presumptions which cannot be easily dismissed. It is therefore not surprising that developing countries worry both that foreigners will invest in them and that they won't; that they are chary of possible exploitation on the one hand and the loss of technology and capital on the other. The dilemma has provoked a growing body of literature on the subject, rich in controversy but, alas, poor in settled conclusions. These controversial issues will now be examined.

Case for Foreign Private Investment

The three-pronged benefits that the host countries are likely to experience from foreign private investment are the initial contribution it makes by way of additions to capital stock, the additional tax revenues it yields and, more importantly, the external effects it confers on the host economies by imparting technical and managerial skills and linkage effects. The essence of the theoretical case for this kind of investment rests on demonstrating that its contribution to the real national income of the country is likely to be greater than the gains appropriated by the foreign investors.

A theoretical demonstration of the benefits of foreign private investment was first provided by G. D. A. MacDougall in his celebrated article on the 'Costs and Benefits of Private Investment from Abroad'.[8] As is true of all idealised theoretical models, Dr MacDougall's exposition also rests on certain restrictive assumptions. The model assumes that there are only two factors of production – capital and labour, that the market structure is characterised by perfect competition and that each factor is paid its marginal product, that is the addition to total product resulting from a unit increment of the factor. Given these assumptions, it is demonstrated that inflows of foreign capital increase total output and augment labour's share of the output and that the host government gains by way of increased tax revenues. Figure 8.1 illustrates the argument. The line GF in Figure 8.1 relates the physical capital stock to the marginal physical product of capital. It is downward-sloping, indicating that as the physical stock of capital increases the marginal physical product of capital declines. Assume that initially the total capital stock of the country is AB. Since it is assumed that profits per unit of capital equal the marginal physical product of capital, total profits accruing to domestic capital are $ABCD$. Total output is $GCBA$ and labour's share of the output is GCD. Now allow for an inflow of foreign capital of the amount BE. The capital stock increases to AE and total profits are now $AEFH$. Total output is $GFEA$ and labour's share is GFH.

When compared to the position before the inflow of foreign capital, labour's share has increased and that of capital has declined. Domestic capital now earns $ABJH$ and foreign capital $JFEB$.

Labour's share has increased partly owing to an increase in labour productivity resulting from the additions to capital stock and partly owing to a redistribution of income from the domestic capitalists to labour. This redistribution occurs because of the decline in the marginal physical product of capital following the addition of foreign capital. The essential point, however, is that inflows of foreign capital augment labour productivity and increase the total output. Furthermore, additional income of the amount of *JCF* accrues to the host country and, more importantly, profits accruing to the foreigners can be taxed.

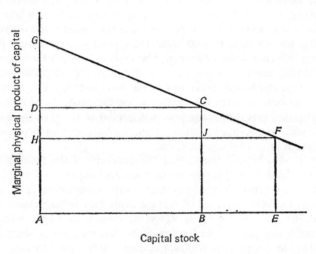

Fig. 8.1

The analysis so far has assumed that the total labour force is fixed. But with the additions to the capital stock, more labour can be employed. This may be a distinct gain to heavily populated countries suffering from unemployment and underemployment. If employment opportunities in the industrialised sector are constrained by a lack of capital, inflows of foreign private capital may permit the transfer of under-employed labour from the rural to the urban areas. This would be a clear national gain, as the newly employed labour, whose marginal product may have been near to zero in their previous occupation, would be contributing positively to the economy. This would be a net gain to the society in the sense that the newly employed labour would be earning a wage rate higher than its marginal product in its alternative occupation; presumably the agricultural sector.

Dr MacDougall's theoretical analysis also emphasises the gains to be had in the form of external effects of foreign private investment. This is a recurring theme in the literature on foreign investment and merits elaboration. Benefits that accrue to the host economy from the operation of foreign firms which they themselves cannot capture in the form of higher profits are the external effects. Important among such benefits are manpower training and productivity gains to the rest of the economy. To be strictly regarded as an externality, the training imparted to the labour force by the foreign firms must be free of cost to the labourers, and it must be available to the rest of the economy. If either the labourers pay for their training by accepting a lower wage rate than they could earn elsewhere over the duration of the training period, or if the foreign firms invest in training just enough to maximise their profits, there would be no external effects on the economy. The extent to which these benefits of training accrue to the rest of the economy depends on the mobility of the labour force out of the foreign firms. The degree of labour mobility in turn would depend on the existence of a number of domestic firms producing products similar to those of the foreign firms, and on the applicability of the techniques and processes of the foreign firms to domestic firms.

It can also benefit the rest of the economy if the foreign firms take the lead in imparting production techniques and marketing expertise to firms that supply them with components and parts. Further, the very presence of foreign firms may induce competition by encouraging new firms to enter the market in a bid to capture the profits enjoyed by the foreign firms, and may also induce existing firms to adopt new techniques and production processes. The resulting competition might also result in lower prices to the consumers. The extent to which these benefits accrue to the host economy clearly depends on the degree of effective competition that can be fostered.

Finally, foreign private investment can also have a positive impact on the balance of payments. Apart from the initial flows of foreign exchange which are contributed, the operations of foreign firms may lead to increased exports and reduced imports. In addition, they might indirectly contribute to export promotion because of their linkage and external effects. On the import side, operations of foreign firms in import substitution industries may curtail imports. Thus the contribution of foreign private investment arises not only from its capital contribution but also from all the additional sales made possible by such investment.

It is also possible that an inflow of foreign private capital may have a favourable impact on the terms of trade of the host country.

If the country's imports are capital-intensive in nature, an inflow of foreign capital used for setting up import-competing industries at home would tend to lower the price of imports. However, if foreign capital flows into capital-intensive export industries it may worsen the terms of trade by lowering export prices. It is, however, difficult to arrive at an unambiguous judgement on the effects of foreign capital inflows on the terms of trade. It depends on the type of industries in which foreign investment takes place, the elasticity of foreign supply of imports and demand for exports, its effects on the distribution of income and the propensities to consume imported goods and exportables on the part of the community. Furthermore, it is possible that even if the relative price of exports to that of imports fell as a result of foreign capital inflows, the import purchasing power of exports (income terms of trade) may improve because of the increase in the volume of exports.

Case Against Foreign Private Investment

The case against foreign private investment is usually an amalgam of both economic and non-economic arguments. A distinction, however, needs to be made between the economic and non-economic arguments, as often opposition to foreign investment based on non-economic grounds is justified on economic grounds. Opposition to foreign investment on non-economic grounds may have its merits. But attempts at justifying such opposition on economic grounds only confuses the issue. If national independence is judged to be worth more than the income sacrificed by barring foreign enterprise the economist has little to say on the matter. But if it is argued that foreign investment itself results in a sacrifice of income or economic welfare, the basis for the argument needs to be examined. The argument that foreign investment results in a reduction of competition and engenders monopolies is a case in point. If there is a genuine concern regarding the pernicious effects of monopolies, the policy maker needs to be wary of both foreign and domestic monopolies. If foreign investment is excluded on monopoly grounds but domestic firms are allowed to enjoy monopoly profits, then clearly the opposition to foreign firms springs from a dislike of foreign firms and not monopolies as such.

This is not to say that there are no genuine economic arguments against foreign investment. The two most controversial economic arguments relate to the effects of foreign private investment on the host country's balance of payments and the distortions it introduces into the host economy.

Balance-of-payments Issue

Evaluating the effects of foreign private investment on the balance of payments of the host countries is a complex task. It involves taking into account both its direct and indirect effects on trade flows. In addition to its initial capital contribution it may directly generate imports and exports. To these direct effects must be added its indirect effects on the trade balance which may be positive or negative depending on whether, on balance, they induce more exports or imports.

Empirical studies which have attempted to take account of all these factors are not lacking. But they are inconclusive and their estimates are strongly influenced by the assumptions they make. In Latin America, for instance, in the year 1966 American foreign subsidiaries exported $4,500m worth of their products and imported $1,300m worth of materials and components. Could it, therefore, be argued that on balance the trade effects of foreign private investment have been beneficial to Latin America? Such a conclusion would be valid only on the assumption that such exports and imports would not have occurred but for this investment. Indeed, basic to the whole issue is the question of whether the production of foreign firms is additional to what is being already produced or whether it is merely a replacement of local output.

The question itself is unanswerable. However, the balance-of-payments impact of foreign private investment has been assessed using models with differing assumptions. The estimated results vary depending on the assumptions made. A study based on the assumption that the production of foreign enterprises was a net addition and no local replacement was possible concluded that foreign private investment had a positive impact on the balance of payments of developing countries. Estimates based on the assumption that local replacement was possible indicated that its impact was negative in the case of Latin America, and neutral for other developing countries.[9] Case studies for India, Iran, Kenya, Colombia and Malaysia made under the auspices of UNCTAD are equally inconclusive about the effects of foreign private investment on the balance of payments of these countries.[10]

The advocates of foreign private investment can take refuge in agnosticism on the issue of its balance-of-payments effects. They could indeed argue that until and unless a full-scale statistical investigation is possible the presumption should be that its effects are either positive or neutral. The critics, however, argue that there is one piece of statistical evidence which shows that foreign investors take out more foreign exchange than they put into these countries.

There is enough evidence for a number of countries and years to show that the outflows of foreign exchange in the form of dividends, profits and royalties on accumulated foreign investment far exceed fresh inflows of foreign capital. Data presented by the United Nations for selected developing countries show that over the six-year period from 1965 to 1970 the annual average inflows of foreign private capital were around $1,355m. Over the same period outflows of income on past investments averaged around $4,496m per year.[11]

Refuting the above thesis has been a favourite pastime of the advocates of foreign private investment. The counter-argument centres on the thesis that the inflow–outflow comparison is too partial in its approach to the issue. In other words, it neglects all the direct and indirect export-generating and import-saving effects of foreign private investment, besides failing to take into account the reinvestment of profits by foreign firms and the technology and skills they impart.[12]

The inflow–outflow comparison approach can be dismissed as unsatisfactory on theoretical grounds alone. It is to be recognised that the balance of payments is a general equilibrium concept. In other words, the problem of balance of payments is an integral part of the total economy. Any positive contribution to the total productivity of the economy *pari passu* improves the balance of payments in the absence of diseconomies and other distortions. Thus C. P. Kindleberger of the Massachusetts Institute of Technology argues that the two sums – the debt service payments and the capital inflows – have nothing to do with one another except in a narrow balance-of-payments context.[13] It is neither inevitable that debt servicing must be made out of new capital inflows nor is it necessary for foreign investors to keep reinvesting their profits. In so far as each act of investment has been productive and contributes to total productivity the problem of debt servicing is taken care of. The problem arises only when past investments have been unproductive or resources have been misallocated, resulting in a loss of production.

That the balance of payments is a general equilibrium phenomenon and is an integral part of the total economy is irrefutable. The advocates of the debt service–fresh capital inflow approach do not deny it. Indeed, they would argue that because it is a general equilibrium phenomenon any significant distortions and diseconomies caused by foreign private investment may have adverse effects on the balance of payments. Further, if the indirect effects of foreign private investment are absent or negative, then the debt service–capital inflow approach, though admittedly crude, may suffice. Paul

Streeten, of Oxford, expresses qualified approval of the debt service –fresh capital inflow approach to an appraisal of the balance-of-payments effect of foreign private investment; this approval appears to rest on the above contention.[14]

Could the distortions and diseconomies following FPI be significant and the much-vaunted indirect effects be weak or negative? It could be negative if FPI either displaces previously employed resources or draws resources away from sectors which were contributing to foreign exchange earnings. It could be argued that even if the investment replaces domestic investment it need not necessarily reduce exchange earnings. It may generate foreign exchange. But, as Mr Streeten argues, the economics of foreign private investment are not the same as the economics of domestic investment. Money crosses the exchanges in the case of FPI, but not in the case of domestic investment. It is in this way that FPI which replaces domestic investment adversely affects the balance of payments. Indeed, empirical studies based on this assumption, referred to earlier, show that this is so.

Is it, however, realistic to assume that FPI would replace previously employed resources in the face of the widespread unemployment prevailing in the developing countries? The assumption of full employment is not strictly necessary to show such a possibility. All that we need to deny is the existence of a Keynesian type of unemployment which would respond to increases in demand. The type of domestic resources which FPI attracts from other sectors may be skilled labour and certain types of raw materials in short supply. If FPI draws away such resources from other sectors it merely replaces an existing investment. If it caters for demand previously met by domestic sectors it displaces domestic investment, resulting in unemployed resources. If these sectors were generating or saving foreign exchange, the introduction of FPI would result in a loss of foreign exchange. It would be so because of the point made earlier that FPI differs from domestic investment in that money crosses the exchanges in the case of the former.

It might appear as though we are playing devil's advocate by indulging in extensive discussion of a position which has so often been criticised. But the devil must have his due. Mr Streeten's thesis does point to the need for weighing the alternatives to FPI in assessing its balance-of-payments effects. The alternative discussed above is domestic investment. It could be readily pointed out that domestic investment in an important sense is not the same as FPI. It may lack the technology and skills that characterise FPI. But Mr Streeten lists the following six alternatives, three of which provide for the importation of foreign technology.[15]

1. Produce the product domestically with domestic capital and resources.
2. Borrow capital from abroad, hire foreign managers and engineers and buy foreign technology through a licensing agreement.
3. Any partial combination of 1 and 2, including management contracts.
4. Joint ventures between foreign investors and local public or private capital.
5. Import the finished product.
6. Do without the product for the time being.

In considering each of these alternatives their net foreign exchange benefits as against those of FPI need to be evaluated. A method of appraising these alternatives has been suggested by another Oxford economist, I. M. D. Little.[16] It is worth pausing to review Professor Little's method if only to show that even this supposedly scientific scheme cannot cope with all the complexities posed by foreign private investment.

The procedure to be adopted in assessing the impact of FPI is to evaluate the benefits and costs of a project assuming that it is domestically financed and then add or subtract foreign financing flows to give the benefits of the project after allowing for foreign financing. The now famous Little-Mirlees *Manual* approach (LM approach) to cost-benefit analysis provides a method whereby the estimation of the benefits and costs of a project implicitly takes into account the balance of payments effects of the project. In the LM approach all material inputs and outputs of the project are evaluated in terms of foreign exchange. In other words, the price imputed to these inputs would be the c.i.f. price of imports if they are importables or the f.o.b. export price if they are exportables. The justification for such a procedure is that international prices represent, through trade and balance of payments, the true social opportunity costs of inputs and outputs in production.

But what if some of the inputs and outputs are non-tradeables? Most goods are tradeable and non-tradeables will be few, like inputs of construction, power, transport and other services. In any case, even the non-tradeables would have traded components in their input structure. Therefore the non-tradeables are to be iteratively broken down into traded and non-traded inputs until one is left only with the traded goods and labour. All traded components of non-traded inputs are valued in their foreign exchange terms as suggested.

How to value labour? In the LM method it is to be valued at its shadow wage rate, meaning its opportunity cost or marginal product in an alternative project. This marginal product is again to be valued in terms of foreign exchange. This will be the employment effect of the project on the balance of payments. In addition, employment of labour in the project may also have a consumption effect on the balance of payments. This is because increased employment may result in increased consumption and worsen the balance of payments. In this case the increased value of consumption in foreign exchange terms has to be deducted from the value added of the project in arriving at its balance of payments.

In essence the LM approach is to value all material inputs and outputs in foreign prices and evaluate non-material inputs in terms of their marginal products valued in foreign exchange terms. The balance-of-payments effect of the project would be the value added of the project (already estimated in foreign exchange terms), minus the production and consumption effect of labour employed on the balance of payments. Now if the project is to be compared with a foreign private investment project, all that needs to be done is to add or subtract the foreign financing flows to give the net benefits after allowing for foreign financing. If the introduction of foreign financing reduces the benefit of the project then clearly FPI is not to be considered.

Mr Streeten's contention that the 'important point for analysis and policy is to envisage the various alternatives, against which any operational assessment has to be made and to assess the benefits and costs of each, measuring what is measurable and judging what is not',[17] can be catered for to a large extent by project evaluation. It permits a net assessment of the benefits of a project, be it foreign or domestic, along with its balance-of-payments effects.

It should, however, be borne in mind that the benefit-cost analysis is only a means to an end. It provides a means of operationally assessing the net benefits of a project compared with its alternatives. The project analysis might well suggest that the net benefits of an FPI project are much less than an alternative arrangement. There is, however, room for subjective considerations to creep into the assessment, and there are problems in judging what is not measurable. Subjective elements enter into the assessment principally in the valuation of labour. It is rightly argued that labour should be valued at its social opportunity cost and not at the market wage rate, as the latter is usually in excess of the former. But how is the shadow wage rate (the social opportunity cost of labour) to be arrived at? Should it be set equal to the marginal product of labour in its alternative occupation, say, agriculture, or should it be valued at the extra consumption cost that increased employment would result in?

If one is intending to maximise the balance-of-payments effect or savings of the project, the latter option would be the one to choose. In this case what is being maximised is the net value added of the project minus the extra consumption incurred by the increased employment. Only those projects where this figure is high will be chosen and these would invariably be capital-intensive projects. If the intention is to maximise current consumption and employment, the shadow wage is set equal to labour's alternative marginal product and the extra consumption costs are ignored.[18] This is only to show that even if project analysis is resorted to, subjective considerations cannot be avoided. Although an FPI project may have a net positive balance-of-payments effect compared to its alternative it may have a negative effect on employment.

This discussion of the balance-of-payments issue points to a need for case studies such as those initiated by UNCTAD. The balance of payments effects of FPI differ from case to case: the crucial need is to assess the alternatives. Cost-benefit analysis provides a method for doing so. Even then, we may be left with a hard choice between the objectives of maximising employment and maximising the balance of payments. But is it an inevitable dilemma? Is there no scope for utilising FPI in both employment creation and export promotion?

Employment Effects of Foreign Private Investment

We have already referred to the opposing positions taken on this issue in discussing the broad case for and against FPI. Its advocates argue that foreign capital flows are likely to absorb domestic labour especially when employment prospects are constrained by a shortage of labour. The opponents' argument, that FPI may be a mere substitute for existing investment and employment instead of being a net addition to it, has also been referred to earlier.

The more often voiced criticism, however, relates to the capital-intensity of the operations of foreign firms and the wage policies they pursue. Foreign firms transplant techniques perfected abroad. These are techniques designed for capital-rich and labour-poor economies and are ill-suited to capital-poor and labour-rich developing countries. In addition, FPI is likely to endanger employment opportunities in other sectors of the economy which may tend to imitate such techniques. Such imitation may be due to a xenophilic preference for foreign technology, or the forcing of local firms to adopt such techniques in order to survive in a competitive milieu. Foreign firms generally tend to pay relatively high wage rates. Such a wage policy may be dictated both by a need for skilled labour and by a desire to appease local national and trade union sentiments against their operations. Such policies may result in an increase in the wage rates in the economy in general, forcing domestic firms to substitute capital for labour.

These issues bear closer examination. The employment effects of FPI differ depending on the nature of the project and the type of investment. Moreover, it is necessary to distinguish between adverse employment effects stemming from the 'foreignness' of the project and effects stemming from the trade and resource allocation policies pursued by the developing countries.

To an extent the claim that foreign private investment tends to be capital-intensive in its operations may be valid. However much some of the foreign investors assert that they are not altogether insensitive to the development needs of the countries in which they operate, it would be too much to expect profit-maximising, cost-minimising entrepreneurs to experiment with new technologies. As the Development Assistance Committee of the OECD puts it, for most of the foreign investors the path of least resistance lies in duplicating developed country systems of manufacture or construction, the result of decades of innovation, for the purpose of substituting more and more intricate, automatic and hard-to-maintain capital equipment for more and more expensive labour.[19] The foreign firms' reluctance to experiment with technologies and products appropriate to the factor endowments, income levels and local conditions of the developing countries may be entirely rational on economic grounds. It is less expensive to transfer abroad a tested and tried technique than invest in a new technique. Moreover, no two developing countries are alike in terms of their resource endowments and socioeconomic characteristics. The foreign firms may be hard put to design differing techniques to suit the differing economic climates in which they operate.

It is, however, possible that the developing countries are no less to blame for the capital-intensive nature of the foreign firms' operations. First, most of the developing countries with their excessive enthusiasm for industrialisation have encouraged foreign firms to invest in capital-intensive manufacturing activities. Secondly, many of the incentives offered to foreign investors by the developing countries tend to encourage capital investment by artificially reducing the cost of such investment. Generous depreciation allowances, lower tax rates for designated industries, tax holidays for new and 'priority' industries and concessionary tariff rates on imports of machinery and equipment are some of the incentives that encourage capital investment. Furthermore, the over-valued exchange rates that most developing countries maintain also favour the importation of capital equipment. All this in essence amounts to granting a subsidy on the use of capital to the foreign firms. Such policies may have on the one hand encouraged further employment of capital in what are already capital-intensive industries, and on the other directed foreign private investment towards the relatively capital-intensive types of activity. Therefore the onus of utilising foreign private investment to encourage employment creation, according to this line of reasoning, rests largely on the developing countries themselves. This they could do by subsidising the employment of labour instead of capital. Further, they could attempt to encourage FPI into labour-intensive sectors of activity.

All this would, however, require considerable changes in the trade and industrialisation policies adopted by most developing countries. Apart from allowing the market prices to reflect the internal scarcities of capital and labour, they may have to relinquish the import–substitution syndrome and actively encourage exports. This would, in essence, mean abandoning the heavily protectionist policies which have tended to encourage foreign firms to enter into capital-intensive industries catering for domestic markets. Without the tariffs and quotas the local markets of the developing countries for capital-intensive manufactures would turn out to be less attractive to the foreign firms. This would, no doubt, run down the amount of foreign private investment that some of the developing countries have been attracting into these industries. But as against this the foreign firms would be encouraged to enter into labour-intensive export-oriented manufactured goods, especially in the presence of a labour subsidy. Of course, the granting of a labour subsidy would to an extent reduce one of the often-preferred benefits of foreign private investment; the excess of the wage rate over the social opportunity cost of labour paid by the foreign firms. Further, care may have to be taken to see that the provision of the subsidy does not result in higher wages. But this could be taken care of by giving a subsidy per man employed and not as a percentage of the wage bill.[20] In any case, the labour subsidy would be an incentive in place of that offered by protectionist policies and foreign private investment would be encouraged to go into export-oriented industries.

The so-called Hong Kong–Puerto Rico type of FPI illustrates the scope for utilising such investment to promote employment and exports. In Hong Kong, South Korea, Taiwan and Singapore, FPI has been utilised to build factories using the abundant supply of cheap labour, and the output is sold in the Western markets through the marketing channels of the foreign investors. Increasingly popular has been a variant of this type of investment, where foreign firms produce labour-intensive components in the host countries but the production of other parts and the assembly of the final product take place in the home countries of the investors. The electronics industry is reported to be in the lead in this form of activity.

Foreign firms are increasingly finding it advantageous to use some of the developing countries as export bases. Such a form of investment is pronounced in the case of Singapore, some examples being investment by the Japanese firm Matsushita in compressors to be incorporated in refrigerators produced abroad, Union Carbide's investment in the production of electrodes to be supplied to their battery-making plants elsewhere, and the investment by the Dutch firm, Philips of Eindhoven, to produce micro-electronic components to be exported back to Holland.[21] These types of high-value-added, low-transport-cost activity have obvious appeal in terms of their employment and export potential.

This type of export-oriented investment appears to provide a means by which the developing countries can participate in the world-wide division of labour in the production of technology-intensive products by the international firms. However, neither the success stories of some of the South Asian countries nor the theoretical attractiveness of this type of investment should divert attention from the preconditions necessary for its success. The characteristic of this type of investment is a combination of foreign technology and cheap domestic labour in the production for the export market.

The cheap domestic labour has to have a certain degree of basic skill to assimilate and utilise the foreign technology. This calls for investment in labour training and education both on the part of the foreign firms and the developing countries. Labour subsidies may have to be granted principally for training labour. Singapore for instance is reported to have set aside $100m, to be managed by her Development Bank, for providing intensive training to enable workers to meet the high standards required by incoming high-technology industries.[22] This type of investment also requires that the developing countries should be able to provide the right 'climate' for FPI by developing the necessary infrastructure and trading conditions. Further, some of the countries which have been successful in attracting this type of investment may be endowed with certain special features not to be found in developing countries in general. Singapore, for instance, is strategically situated in South Asia and the resilience of the Chinese labour force in most of the South Asian countries cited is well known. It is also to be noted that Hong Kong, Singapore and Taiwan all have strong political ties with the West and are strongly oriented towards the development of private enterprise.

Despite all the economic advantages of such investment, political and nationalist sentiments have to be reckoned with. The developing countries may not want to be relegated to the role of component and spare part manufacturers for the international companies. Singapore itself is reported to be becoming selective in the type of investment it wants. 'We no longer want nut and bolt operations industry for its own sake, we want something with a future, like radios now and televisions and computers later, something that needs a balance of operating skills.' This comment of one of the officials of the Singapore Economic Development Board sums up the changing attitude towards such investment. However, in spite of all these qualifications, a policy of subsidising labour and attracting FPI into export industries appears to provide one way out of the dilemma posed by the capital-intensity of FPI.

Employment Potential of FPI in Natural Resource-based Industries

It would be fallacious to conclude from the foregoing that foreign private investment in all export-oriented industries is necessarily employment-generating. Although FPI in agro-based and extractive industries also tends to be heavily export-oriented, the employment potential of such investment may not be very high. The plantation industries and extractive industries present a contrasting picture in this context. Plantation industries like tea, coffee, tobacco and sisal are relatively labour-intensive and require less capital equipment and material inputs.

Mineral-based extractive industries not only tend to be relatively capital-intensive but also offer more scope for mechanical innovations.[23] Rapid advances have occurred in mining technology resulting in widespread displacement of labour by machinery. A case in point is the innovation made in drilling equipment in the Zambian copper-mining industry. Around 1950 the forged steel-tipped drill with a drilling life of 42 inches was replaced by the tungsten carbide-tipped drill with a mining life of 35 feet. This innovation not only resulted in an increase in underground productivity but also cut the size of the European miner's gang of African workers from sixteen to twelve.[24] The scope for such mechanical innovations in plantation industries may not be very high. It is difficult to foresee the annual plucking of two leaves and a bud in the tea industry being replaced by mechanical devices.

The indirect employment-generating effects are also likely to be greater in the case of plantation industries than in the case of extractive industries. Such indirect effects arise from the input demand and outlays made by productive agents in these industries. A high proportion of the outlays made by plantation industries is likely to generate demand internally in the host economies. Because of the labour-intensive nature of these industries there would be a substantial amount of demand for food and other basic consumer goods. Further, these industries may also give rise to employment in the industries processing and packing the plantation products. In the case of mineral industries, however, such effects may be limited. Because of the relatively capital-intensive nature of their operations much of the income generated will accrue to profit-earners and skilled labour. To the extent that profits are repatriated abroad and the consumption pattern of skilled workers, most of whom may be expatriates, is foreign-oriented, very little effect on demand is likely to be felt internally.

Although the employment-generating effects of the mineral industries may not be very high, they are likely to have a much more favourable impact on the creation of labour skills. Because of the capital-intensive nature of their operations their demand for skilled labour is likely to be high. The returns to investment in labour training for the foreign firms could, therefore, be considerable. However, such benefits would tend to be confined to a small section of the population with little spread effects.

A study of the copper-mining industry in what was then Northern Rhodesia for the period 1920–60 by an American economist, Robert Baldwin, amply illustrates the foregoing observations.[25] Because of the nature of the production process characterising the copper-mining industry, the direct employment and skill-generating effects of FPI on African labour were comparatively slight, as were the repercussions of cash-spending by the workers. A large part of the capital needs of the industry consisted of complex machinery whose production in turn required skilled labour and complicated capital goods. A large proportion of these items had to be imported. There were, however, some important demand effects set off by the needs of the copper industry for non-labour inputs. These related to demand for transport services and electricity. Although such demands permitted industrial growth in these sectors their employment effects were not very high.

What then should be the policy of developing countries towards FPI in extractive industries? Discussion of FPI in such industries easily arouses passions. The colonial experience of these countries with such investment has given rise to various fears of exploitation and prejudices. Exploitation of natural resources in the physical sense is often equated with exploitation in the economic sense. It is then argued that it is not in the nation's economic interest to allow foreigners to exploit its natural resources. But Professor Myint, of the London School of Economics, argues that the only meaningful way of defining a nation's economic interest is in terms of its economic gains and losses affecting the size of its national income and the rate of its economic growth.[26] National economic interest requires that highest economic gains be procured by exploiting the resource endowments of the country by whichever form of economic organisation does it best. If foreign investment and management are technically more efficient in exploiting such resources, the rational course of action would be to allow them to do so and protect the national economic interest by charging them the full economic rent.

Charging a full economic rent implies levying the maximum possible taxes on the incomes of the foreign enterprises and fixing appropriate royalties for the use of the nation's irreproducible natural resources. The height of such taxes and royalties would, of course, depend on the type of resources with which the country is endowed. The general point, however, is that it would be injudicious of the developing countries to try to impose conditions on the use of local labour and labour welfare on the foreign firms. Instead they should attempt to transfer the maximum possible income direct from the foreign firms to the national economy.

In most extractive industries factor proportions are fairly rigid and there may not be much scope for adopting labour-intensive methods of production. Moreover, imposing conditions on the use of labour and labour welfare on the foreign firms may even prove detrimental to the development effort. Indeed foreign firms may only be too willing to pay high wage rates, introduce shorter working hours and adopt extensive social welfare services. It promotes better labour relations, begets a dedicated labour force and strengthens the position of foreign firms in bargaining for tax concessions. But such policies may benefit only a small section of the labour force, breed a labour aristocracy and aggravate social inequalities in the economy. Further, the foreign firms may absorb the high wage costs by raising the prices of the products they produce. These may be transmitted to the rest of the economy resulting in a general rise in the price level. Thus, 'it is not sensible to transfer income by attempting to transform the MPE [multinational producing enterprise] from what it is – a profit-seeking animal – into something it is not – a public service.'[27]

There are, however, problems in adopting direct methods of income transfer. Some of these are inherent in the nature of the problem and some stem from the unhealthy competition between the developing countries for foreign capital. In their bid to attract foreign private investment many of the developing countries vie with each other in offering tax holidays, concessions and generous depreciation allowances to foreign firms. Such action only results in their unnecessarily giving away income to the foreigners. In this context many economists have long urged a common code of action on the part of the developing countries. One of the radical solutions proposed in this context is that international firms should be incorporated under international law and be subjected to a single international income tax.[28] Such a solution would eliminate problems arising from differing tax structures and the granting of competitive tax concessions.

There are also problems inherent in taxing the foreign firms. They are more often than not better placed than local firms to avoid fiscal levies. Over-statement of the book value of capital in a bid to earn higher depreciation allowances, under-statement of the rates of return earned on capital and, more important, charging prices much above the ruling market prices for components and equipment imported from the parent firms – these are some of the expedients available for avoiding the tax net. These are again problems which may be amenable to international action. Discussion of this issue will be continued in the next section.

The conclusions of this section of the argument are:

1. Although FPI may be relatively capital-intensive the policies of the developing countries may have not only encouraged it to move into capital-intensive sectors of activity but also provided incentives for the substitution of capital for labour. This is particularly so in the case of FPI in import-substitution industries.

2. FPI can be utilised to generate employment by adopting rational policies of resource allocation and labour subsidies, with the accent on export-intensive manufacturing industries. The Hong Kong–Puerto Rico type of FPI illustrates the success of such policies.

3. FPI in natural-resource-based industries is inevitably capital-intensive because of the production conditions that obtain in these industries, although plantations may be an exception. The judicious policy in the case of such investment is to adopt direct methods of income transfer from the foreign firms to the national economy rather than impose conditions on the use of labour or bar such investment altogether.

Monopolistic Exploitation

The argument that FPI entails monopolistic exploitation of the host countries has been a long-standing one. Indeed, all the other criticisms discussed thus far form a subset of this general theme. For instance, the argument regarding the adverse balance-of-payments effects of FPI used to be referred to as the suction pump thesis. FPI pumps out more from the economy in the form of dividends and profits than it puts in by way of fresh inflows of capital. The same argument has been presented in recent years in the form of the 'high profits' thesis. The profits made by foreign firms are reckoned to be high in the sense that the measured rates of return on their capital tend to be higher than those earned by comparable domestic firms.

The critics contend that the high profits earned by foreign firms *ipso facto* amount to monopolistic exploitation and a regressive transfer of wealth from the developing to the developed countries. It is further argued that reinvestment of such high profits may lead to the eventual domination and control of the economy by foreigners. If the rate of return on foreign capital exceeds the growth rate of national income, and if initially very little local capital exists, before long the entire domestic capital may be owned by foreigners. A variant of this proposition has come to be known as the 'Streeten Dilemma'. If fresh foreign capital inflows do not exceed the rate of return on past capital the country will be faced with a balance-of-payments problem; if it does grow at a faster rate and since the rate of return on existing capital is greater than that on domestic capital an increasing proportion of the country's capital stock will come to be owned by foreigners.[29]

This particular dilemma is easily disposed of by invoking the same kind of arguments that were invoked against the inflow-outflow approach to the balance-of-payments issue discussed earlier. Such arguments fail to take account of the indirect effects of FPI on trade, production and employment of the host countries. Further, they ignore the possibility that developing countries can take action through exchange rate variations and fiscal and monetary policies to redress the balance of payments. In addition they tend to ignore the fact that in the face of host countries' taxes on foreign profits, the profit rates earned by foreign firms would have to be substantially higher than those on domestic capital if they were to dominate the domestic economy.

But apart from the dramatic possibility of total foreign economic domination what is the theoretical and empirical rationale for the charge of monopolistic exploitation? Empirical evidence on comparable rates of return between foreign and local firms is hard to get. The only available evidence relates to rates of return on FPI in developed and developing countries. It is estimated that the average rate of return on book value of capital earned by American firms was 11 per cent (excluding petroleum) in developing countries and 9·6 per cent in developed countries. Comparable figures for Britain are put at 9·8 and 9·3 per cent respectively.[30] The figure of 11 per cent for American subsidiaries quoted above refers only to profits. If the royalties, rentals and service charges earned by foreign firms are included in the rate of return it goes up to 14 per cent.

These are aggregate figures. There could be wide variations in earnings between different countries and sectors in which FPI operates. These figures, however, do suggest that FPI in developing countries earns higher rates of return than in developed countries and that a total rate of return of 14 per cent could be substantially higher than that earned by domestic capital in these countries. But do these relatively higher rates of return prove monopolistic exploitation? Exploitation is an emotionally charged expression. Strictly interpreted, economic exploitation arises when the firms' profits are far in excess of what their contribution to the economy merits.

Whether or not the profits earned by foreign firms are high needs to be adjudged in terms of their contribution to the economies of the countries in which they operate. As has been repeatedly pointed out a major contribution of FPI is in terms of the technology and skills that it imparts to the host countries. It would be hard to counter the argument that the so-called 'high profits' earned by foreign firms are economically justified as representing a return on the scarce technology and skills these firms possess and as being a fair reward for risk-taking. The high profits they earn may thus represent a return on the past investment they have made in the production of knowledge, which does not appear on the firms' books as an addition to material capital.

Such a thesis, however, raises complex policy issues. Should not new knowledge be a free good to be utilised in furthering society's welfare instead of being a monopolistic preserve of the possessor of such knowledge? But if one takes such a stand it is difficult to see how the production of new knowledge can progress. Unless the producers of knowledge expect to make a private profit there would be no incentive for them to engage in such production. A way out of this dilemma is suggested by Harry Johnson. He advocates lump sum payments by the governments of the host countries to the knowledge-producers and the placing of this knowledge at the disposal of all firms in the economy.[31] In this context the suggestion that part of the official aid funds could be used to finance research by international corporations and scientific institutions for the production and dissemination of appropriate technologies to the developing countries merits consideration.

The above line of reasoning, though theoretically sound, may not provide a complete explanation of the difference in rates of return earned by foreign and domestic capital. Even conceding that FPI is technologically superior, why should it earn higher rates of return in developing as opposed to developed countries? It cannot be denied that there may be a monopoly element in the profits earned by foreign firms in the developing countries. The advocates of FPI would concede that much. But they would argue that such monopoly profits are a consequence of the trade and resource allocation policies pursued by the developing countries. It is not the 'foreignness' of FPI that is to blame for such high profits but the policies of developing countries that have facilitated the earning of monopoly profits by foreign firms.

High among the list of such policies are the tariffs and quotas imposed on imports and designed to facilitate industrialisation through import substitution. Such policies result in highly profitable domestic markets sheltered from international competition. The prevalence of such profitable markets provides a strong incentive for foreign firms to establish production facilities behind these tariff walls. Further, the industrial licensing and resource allocation policies pursued by many developing countries limit competition from domestic firms also, providing a monopolistic haven for foreign firms.[32]

It is clearly to the advantage of foreign firms to operate behind such tariff walls. Indeed, one of the advantages claimed in favour of protectionist policies is that they attract FPI. Even if this is so, it is not at all evident that FPI in import-substitution industries is socially beneficial to the host countries. In fact, there is enough evidence to argue the contrary. While such FPI may be highly profitable to the foreign firms it may be inefficient from the point of view of the host countries. Several instances have been cited in the cases of India, Pakistan and recently Brazil, where the operations of the foreign firms have resulted in 'negative value added'.[33] In other words, when the outputs and inputs of these firms were both valued at international prices the value of their inputs was found to be higher than that of their outputs. What this phenomenon reflects is that the investment was inefficient from the point of view of the host countries though profitable to the foreign firms. These countries would have been better off importing the final product than having it produced by foreign firms, or for that matter by domestic firms, operating behind tariff walls. The point to note, however, is that but for the protectionist policies of the developing countries, which enabled these firms to charge prices higher than the ruling international prices, their operations would not have been economically viable.

The protectionist policies of the developing countries thus result in a subsidisation of the foreign firms' activities by the host countries. This not only leads to a wasteful use of capital from the society's point of view but also imposes a balance-of-payments burden by committing the country to the payment of dividends and profits in foreign exchange. Clearly, in these cases, monopolistic exploitation exists. The onus of avoiding such exploitation, however, rests on the developing countries.

An additional source of worry in this context is the inability of most countries to regulate the transfer of additional profits by the foreign firms through their pricing policies. We have referred earlier to the practice of charging prices higher than the world market prices for inputs bought from the parent firms. Foreign firms may deliberately inflate the prices of the inputs they purchase not only to minimise tax payments but also avoid the odium attached to enjoying high monopoly profits and to forestall host country action designed to curb such profits. Such practices, whereby prices of inputs purchased by foreign affiliates from their parents are inflated, are known as transfer pricing.

Several examples of profit transfers through transfer pricing have been cited in case studies on FPI. For instance, one study estimates that intermediate inputs imported by foreign subsidiaries in the Colombian pharmaceutical industry were overpriced by 155 per cent, by 40 per cent in the rubber industry, by 26 per cent in the chemical industry and by 16 to 60 per cent in the electronics industry.[34]

Although it cannot be generalised from these cases that foreign firms systematically pursue a policy of transfer pricing, in certain cases profit transfers through this mechanism may be substantial. This is a problem which calls for effective enforcement of tax laws and policing of pricing policies. But few developing countries possess the high degree of expertise, the extensive information and the administrative personnel required. This is clearly an area for international action designed to curb such practices and to disseminate information to the developing countries.

Question of Control

One of the primary objections to FPI relates to the control that foreign firms exercise over operations. Nationalistic resentment of such control apart, there is the worry that the operations of foreign firms may conflict with domestic economic objectives. The advent of the international corporation has added new dimensions to this problem. Their ability to move resources from one country to another and the ease of their access to funds and information may thwart domestic monetary and fiscal policy objectives.

In addition, there is the concern that FPI may aggravate social and economic inequalities. Indeed, one writer has argued that foreign firms are able to earn high profits because of an unholy alliance that exists between foreign investors and the political power groups in the developing countries. These power groups, according to the writer, are shaped, nourished and sustained by foreign economic power, an external constituency whose interests coincide with the interests of indigenous ruling groups.[35]

It may be true that FPI confers significant benefits on a small section of businessmen and civil servants. It is not uncommon to find retired civil servants in many of the developing countries on the boards of directors of foreign firms. In return for the high salaries paid to these civil servants the foreign firms can expect a smooth passage in their dealings with the bureaucracy. To the extent that foreign firms raise equity capital on the domestic capital markets, the local élite who can afford to buy such equity may gain from the operations of the foreign firms. Profits to domestic firms participating in joint ventures may be paid in foreign exchange abroad, providing a convenient method for transferring funds overseas in the face of stiff exchange regulations.

No doubt there may be vested interest groups gaining from the operations of foreign firms. But to allege a conscious alliance between foreign firms and local élite groups appears to be too radical. Even if such unholy alliances do exist it is the internal political and income structure in the developing countries that is to be held responsible for such exploitation.

The problem of control, however, is a vexed one. It is a question of reconciling conflicting objectives – the desire to be independent of foreign control over decision making and ownership of productive assets on the one hand; and the desire to garner the benefits of technology, skills and capital that FPI provides, on the other.

The economist may argue that while the desire for economic independence is an understandable nationalist sentiment, it is non-economic. Nationalism has its costs. These costs are the income forgone by barring FPI. If nationalism and economic independence are of paramount importance these countries have to pay this cost. They cannot, however, hope to have the cake and eat it too.

Most developing countries, however, seem not to have been impressed by such cold logic. They have responded to the challenge posed by FPI by attempting to regulate it and by seeking out alternative channels of foreign enterprise and technical participation.

Response of the Developing Countries

Many developing countries have attempted to regulate FPI by restricting it to certain areas of activity, by insisting that foreign firms increasingly absorb local labour and capital by fixing ceilings on royalties and technical fees and by urging foreign firms to be export-oriented. They have at the same time attempted to attract FPI by offering tax concessions, guaranteeing repatriation of dividends and profits and by extending assurances regarding compensation in the event of nationalisation. The alternative channels they have sought out are joint ventures, technical collaboration agreements and management contracts. These have been defined earlier in this chapter.

Such regulations on FPI have been criticised as short-sighted second-best solutions. They amount to an interference with market forces and as such tend to lead to misallocation of resources and additional economic costs. For instance, most countries exclude FPI from industries producing luxury goods on the grounds that such products are socially undesirable. It is argued that this is a second-best solution. The best solution would involve changing the underlying income distribution by fiscal levies. It is the unequal income distribution that gives rise to demand for such goods in the first place. Similarly, the restriction that FPI must be export-oriented is criticised on the grounds that the balance of payments is a macro-economic phenomenon and as long as FPI adds to the productive capacity of the economy it is bound to improve the balance of payments. The stipulation requiring foreign firms to employ local personnel in managerial and supervisory positions can likewise be questioned. Such stipulations only result in inefficient operations in so far as local personnel of requisite calibre are not available.

No doubt many of the restrictions and regulations relating to FPI are second-best solutions. But often first best solutions may be possible only in theory. If the market fails to give the correct signals and the reasons for market failure are too deep-seated to be corrected speedily, second-best solutions may have to be adopted. Not all of the restrictions and regulations may be well thought out and judiciously designed. But this is no reason for urging total non-interference on the part of the developing countries.

Alternatives to Foreign Private Investment

Joint ventures and technical collaboration agreements are the currently fashionable alternatives to FPI. They are both recommended to and increasingly sought by developing countries. The main advantages claimed for such arrangements is that they do not involve foreign control. In the case of joint ventures neither of the two partners exercises complete control over operations. There is a commitment of resources by both partners. Further, by allowing domestic capital and managerial participation they provide for training effects.

Although joint ventures are attractive in theory they are fraught with practical problems. The main drawback of joint ventures is that instead of resulting in a harmonious blending of interests they may often lead to a conflict of interests between the partners. The foreign partner may be interested in the long-run growth of the enterprise, whereas the local partner may be interested in quick returns. Professor Kindleberger says, 'it may be difficult for the local investor to appreciate the profitability of the prospective enterprise, so that he would be unwilling to make his monetary contribution which accorded with the foreigner's view'.[36] Furthermore, when the contribution of one of the partners is in kind rather than in cash it may be difficult to evaluate his contribution properly in monetary terms.

A Reserve Bank of India study which analysed the reasons for the failure of proposals for joint ventures showed that in 36 of the 76 cases investigated non-acceptability of terms to either party was the major reason for failure.[37]

The absence of complete foreign control over operations may also be more apparent than real. The very fact that the foreign firm holds the reins over technology may enable it to exercise effective control over operations. It is possible that more often than not the foreign firm is the senior partner.

The shortcomings of technical collaboration agreements are even more pronounced. In essence they represent an attempt at taking the FPI package apart. The developing countries are urged to import the technology under such agreements, borrow the required foreign exchange for the project on international capital markets and raise the needed domestic finance on local capital markets. The supposed merits of this solution are that it eschews the most detested aspect of FPI – foreign control – and yet it begets foreign technology.

But both these suppositions are open to question. Capital investment is not always a necessary condition for control. Effective control is defined to mean the ability of the foreign firms to influence the future course of operations of the technology-importing firms. The foreign firms may be able to achieve this by controlling the sources of supply of materials and components, market outlets, production standards, and so on. A feature of the technical collaboration agreements is the restrictions on exports, sources of raw materials and pricing policies that foreign firms impose on the recipients of technology. Even if the governments of developing countries are able to restrict the imposition of formal controls in the agreements, the foreign firms may be able to enforce such restrictions under informal agreements with the recipient firms. Thus, even in the absence of capital ownership foreign firms may exercise effective control over operations.

Apart from the objection that the foreigners retain control, the viability of these agreements as technology transfer mechanisms is often in doubt. The absence of long-term interests of the kind involved in a direct investment venture may itself limit the commitments of the foreign firms. The gains to the foreign firms from a technical collaboration agreement are ephemeral. Once the project comes to fruition the agreement is likely to expire, resulting in the cessation of royalty and technical fee payments. Moreover, the acquisition of the knowledge by the recipient firms implies an erosion of monopolistic control over technology by the foreign firms. Hence the foreigners' willingness to transmit technology may be limited. This may be so even if they are transmitting knowledge which is to them obsolete but is not to the developing countries in view of the factor proportions that prevail there.

A possibly greater impediment to the success of these agreements is the inability of the recipient firms to make effective use of the imported knowledge. Much of the knowledge transmitted under these agreements is in the form of blueprints and designs. Utilisation of such knowledge requires 'human capital' on the part of the recipient firms, especially if the technology is to be restructured and tailored to local conditions. It also involves the availability of complementary factors at home including components and spare parts.

The often-quoted Japanese success story with regard to licensing agreements is relevant in this context. Japan's success with such agreements is largely due to the availability of human skills adept at imitation and restructuring of imported know-how, her ability to raise savings and her government's initiative in promoting indigenous research efforts complementary to imported know-how. Few of the present-day developing countries possess these prerequisites.

All this is not to say that technical collaboration agreements have no role to play in the development process. They could be fruitful if the right conditions are found. But as long as the host countries are relatively underdeveloped they may have only a limited role to play.[38]

Conclusions

Foreign private investment is perhaps the most sensitive and challenging issue in the field of international economic relations. The problem is how best to reconcile the conflicting objectives of remaining independent of foreign control and taking advantage of foreign technology, skill and capital.

Even the most trenchant critics of FPI would concede its potential for transmitting technology and know-how. When due allowance is made for the transfers of managerial and technical skills – factors of production which are probably even scarcer than physical capital in developing countries – the social benefits of FPI must be relatively high. This is not to say that this is invariably so. There are cases where the private rate of return to FPI may be substantially higher than the social rate of return. Individual cases of FPI may have ranged from the enormously beneficial to the disastrous. But in cases where it has been disastrous it is perhaps true that it was the policies of developing countries that were at fault.

In the same vein, generalisations about the balance-of-payments and employment effects of FPI are hazardous. They differ according to the type of FPI and the assumptions made in discussing these issues. These, however, are macro problems. Partial approaches which fail to take into account the external and indirect effects of FPI would lead to erroneous conclusions.

In general FPI must be judged on the basis of its total contribution to the incomes of the host countries and its effects on the productivity of the economy. These may not always be quantifiable. Indeed many of the effects of FPI are in the nature of imponderables. In the present state of knowledge it is probably impossible to provide a quantitative estimate of its impact on the host countries. But this is no reason to deny that it can be a potent force in the development process.

The economist can rest content in the knowledge that FPI can have a beneficial effect on the productive capacity of the host countries and that there are good reasons to believe that it does so. But FPI invariably brings with it problems of control and foreign economic domination. This perhaps is the fundamental objection to FPI.

Economists may argue that fears of foreign domination and control stem from nationalistic considerations and irrational sentiments unworthy of rational man: such nationalism is understandable but it is non-economic. Equally, it has become almost trite to say that these issues in any case fall outside the domain of the economist.

But these issues are the crux of the challenge posed by FPI. Unworthy of rational man or not, economic nationalism in the new nation states of the Third World is a reality. The challenge is to make FPI acceptable to these countries and suggest ways and means of harnessing the beneficial effects of such investment and at the same time limiting its pernicious effects.

Currently fashionable alternatives to FPI, such as joint ventures and technical collaboration agreements, are of limited significance. FPI is an integrated package of technology, skills and capital. Not much can be gained by attempting to take the package apart. There are, however, three main areas of action to make FPI itself more effective.

The first is the need to strengthen the bargaining position of the host countries *vis-à-vis* foreign firms. Bargaining power is not a function of political considerations alone. It also depends on the nature of the resource endowments of the individual developing countries and the type of international markets that exist for the commodities produced. In cases where the international marketing network and management provided by the foreign firms are indispensable, the host countries may find themselves in a weak bargaining position. Some products, like oil, copper and bauxite, are marketed in narrow channels by the foreign firms. There is a close nexus between the foreign firms producing such products and those selling them abroad. In these cases the host countries may find it difficult to break into the production or marketing of such commodities on their own or to initiate competition among the foreign firms. At the other end of the scale are products like coffee, sugar and cotton. The entry of new producers into these industries is relatively easy and the possibility of making a larger proportion of sales on the open market is high.

There are difficulties inherent in strengthening the bargaining position of the developing countries. But these difficulties should not divert attention from the need to do so. The need is for collective action on the part of the developing countries. Most developing countries today may be giving away income to foreign firms by engaging in unhealthy competition among themselves for foreign capital. The developing countries need to frame a common code of action. The success of the oil-producing countries in wresting a greater share of the profits of the foreign firms and in becoming more closely involved in their production and pricing policies is illuminating. So, even more, is their recent dramatic success in quadrupling the price of oil.

It is, of course, true that oil is a special case and not all developing countries are in the fortunate position of possessing such a vital resource. But the operational method by which the oil producers were able to strike favourable bargains has lessons for the developing countries. The joint efforts of the oil countries through OPEC illustrates the need for collective action among the developing countries. Further, developing countries may also be able to develop market networks of their own, as Iran has done with her National Iranian Oil Company.

The second area of action relates to the trade and resource allocation policies of the developing countries. Their protectionist policies may have tended to give income away to the foreigners. A more rational policy of resource allocation and factor subsidisation may result in greater benefits from FPI although it may somewhat reduce the volume of capital inflows. Further, many of the developing countries also need to provide a better 'climate' for FPI if they are to benefit from it. By a 'climate' for FPI is meant not only the provision of overheads and infrastructure facilities but also the adoption of a less bellicose stand towards private enterprise in general. In fact, a 'climate' for FPI may hold out greater attractions to foreign firms than tariffs on imports. The contrasting experience of Malaysia, Mexico and Singapore on the one hand and India and Pakistan on the other illustrates this point.

There is a third fertile area for international action. A body of international regulations designed to curb practices such as transfer pricing on the part of foreign firms belongs in this area. More significantly, international expertise in designing and implementing effective tax structures could be of immense value in transferring the maximum amount possible from the foreign firms to the host countries.

NOTES

1. Peter Ady (ed.), *Private Foreign Investment and the Developing World* (New York: Praeger, Special Studies in International Economics and Development, 1971) p. 3.

2. John H. Dunning, *Studies in International Investment* (London: Allen & Unwin, 1970) pp. 4–5.

3. See Richard E. Caves, 'International Corporations: the Industrial Economics of Foreign Investment', *Economica*, February 1971. Also Mac-Bean, 'Economic Aspects of Direct Investment,' *Kajian Ekonomi Malaysia*, December 1972.

4. J. W. C. Tomlinson, *The Joint Venture Process in International Business, India and Pakistan* (Cambridge, Mass.: MIT Press, 1970) p. 44.

5. J. S. Fforde, *An International Trade in Managerial Skills* (Oxford: Blackwell, 1957).

6. Pearson Report, *op. cit.*, p. 155.

7. Grant L. Reuber *et al.*, *Private Foreign Investment in Development* (London: Clarendon Press, 1973) p. 251.

8. G. D. A. MacDougall, 'The Benefits and Costs of Foreign Private Investment from Abroad: a Theoretical Approach', *Economic Record*, Special Issue, March 1960.

9. G. C. Hufbauer and F. M. Adler, *Overseas Manufacturing Investment and the Balance of Payments* (Washington: United States Treasury Department, 1967).

10. Streeten and S. Lall, *Main Findings of a Study of Private Foreign Investment in Selected Developing Countries* (Geneva: UNCTAD, 1968).

11. *Multinational Corporations in World Development* (New York: United Nations, 1973). It is reported that over the period 1960–68 while $1,000m or so of fresh capital was being transferred to American-controlled subsidiaries in the developing countries, something like $2,500m was being withdrawn annually in the form of income alone. Again, Michael Kidron's estimates for India show that over the fourteen-year period ending in 1961 foreign investors had taken out of the general currency reserves three times as much as they contributed directly. See Michael Kidron, *Foreign Investment in India* (London: Oxford University Press, 1965).

12. Pearson Report, *op. cit.*, p. 101.

13. Kindleberger, *American Business Abroad* (New Haven: Yale University Press, 1969).

14. Streeten, 'New Approaches to Private Overseas Investment', in Ady (ed.), *op. cit.*, pp. 54–5.

15. Streeten, 'Costs and Benefits of Multinational Enterprises in Less Developed Countries', in Dunning (ed.), *The Multinational Enterprise* (London: Allen & Unwin, 1971) p. 250.

16. See Little, 'On Measuring the Value of Private Direct Overseas Investment', in Ranis (ed.), *The Gap between the Rich and Poor Nations* (London: Macmillan, 1972).

17. Streeten in Ady (ed.), *op. cit.*, p. 250.

18. As neither of these objectives can be given exclusive priority, Little and Mirlees suggest a compromise solution where the shadow wage rate lies in between the two alternatives discussed above. But the point is that in deciding on the wage rate subjective elements are unavoidable.

19. *Development Assistance: 1970 Review* (Paris: OECD, 1970) p. 17.

20. For a lucid discussion of the case for labour subsidies in general, see Little, Scott and Scitovsky, *op. cit.*, pp. 331–2.

21. *The Times*, 2 May, 1973.

22. *Ibid.*

23. The number of labourers employed per $1,000 of output per year was 6 in the Ceylonese tea industry, 2 in the Malayan rubber industry and 1·6 for tobacco farming in Southern Rhodesia. In the case of mineral industries it was 0·033 and 0·026 in oil in Venezuela and Saudi Arabia respectively, 0·13 in the Rhodesian copper industry and 0·31 for iron ore production in India. Data cited by R. E. Baldwin, *Economic Development and Export Growth* (Berkeley, University of California Press, 1966) p. 61.

24. *Ibid.*, p. 94.

25. *Ibid.*, pp. 214–5.

26. Myint, *South East Asia's Economy, Development Policies in the 1970s* (Penguin, 1973) p. 90.

27. Streeten, *op. cit.*, p. 245.

28. Edith Penrose, *The Large International Firm in Developing Countries* (London: Allen & Unwin, 1968) p. 273.

29. Streeten, *op. cit.*

30. United Nations, *op. cit.* p. 170. Estimates by J. H. Dunning put the UK figures at 9·1 per cent and 7·1 per cent for the period 1960–65. See Dunning, *op. cit.*, p. 57.

31. For a detailed analysis of this issue see H. G. Johnson, 'The Efficiency and welfare implications of the International Corporation', in C. P. Kindleberger (ed.), *The International Corporation* (Cambridge, Mass.: MIT Press, 1970).

32. For an extensive discussion of such policies in the Indian context see T. N. Bhagwati and P. Desai, *India: Planning for Industrialisation* (London: Oxford University Press, 1970).

33. Little, Scitovsky and Scott, *op. cit.* (London: Oxford University Press, 1970).

34. Constantine V. Vaitsos, *Transfer of Resources and Preservation of Monopoly Rents* (Development Advisory Service, Harvard University, 1970). For other such examples see M. Kidron, *op. cit.*; and Raymond Vernon, *Sovereignty at Bay* (New York; Basic Books, 1970).

35. R. B. Du Boff, 'Transferring Wealth from Underdeveloped to Developed Countries via Direct Foreign Investment', *Southern Economic Journal*, Vol. xxxviii, July 1971.

36. C. P. Kindleberger, *op. cit.*, pp. 27–9.

37. Reserve Bank of India, *Foreign Collaboration in Indian Industry: a Survey Report*, Bombay, 1968, p. 89.

38. For a detailed discussion of the issues relating to technical collaboration agreements, see V. N. Balasubramanyam, *International Transfer of Technology to India* (New York: Praeger, 1973).

CHAPTER NINE

Myths and Realities in Development: Prescriptions for Policy

Both the theory and the practice of development policies have bent and swayed to the dictates of fashion since the early 1950s. Often a basically reasonable idea has been pushed to absurd extremes. The accumulation of capital is a necessary part of the development process but without able managers and skilled workers injections of capital are of little avail. Despite this obvious objection stressed repeatedly by economists such as Peter T. Bauer, Sir Alec Cairncross and Jacob Viner, the central core of development literature continued to treat capital as the only scarce factor. So long as the fixed marginal capital/output ratio models remained within the confines of academic journals little harm would have been done, but countless development plans were built upon such naïve models and they remained implicit in a great deal of official thinking on development, including policy documents of the United Nations. Aid requirements were solemnly predicted on the basis of savings gap and foreign exchange gap models which once again assumed fixed capital/output ratios in addition to fixed savings and import coefficients. Aid donors actively encouraged these exercises.

The effect of this excessively macro-economic approach was to make planning and policies over-concerned with attracting aid and foreign investment, and with squeezing savings out of the nation's population. This diverted attention from the issues of the quality of investment and the need to maintain incentives to efficiency. Most of the Latin American nations, South Asia, Ghana and Egypt struggled hard to raise investment by squeezing resources out of their agricultural sectors and borrowing heavily from international sources, both official and private. These resources were then invested largely in infrastructure and industrialisation with too little attention to the choice of projects in relation to their international competitiveness or their pay-off periods. Their poor showing in these terms, the high costs of continued imported inputs for these industries, the servicing costs of debt incurred for unproductive investment and the misfortune of declining commodity prices, falling from their Korean War peaks of the early 1950s, produced balance-of-payments crises, hastily imposed foreign exchange controls on top of high tariffs for tardy infant industries, and inflationary pressures. These difficulties were exacerbated by lagging agricultural sectors, depressed by low prices for food controlled at low levels to keep urban workers happy; and heavily taxed primary exports.

Industrialisation

The enthusiasm for indiscriminate investment was supported by the industrialisation fetish. There were excellent reasons why many developing countries should, fairly early in the course of their development, establish certain types of processing or manufacturing industries. They already possessed or could soon acquire a comparative advantage, or high international transport costs and/or a low tariff would have been sufficient to enable them to compete in home markets against imports.

What was damaging was the identification of development with industrialisation, and a tendency in a number of countries to take the Russian example of early investment in heavy industry as the main path to rapid growth. Eager salesmen from the capitalist West and the Communist East happily encouraged the indiscriminate construction of massive steelworks and extraordinarily complex heavy electrical and industrial engineering projects. These swallowed imported capital goods without any impact on real standards of living. Few ever approached their planned levels of output, many plants spent much of their time idle for lack of demand for their products or lack of imported inputs.

But to support these mammoths the poor peasants paid dearly. High taxes, high tariffs and over-valued exchange rates made consumer goods dear and agricultural inputs scarce and expensive. At the same time farm prices were held low by export tariffs, compulsory purchases of grain at low fixed prices and the dumping of United States' PL 480 surplus grains and soya oil in their markets under food aid programmes. The over-valued exchange rates also reduced demand for traditional exports, mainly based in the agriculture and mining sectors of their economies.

Denial of the Gains from Trade

Much of the economic literature of the 1950s was devoted to explanation of why the price mechanism did not work in general, and in particular in the context of developing countries. Elasticity pessimism was rife in the literature, hardly surprising in the late 1940s and early 1950s. A world newly emerged from the most destructive war in history, structurally distorted, with strict controls and rationing dominating many economies, is not an environment in which fine alterations in prices would bring about smooth marginal adjustments in supply and demand. The imbalances were too great and were held in check by rigorous controls on trade at home and abroad. When the economists of the day turned their attentions to the problems of the newly emergent nations it was not unnatural that their early training and experience in the sick world economy of the 1930s and the controlled economies of the war and postwar reconstruction era should carry over into their analyses and prescriptions for developing countries. It is not only generals who fight the new war with the ideas and weapons of the previous one.

At the same time the plunging prices of primary commodities over the decade of the 1950s was taken as evidence of a long-term trend against primary prices instead of the short-term phenomenon which it was. This reinforced the pessimistic view of the prospects of increasing national incomes through trade. Pessimism about prospects for exports as an argument for autarky was reinforced by doubts about the gain from trade accruing to developing countries. Many authors maintained that trade, which had been an engine for progress in the nineteenth century, would not work for developing countries today. They stressed the enclave nature of much of the export development. Profits and managerial rewards were largely repatriated to overseas owners. Relatively little of the value of the exports accrued to the developing countries. The positive spread effects though the rest of the economy were weak, and some negative 'backwash' effects tended to retard development of the rest of the economy – drawing capital and the best labour and entrepreneurial spirits into the trading sector. The destruction of indigenous industry by imports and the demonstration effects of foreigners' consumption patterns in reducing domestic savings were other adverse effects laid at the door of *laissez faire* trade relations.

All these ideas became, and even today remain, very fashionable. They helped provide rationalisations for the actions of politicians in creating prestige industries with little concern for their present or future competitiveness. The criteria for selecting industries put forward in much of the literature stressed externalities rather than the generation of surpluses of revenue over costs. But these external economies of benefits to other industries in the form of trained labour, experienced managers, financial know-how and so on are all extremely difficult to quantify. The very vagueness of such criteria makes it difficult to challenge the economic justification of projects based upon them. They lend themselves to inefficiency and corruption. A politician can justify the location of a sugar mill in his constituency, even though no sugar is grown within miles of it, on the grounds that it will create demands for sugar cane farming, introduce cash farming to a subsistence cropping area, train mechanics for running tractors and create a need for irrigation systems. The fact that it will never show a net profit is regarded as being of little importance.

All of the themes outlined in the foregoing paragraphs amount to a denial of the importance of the price mechanism and market forces in allocating resources so as to increase welfare and growth. Inequality in income distribution seems not to have been a major part of their criticism of the result of market forces. Indeed most of their recommendations and the policies which flowed from them made the distribution of income very unequal, largely because the vast majority of the population in most developing countries live in rural areas and derive most of their income from agriculture. For reasons outlined above, the focus on capital formation in industry as the main driving force of development caused agricultural incomes to stagnate while incomes in the urban areas rose rapidly.

Surplus Labour

If resources are heavily under-utilised their opportunity cost is not measured by their price in the market. Many thought that this was the case in developing countries. Labour was considered to be seriously under-employed in the non-capitalist sectors of the economy: subsistence agriculture, petty trading and domestic service. From this it was deduced that the marginal opportunity cost of labour was zero or close to zero so that labour could be moved into industry without sacrificing output of other goods, especially food. Subsequent experience has shown this not to be so. Many costs do arise when labour is moved out of agriculture and into industry. Firms do have to pay quite high wages for workers and many social costs are incurred in the growth of urban areas around the factories. Unless efforts are made to prevent it, agricultural production fails to keep up with demand and food has to be imported to prevent a politically embarrassing rise in food prices.

Put together, all these arguments tended to support policies aimed at rapid capital accumulation and capital- (and import-) intensive industrialisation.

Education and Growth

Subsequent literature identified the importance of education and human capital as a key factor in economic growth in the United States, Western Europe and Japan. Once again the ideas were transferred uncritically into the context of the developing countries. Many invested heavily in education without much consideration of the type of training which would be relevant to their mainly rural societies. At one time Tunisia was investing a higher proportion of national income in education than the United States. Having reached a state where primary education was nearly universal, with a strong French academic bias, the Tunisian Government found the demand for unlimited entry into secondary education well-nigh irresistible. Heavy unemployment of school leavers is a common symptom of the urban areas of developing countries. Several have serious unemployment among university graduates. Their education systems have been much criticised for biasing the young away from manual work, making them contemptuous of a life in agriculture and drawing them into urban unemployment or the unproductive life of the petty bureaucracy.

Technology

More recently there have been other enthusiasms insufficiently based in either logical analysis or empirical verification. There is a strong tendency for well-intentioned members of the 'aid community' to exaggerate both the defeats and the successes of the Third World. Food production is one area in which they have turned full circle in a matter of a few years. In the early 1960s there was nothing but gloom and despair over the possibility of the growth of food being sufficient to match the growth of population. The world, it was said, was heading straight for famine. Then, all at once, the 'miracle' wheat and rice arrived upon the scene and were hailed as the salvation. Countries which had suffered food deficits for years were suddenly advised to start worrying about the problems of exporting their expected food surpluses. (Journalists seeking headlines and the public relations officers of the aid agencies need drama to keep up public interest; but they may do a disservice by encouraging disillusionment and cynicism in the longer run.)

The new varieties were a great technological advance, perhaps the most important result of any technical assistance programme in the history of aid, but even so they have their limitations. Scientific writers were quick to point this out: their dependence on irrigated land and massive doses of chemical fertilisers, their problems of palatability, their vulnerability to disease and attack by insects when transferred to new environments and the great risks of planting large areas with a single variety open to devastation by a single fungus. But such warnings did not deter the proclamation of the 'Green Revolution' as the solution to the food problems of developing countries.

Few noticed that the main causes of the rise in wheat yields in Mexico, the pioneer of the new dwarf varieties, were the shift of wheat production from infertile non-irrigated land to irrigated land, the increased use of fertilisers, and government policies of payment of subsidies to wheat producers.[1]

In fact there has been no miracle. Sensible policies involving proper incentives and making a package of inputs available to the farmers have raised grain output in many regions, but it is not easy and there are vast areas where the new varieties for one reason or another cannot be used. An unforeseen result was that the larger farmers garnered most of the benefits of the new varieties, but food output as a whole actually fell in 1972 and 1973.

The Green Revolution was but one example of the general myth that there exists a technological solution to all problems. The well-meaning technological interventions of aid agencies were a major factor in the destruction of the grazing lands of the Sahele. By programmes of well construction, particularly of artesian wells, the herders and their livestock were encouraged to overgraze and trample the grasses by remaining too long in one spot. Campaigns in animal health which succeeded in controlling rinderpest and other endemic diseases, caused livestock numbers to grow well beyond the equilibrium population which could have maintained an ecological balance. As a result overgrazing and soil erosion were apparent in the Sahele even before the onset of the years of drought which brought disaster in their wake.

It seems likely that each year more land goes out of production as a result of badly designed irrigation schemes than is brought into use by new ones. Poor drainage leads to saline soils particularly with the high evaporation rates of the tropics. In parts of Africa and the Middle East bilharzia, a debilitating parasitic disease, is spread by irrigation canals which provide an ideal breeding ground for the snails which act as a host for the parasites. The Sennar Dam in the Sudan was reported to have brought about an explosion in the incidence of the disease within three years of coming into operation. The Aswan Dam in Egypt is likely to do the same. But it may prove to have even more serious defects. Throughout history the Valley of the Nile owed its great fertility to the inundations of the river and the rich silt deposited each year in the farmers' fields. Now this silt settles in the lake behind the dam. Already, there is evidence of a lack of silt carried by the Nile into the Mediterranean in lower plankton levels and fewer fish in its vicinity. The Egyptian shoreline is also showing signs of erosion from the changed flow of the Nile.[2] The absent silt has to be replaced by chemical fertilisers if crop production is to keep pace with needs, but the energy crisis has pushed up the price of nitrogen, and the price of phosphates has increased by even more than the price of fuel. Large-scale irrigation schemes throughout the developing world have yielded disappointing results, often because of over-confident technology and insufficient concern for human response.

The fashionable demand for the development of intermediate technology may be another over-stressed notion. If factor prices do reflect real opportunity costs, then in countries where labour is plentiful and capital is scarce entrepreneurs will tend to produce things which make more use of the cheaper factors of production. Provided they are operating in an open economy there is no need or incentive for them to produce goods which require capital-intensive production methods. These can be obtained more cheaply through trade. Indeed if trade is relatively free, local entrepreneurs would be unable to compete in these lines of production. Even if all production coefficients were technically fixed there would be no need for a labour-abundant country to have capital-intensive industries (save for strategic or political reasons). It is only if a good cannot be obtained through trade and a demand for it exists that the question of choice of technology becomes important. Even then the spectrum of possible combinations of capital and labour which can be used in the production of most goods and services is much wider than is normally thought; and under the stimulus of a profit incentive considerable ingenuity is already put into substituting labour for capital. Shift working is the most obvious method of increasing the labour-to-capital ratio in manufacturing industry but there are many other examples.[3]

In Pakistan the rush to sink tubewells led to the development of an indigenous innovation in which iron rods with spacers and wrapped in coir rope were substituted for expensive imported brass tube strainers and a locally produced archaic diesel engine was substituted for expensive modern ones. The methods of sinking wells used by these private enterprise gangs were much more labour-intensive than those used by the Agricultural Department or the Water and Power Development Authority.

The principal offenders in the use of excessively capital-intensive technologies have generally been public-sector enterprises or large-scale industries with heavy subsidies and protection which encouraged them to do so.

Of course it would greatly increase the flexibility of a developing country's economy, enabling it to produce efficiently for itself a

wider range of goods, if there were a broader spectrum of technologies available. But these are unlikely to come from research insti-
tutes in the West. More probably they will be developed locally by
research and development which is much closer to the point of
production. One must also beware of taking too narrow an approach
to labour intensity. The use of a tractor to plough land quickly may
enable an extra crop to be grown and raise employment in an additional season. A capital-intensive project like a bridge or an irrigation scheme may make a major contribution to raising employment
by opening new possibilities in marketing or growing crops.

Current Fashions in Economics

The analyses and policy suggestions put forward in the foregoing
chapters of this book probably reflect fairly closely the views of
development economists of the 1970s. Much of what has been said
reflects the work of economists such as Ian Little, J. A. Mirrlees,
Tibor Scitovsky and Maurice Scott in their OECD publications on
industry and trade and on cost-benefit analysis in developing countries. Other writers, such as Harry Johnson, Hla Myint, Gustav
Ranis and Jagdish Bhagwati, share many of the views which have
been outlined here. The fashions of yesterday have been attacked;
but what grounds are there for thinking that the current consensus is
any nearer the truth? No one can be sure of that. Economics is
not an exact science. Keynes's oft-quoted remarks on this topic
remain true today. 'The Theory of Economics does not furnish a
body of settled conclusions immediately applicable to policy. It
is a method rather than a doctrine, an apparatus of the mind, a
technique of thinking, which helps its possessor draw correct conclusions.'

Despite some awareness of the historical development of the subject, and especially of how sensitive conclusions are to the explicit
and implicit assumptions made in the theories used to reach them,
some factors may give a modicum of support to the view that the
general diagnosis of the problems is not too far out.

Firstly, there is the fact that the literature of the 1960s and 1970s
has been based on much more detailed study of what has happened
in developing countries than was true of the theorising of the 1950s.
Second, there is a great deal more understanding of the economics
of centrally-planned economies as a result of the socialist experi-
ments in Russia and Eastern Europe. There is a much greater awareness of the advantages of decentralised decision making and of the
use of accounting prices to reflect social choice and opportunity costs
in both centrally-planned and mixed economies. Third, there is a

great deal more experience with comprehensive planning and with operation of public enterprises in developing countries than was possible earlier.

The present authors are not arguing that the adoption of equilibrium exchange rates, the removal of controls and high tariffs, and the restoration of free markets would achieve the best of all possible worlds. For one thing, the price signals which would result from that would reflect the existing distribution of income and in many countries that would be undesirable. For another, regional imbalances within nations, structural distortions, existing monopolies, and factor immobilities are likely to require more direct government intervention to achieve desirable changes. What the present authors do believe, however, is that it is important that the incentives created by existing prices do, as far as possible, work in the correct direction. If capital is scarce, interest rates should be high to all borrowers. If some uses of capital must be protected from the cost of high interest rates this is better done by an explicit subsidy. If unskilled labour is abundant then wages should be low and barriers to entry into all markets for labour should be eliminated. If it is politically impossible to keep wages down then it is important to find ways of subsidising firms to employ more labour, which will not merely add to profits or drive up wages still further. Of course, the potential importance of external benefits and costs should be recognised and where necessary taxes and subsidies should be adjusted to allow for them. Included in that would be the case for infant industries. With these thoughts in mind some recommendations will be made for policies to promote more rapidly rising standards of living in developing countries.

Positive Recommendations

The major issue in the development of the Third World today is how to combine growth with a fair distribution of the benefits. Although many developing countries achieved very creditable growth rates in the last decade the problem of unemployment has increased and income distribution has worsened in most of them. The continuing rapid expansion of population is a key factor in explaining low per capita growth, unemployment and inequality of income distribution. These last two are the main sources of the evils of hunger, malnutrition and the resulting physical and mental damage to generations of children in Asia, Africa, and Latin America. Although food production in developing countries should certainly be increased, it is not overall scarcity of food that is the main cause of hunger. Unemployment and lack of income are the basic causes. The trend of food production has, in most countries, kept pace with or exceeded population growth. The knowledge is readily available to keep it that way.

If it is accepted that unemployment and income inequality are the principal evils in the situation, policies must be designed to combat these directly. In general, this would involve little if any conflict with the growth objective.

Population

The real objective of population policy is not to avert famine but to raise standards of living. The stress on world hunger as the motive for population control has had the unfortunate side-effect of making countries in Latin America such as Brazil, and African countries, which have no shortage of land, consider that they have no need to lower birth-rates.

There is a powerful economic case for birth control in almost all developing countries. High fertility combined with lowered death rates, especially among children, has produced heavy dependency rates in the developing countries. Most of the population in many developing countries are under 18 years old and high pregnancy rates combined with an aversion to women working outside the home makes for low female participation in the labour force. The combination of these factors results in a situation in which a small number of producers have to support a large number of consumers, compared with the industrially developed countries. Rashly undertaken commitments to universal primary education and the consequent demands for secondary and higher education have committed much larger sums to general education than most developing countries can afford.

The private and public consumption expenditures generated by this age structure have increased the difficulty of raising domestic savings. The flood of young people entering the labour market each year has added constantly to the unemployment problem. Moreover, the tendency for many of these young people, with some basic education, to migrate to the towns, creates severe social and political difficulties. They form an unstable, dissatisfied section of the community. Young people with little or no personal income living in the urban areas where the consumption of those who are employed in industry and government is far above average are subjected to stresses which make it likely that some will turn to crime and even more to revolution.

Policies to reduce age-specific fertility through contraception or abortion will not reduce population growth for some time yet, even if highly successful. The reason is that ever larger numbers of girls are entering the child-bearing age groups. This adds to the urgency of the problems. Changes in social custom towards later marriage could make a significant contribution, as was demonstrated in Ireland in the past and by China today.

Technology is clearly one factor in solving the problem, but motivation is probably still more important. Western Europe and the United States both lowered birth rates in the nineteenth and twentieth centuries by very primitive methods compared with those available today. It takes some time for recognition that the probability of children surviving to adulthood and old age is now reasonably assured and that the need to have large numbers of children to ensure this no longer obtains.

Policies have to be directed towards much better marketing of contraception. This involves motivational analysis and skilful advertising. Distribution points have to be multiplied and taken out of the hands of state organisations. Contraceptives have to be both cheap and widely available. In the past, few of these objectives have been achieved in official programmes. Many people who actually wanted contraceptives could not obtain them locally. Citizens of India at one time were actually crossing the border into what was East Pakistan to obtain contraceptives in the Commilla district where a special programme made them available.

Research and development of better technology is also important, particularly in producing types of contraception more acceptable and less demanding on unsophisticated users. But excellent methods will be of no avail if the mass of the population do not want contraception, or do not know enough about it, or cannot gain access to advice and materials.

All of these areas are ones in which donors are capable of providing assistance. The Swedish agencies have an admirable record, and their example should be widely imitated. But the political will necessary for success has to be shown by the governments of developing countries themselves.

Success in reducing the rate of population growth would bring great benefits in terms of higher savings rates, greater investment, and reduced pressure on labour markets.[4] Probably more would be achieved by success in this one area of policy to reduce unemployment and raise wages than through any other.

Trade

The objectives of increasing employment and decreasing inequality of income support strongly our recommendations in trade policy made for other reasons. Our view is that the major drive in trade policy should be to expand exports of manufactured goods from developing countries, agricultural commodities and processed raw materials. This is in line with both the current comparative advantage of developing countries and the way comparative advantage is likely to evolve from trends in developed and developing countries alike. Provided the industrial nations permit entry of exports from the developing countries this should be the next biggest contribution to raising employment in developing countries.

The alternative proposal of the New International Economic Order of wide-ranging introduction of international commodity agreements and the chimera of indexation, means restricting the quantities of goods produced in an attempt to hold up prices. That will reduce the level of employment in primary export production. Any gains in foreign exchange will accrue either to governments or to the businesses engaged in such exports. If the commodities involved are considered (coffee, cocoa, tea, sugar, bananas, copper, bauxite, tin, other non-ferrous metals, and fibres) it seems rather unlikely that many of the benefits from increased commodity revenues would filter down to the ordinary workers or peasants engaged in producing them.

The opposite policy in the commodity field is one of attacking all barriers to primary exports of developing countries. Increasing exports would increase the demand for labour, raising employment and incomes among the lower-income groups. The main difficulty to be overcome is the opposition of the farming lobbies in the industrial nations.

Increased exports of labour-intensive manufactures and processed raw materials could have the same effect of increasing employment and raising incomes of workers and their families. Moreover, such a policy would increase internal markets for the kinds of goods wanted by the masses. The past policies of import-substituting industrialisation have not created the jobs required, in large part, because they were often the wrong industries and they were capital- and import-intensive. The profits which accrued often went into overseas investment or luxury consumption, which increased imports or stimulated the creation of inappropriate industries producing luxury goods such as air-conditioners and private cars.

Should the aims of increasing manufactured exports and processed raw materials mean pressure for extension of the Generalised System of Preferences or for dismantling of tariffs and quantitative restrictions on a most favoured nation basis? There are arguments for both approaches. The Generalised System of Preferences up to now has given limited benefits affecting a rather small share of developing countries' exports. As exceptions to this system are the very goods which the poorer developing countries have prospects of exporting, most of the benefits go to the countries which are already nearer the top of the list in terms of GNP per capita and level of industrialisation. Because of the uncertainty attending the imposition of quotas under 'market disruption' clauses, whose application is entirely at the discretion of the nation conceding the preferences, few developing countries can risk creating new export industries specifically for the purpose of taking advantage of concessions granted under the Generalised System of Preferences.

For these reasons some economists argue that a MFN approach to reduction in trade barriers could be superior. Many developing countries have already shown that they can produce quite a wide range of manufactured exports.[5] As population expansion, migration to the urban areas and unemployment are likely to persist for a very long time in most of the developing countries, wage levels are likely to stay very low. Because similar capital equipment and technology as is available in developed countries is generally available to them they are likely to have a large comparative advantage in many kinds of manufactures, provided their own policies do not discriminate against exporting, for example by maintaining overvalued exchange rates and excessive protection of their home markets. It seems unlikely that supply of manufactured exports will prove to be the problem.[6] The main difficulty in expanding developing countries' exports of manufactures is certain to stem from the reluctance of developed countries to adjust to large quantities of imports of labour-intensive manufactures.

The problem lies in the fact that the cost to workers and owners in labour-intensive industries in the industrial nations from a surge in imports is very great, and concentrated heavily on them, while the benefits of cheaper manufactures are spread widely over the rest of the community. Often such industries are concentrated in regions of the industrial nations which are already lagging behind the rest of the economy. This can mean severe local unemployment among workers who have no skills, or have skills which are peculiar to these industries. Often general education standards are low among such groups. All of these factors militate against an easy and rapid transfer of such workers into the technologically more advanced industries and services which are the growth areas in the developed economies. This calls for very special efforts on the part of governments to ensure that these workers are fully compensated for loss of employment and given generous assistance to re-equip themselves for better jobs. If this is not done the opposition to freer trade will grow irresistible and governments will find themselves re-erecting barriers to imports from developing countries.

Governments in the industrial nations should, in their own interests, be anticipating these problems and acting before industries and areas become so run down that the more vigorous managers and workers who could be used to build new industries will have already left. The pursuit of full employment policies generally seems to be important in providing new opportunities for entrepreneurs and workers, as evidenced by the experience of the Ruhr, Lancashire and Japan in making adjustments to the rundown of major industries.[7] The problems of 'adjustment assistance' are sometimes very great. Past experience shows that many workers have suffered severely in loss of security, unemployment and acceptance of an inferior job.

Policies are needed which make sure that the gainers from free trade do effectively compensate these losers.[8] However, it should be noted that the gainers are enormously more numerous than the losers. Exports from developing countries are likely to be less concentrated on textiles and leather goods than in the past so that the expansion of trade may be as much intra-industry as inter-industry, or more. (Japan and the United States export television sets and automobiles to each other, as do most of the Western European nations.) The effects of trade expansion then become much more widely diffused. At the same time as exports from developing countries to advanced countries increase it would seem logical that their imports would also rise. There is no reason to expect the developing countries to accumulate foreign exchange reserves. The expansion of developed countries' exports could maintain a buoyant demand for labour unless there were a substantial difference in the labour intensity in the firms producing their exports. Were that the case there would be a tendency to some relative decline in real wages in the industrial nations, but this would be swamped in the overall rise in productivity due to more efficient allocation of labour and the stimulus to efficiency from increased competition.[9]

The problem of disruption to sluggish economies such as Britain's tends to gain exaggerated importance in times of relatively high unemployment such as Britain is experiencing in the mid-1970s. Balance-of-payment difficulties combined with stagnation tend to strengthen the hand of protectionists, but in the longer run, once these short-term difficulties have been overcome, the probability is that the structural adjustments which would result from expanded imports from developing countries would not be very great and would in any case help to push the British economy towards a better use of its resources.

Aid

The issues of employment and income distribution suggest certain recommendations in the field of economic aid. Clearly assistance to all developing countries which wish help to restrict births is an imperative. It should be possible to make certain changes in aid programmes generally, which would help to improve employment and equality. Most bilateral aid is still given for the foreign exchange costs only of selected projects. This can bias the type of projects put forward by developing countries for aid towards those which have a high foreign exchange component; and, where there is a choice in technique, that which involves the higher import content may be chosen simply to get as much aid as possible and to reduce the local costs which have to be borne by the government's budget. The tendency then is for projects and techniques selected to be intensive in the use of imported capital goods and imported technology. The effect is likely to be that the stimulus to local employment which could have been effected by the aid is much smaller than its potential.

This tendency could be combated by meeting more of the local costs, and by giving more aid to sectors of the economy which do naturally use more labour-intensive methods, such as agriculture and its ancillary service industries, and labour-intensive manufactures. Aid can be directed to smaller rather than larger projects and preferably in rural areas where per capita incomes are lower than average. This may involve channelling the aid through local development banks as the World Bank has done on a number of occasions. Where shortage of materials or spares are responsible for lower utilisation of existing plant it should be recognised that assistance for these can be a very productive use of aid, expanding employment and wage incomes as well as raising GNP and enabling higher domestic savings. The World Bank and its associated institutions have expressed their intention of moving in these directions, and there is some evidence of their actually having done so. This strengthens our recommendation that a great deal more aid should be directed through multilateral channels. Few bilateral donors are likely to move very far in these directions. The pressures upon their aid agencies to serve the commercial interests of their nation militate strongly against local cost aid and aid directed to more labour-intensive projects which involve less use of imported machinery.

The general aim of encouraging more labour-intensive development should not be pursued too narrowly. First, there is a risk that in a given project the choice of labour-intensive methods of construction may actually have a smaller effect on reducing unemployment and raising low incomes than would a capital-intensive method. For example, a road designed to link a backward region to metropolitan markets might take a year to construct by means of heavy construction machinery, but two years by the use of a huge army of unskilled workers. The labour-intensive method would provide more jobs to an underprivileged group and might even be cheaper, but the benefits flowing from the project could be delayed for a year. These benefits might include a considerable expansion of marketable output and employment in the area brought into contact with the metropolitan market. Even looked at purely in terms of employment, the capital-intensive method could have created far more employment in the economy at large than the labour-intensive approach created directly. Project evaluation must always be carried out with a careful eye to the wider repercussions on the whole economy.

It should also be recognised that labour-intensive approaches are often very difficult to organise and manage. The use of huge armies of workers milling about in confined spaces such as irrigation ditches tends to be an impossibly inefficient method of construction. All that can be asked for is that aid analysts constantly bear in mind the possibility of using labour-intensive methods wherever this is technically feasible and economically viable.

In countries where per capita incomes are fairly low a redistribution of income to peasants and unskilled workers should increase markets for labour-intensive products such as food, clothing and materials for house construction. The income elasticity of demand for these is likely to be high at low income levels. In better-off countries like Mexico, Chile or Columbia this may be less so. For them extra income among lower income groups may go on better housing, radios, bicycles and scooters, and durable consumer goods generally, which tend to be produced by relatively capital-intensive methods. However, the vast majority of the citizens of developing countries live in Asia and Africa with very low incomes. For them, redistribution is likely to stimulate internal markets for the kinds of goods which their resource endowment enables them to produce most economically for themselves. Accordingly, policies to generate employment and income equality should provide the home markets necessary for expansion of domestic production of a wide range of consumer goods.

If the policies advocated for improving the trade prospects of developing countries are successful then there will be a case in equity for directing more aid towards the poorest countries: those in the United Nations category of the Least Developed Nations. They are the ones least likely to benefit from opportunities to expand manufactured exports. They are generally in need of a great deal of technical assistance to raise their capacity to make efficient use of financial aid. They may also have more need of basic infrastructural investment in communications, education and health. That aid can help them is evident from case studies, such as Kathryn Morton's carefully researched report on aid to Malawi.[10]

Foreign Private Investment

There is a tendency for foreign firms to use capital-intensive technology in their subsidiaries in developing countries. Whether they are actually prone to do so more than similar indigenous firms operating in the same industry is open to question, but is nevertheless widely believed and seems plausible on *a priori* grounds. The foreign firms are familiar with the technology of their home environment which is one of expensive labour and relatively cheap capital. Inertia would favour use of the same methods abroad. But inertia is reinforced by the fact that the actual prices they have to pay for capital and labour often bear little relation to the social opportunity costs of these factors in developing countries. They have access to capital from abroad and are often privileged borrowers even in the developing country. Since they have prestige and a reputation for financial sophistication, local banks and government development institutions are often willing to supply them with capital at relatively low rates of interest.

The price they have to pay for local labour is often inflated well above local norms. Foreign companies are fair game for local trade union and political pressure to pay high wages. Often they have to be model employers, providing various fringe benefits to workers which would often be provided by the state in richer nations. These high labour costs reduce the incentive to seek less capital intensive methods of production. Often labour will, in any case, be of low productivity, certainly initially, but often also on a longer-term basis. Absenteeism through ill-health of the worker or his family is common. Often the discipline of fixed hours in a factory is novel and irksome to workers in developing countries and is an additional cause of casual absenteeism. Foreign firms may also be unwilling to become involved with the difficulties of handling large masses of labour. They may not have the staff at foreman level who could operate in these ways. They may consider that the shortage of skilled labour and the costs of training them from among a labour force lacking basic literacy may justify substituting more advanced machinery which eliminates the need for skill in the ordinary workers.

Some of these reasons will affect all firms whether local or foreign, but one which particularly influences some foreign companies may be that they expect to make their major contribution to the share capital of the firm by providing the machinery and the main management team. Sometimes they may even be making a substantial profit by the intra-firm sale of equipment. This greatly reduces any incentive to reduce dependence on imported capital and technology.

Of course if factor prices in developing countries really reflected true social opportunity costs a large part of this problem would disappear. Only firms which saw prospects of profits when operating in accordance with the local factor costs would choose to locate there. As a short-term solution that is no answer, but at the very least developing countries should scrutinise their systems of incentives to foreign private investors. If subsidies and tax privileges are necessary, they should be chosen so as to attract more labour-intensive industries and, where various production methods are feasible, to encourage the choice of the more labour-intensive. The basic recommendation in this, as in all the other policy fields, is to ensure that exchange rates are not over-valued and tax/subsidy policies do not distort prices too much from the basic opportunity costs of the resources of the economy.

The high wages and the welfare schemes extracted from multinational corporations by developing countries may simply be a method of ensuring that a larger proportion of value added accrues to the host country. The same objective, however, can be achieved much more efficiently by taxation of profits. This would not put up the cost of labour and encourage capital-intensive methods of production.

Rather than regulate foreign private investment so as to direct it into specific sectors, governments would be better advised to correct the basic incentives of the price mechanism. If particular goods are not wanted, such as luxuries, a high excise tax which will deter imports or domestic production, whether by foreign firms or local ones, is superior to administrative controls. The limiting of foreign companies to specific sectors prevents one of the most important forms of competition, the possibility of entry into any market. This lowers efficiency and creates monopoly profits.

There is a case for policies designed to encourage links between multinational corporations and local firms. The sub-contracting of production of components assures small indigenous firms of a steady demand and may bring them some technical assistance to ensure quality and consistency of output. Connection with a large foreign firm may also ease their problems of obtaining credit.

For rather similar reasons governments might encourage joint ventures between local and foreign firms. The pooling of the foreign companies' knowledge of technology with the local firms' knowledge and experience of local conditions should make for vastly more efficient undertakings than either could be on their own.

Industrialisation Policies

The new thinking on development has been severely critical of much industrial development in South Asia and Latin America. Calculations for Brazil and Pakistan show that the misallocation resulting from over-valued exchange rates and excessive protection cost them a significant proportion of GNP. Nevertheless, the industries which they did install have served some purpose. They form the base from which both Brazil and Pakistan are now successfully venturing into export markets. A number of their infants have turned from ugly ducklings into swans, achieving hoped-for internal economies of scale and successfully passing through the learning stage necessary to their development. The route which they chose probably involved delay in achievement of benefits, generated less employment, and worsened the distribution of income more than would an alternative, less autarkic line of development. But they could certainly claim historical precedents for the general strategy which they pursued. Germany, the United States and the Soviet Union had followed rather similar ones in the nineteenth and early twentieth centuries.

It should be noted that the countries which have adopted extreme import-substituting industrialisation were very large nations. Those which have shone as export-oriented development successes were relatively small economies such as Hong Kong, Singapore, North Korea and Taiwan (and with other special characteristics such as high literacy rates and immigrant populations). A large economy such as India or Brazil will eventually end up with a huge internal market supplied mainly from home industry, and foreign trade will always remain a small proportion of national income. In the long run, such an economy is unlikely to set up industries which do not eventually become viable. The internal market will become large enough to yield the economies of scale required even by industries such as car manufacturing or petrochemicals. Errors in choice of industry then become errors of timing rather than errors involving total non-viability. Even the former is costly, but it is not irredeemable. Small economies could never have a large enough internal market to do this. They are soon forced to look outwards for markets as they use up the simpler import-substituting possibilities.

The successes among them have made a virtue of this necessity.

The results of past capital- and import-intensive development defying comparative advantage, in countries like India, have been painful. They have created pernicious monopolies, urban, rural and regional imbalances, relative neglect of agriculture, unemployment and increased inequality of income. Elimination of over-valued exchange rates and reduction of import licensing and excessive tariffs will not be easy in the wake of the enormous balance of payments deficits produced by the quantum jump in petroleum and fertiliser import prices. Steps towards liberalisation in Pakistan in the early 1960s were only achieved with the assistance of substantial programme loans and grants from the Consortium of Development Assistance Committee agencies. Perhaps now is the time to introduce the famous 'Link'.[11] If special drawing rights (SDRs) were created and distributed through International Development Association loans to developing countries, the latter's ability to relax import controls would be enhanced and could be a condition of such lending. Given the great under-utilisation of industrial capacity in the world today the effects could hardly be inflationary in the sense of causing excess demand.

It is impossible in a relatively short book with a fairly broad coverage of problems to go into detailed suggestions for reform of industrial policies. That is a specialised topic requiring a book of its own.[12] However, over-centralised decision making, with its need of physical targets, has been identified as a major cause of inefficiency in many countries. Public-sector industries have to be given clear financial and economic criteria so that their actions can be judged. A vague requirement to cover costs is totally inadequate, particularly where they possess monopoly power and can always raise prices at the cost of output. Where public enterprises have to be used for social policy, for example in urban transport, subsidies should be explicit and geared carefully to their objective, and not be allowed to fudge the profit and loss account.

Concluding Remarks

Small books on big problems are apt to over-simplify. No doubt this work is guilty of that sin. In these last few lines the author's views have been stated boldly. The clamour for a New International Economic Order should not divert attention from the main challenge of poverty in the world of the 1970s. That challenge is to the leadership of the Third World. The one single act which could do more to improve economic prospects for the mass of their people is to slow the growth of population. The task can only be done by national governments in developing countries. Assistance from the rest of the world for population control would be useless without the enthusiastic support for birth control policies from the host governments.

It is much more difficult to decide what is the next priority. The particular circumstances of individual nations will mean that their ranking of policies will differ for sound economic reasons. The importance they set on a more equal distribution of income will clearly affect their choice.

In the recommendations which have been made in this book there is, however, one common element. This is that the likely effects of policies should be appraised in terms of benefits and costs valued at their social opportunity cost. This does not establish a preconception in favour of agriculture as against industry, of consumer goods as against capital goods, or of exporting as against import substitution, or even of labour-intensive as against capital-intensive techniques of production in any particular activity. What determines these choices is the ranking which emerges from the benefit-cost analysis after taking into account the objectives of the society and the real costs of resources there. On such a calculation it is quite possible for certain types of heavy industry to emerge as viable. If a particular heavy industry is labour-intensive (as quite a few are), if the technology can be acquired at reasonable cost, if there is a market for the output and the plant can come on stream within a reasonable time, then it could be ranked highly by benefit-cost analysis.

As Ian Little, Tibor Scitovsky and Maurice Scott have shown, many industries have already demonstrated their viability in developing countries and rigorous cost-benefit analyses have shown the potential for many more.

The main contribution which the rich industrial nations of the world can make to meet the challenge of poverty in the Third World is to open their markets to the products of the developing nations. It is in their own long-term interests to do so. The sooner policies are worked out to cushion the shock and aid internal adjustment the better. The rich nations should seize the opportunity offered by the current Multilateral Trade Negotiations in the GATT to make wide-ranging trade concessions on exports of importance to developing countries. Most of the gains from such a policy would, however, accrue to the better-off Third World nations. This means that aid should not only be more generous, but also more concentrated on the poorest countries.

NOTES

1. See W. Paddock and E. Paddock, *We Don't Know How: an Independent Audit of What They Call Success in Foreign Assistance* (Ames: Iowa State University Press, 1973) pp. 211–4.

2. *Ibid.*, pp. 239–40.

3. Ranis, 'Industrial Sector Labour Absorption', *Economic Development and Cultural Change*, April 1973.

4. G. C. Zaidan, 'Population Growth and Economic Development', *Finance and Development*, No. 1, 1969.

5. Hughes (ed.), *op. cit.*

6. *Ibid.*, p. 270, where it is expected 'that manufactured exports which accounted for less than 20 per cent of total manufactured output at the end of the 1960s will represent more than 40 per cent of such output by 1980'. In all probability, the oil crisis has set that back a few years but the general trend is likely to remain correct.

7. See Caroline Miles, 'Employment in the Industrialised Countries,' in Hughes (ed.), *op. cit.*

8. See Nathaniel Goldfinger's 'Comment' on Miles, *ibid.*, pp. 118–24.

9. See W. M. Corden's 'Comment' on Miles, *ibid.*, pp. 125–7.

10. Morton, *op. cit.*

11. Various proposals to link an expansion of international liquidity to aid have been put forward since 1960.

12. See Sutcliffe, *op. cit.*

Selected Bibliography

Set out below is a selected bibliography relating to the various development problems of the Third World. In no sense is this list meant to be comprehensive. Having been prepared for general as well as specialist readers, it has been confined to books and monographs; journal articles, where relevant, have been cited in the notes and references at the end of each chapter. In addition to a selection of general titles on development, there are sections covering international trade and development, planning for development, aid, industrialisation and employment, foreign private investment and the transfer of technology, and agriculture, food and population.

General

JAGDISH BHAGWATI, *The Economics of Underdeveloped Countries* (London: Weidenfeld & Nicolson, 1966).

WALTER ELKAN, *An Introduction to Development Economics* (Harmondsworth: Penguin, 1973).

HLA MYINT, *The Economics of Developing Countries* (London: Hutchinson, 1965).

These three books represent brief general introductions to the study of development problems in the Third World. Elkan's is more up to date, aimed a little more at the undergraduate and gives particularly good summaries of many of the main debates with shrewd, balanced comments.

PETER BAUER and BASIL YAMEY, *The Economics of Underdeveloped Countries* (Cambridge: Cambridge University Handbooks, 1957).
This is an uninhibited defence of the price mechanism as the best allocator of resources in the less developed countries. Professor Bauer draws on his earlier studies on Malaysia and West Africa.

PETER BAUER, *Dissent on Development* (London: Weidenfeld & Nicholson, 1971).

A monstrous blast against the regimen of what might be characterised as UNCTAD-type doctrines on aid, trade and development.

LESTER R. BROWN, *World Without Borders* (New York: Random House, 1972).

Combined here is a concern for the problems of raising living standards in developing countries with concern for the preservation of the environment. It also stresses the interdependence of nations and urges Americans against isolationism.

SIR ALEC CAIRNCROSS, *Factors in Economic Development* (London: Allen & Unwin, 1962).

A collection of stimulating articles on controversial topics.

ALEXANDER GERSCHENKRON, *Economic Backwardness in Historical Perspectives* (London and New York: Praeger, 1962).

A series of essays of great historical sweep and insight into economic development of nations. Detailed study of aspects of Soviet development.

BENJAMIN HIGGINS, *Economic Development: problems, principles and policies* (London: Constable, 1949).

A massive well-balanced treatment of the problems of developing countries, and of theories and policies related to their development, perhaps a little dated now.

HARRY G. JOHNSON, *Economic Policies Towards Less Developed Countries* (London: Allen & Unwin, 1968).

An excellent study, for the Brookings Institution, in Washington, of the claims of the 1964 UNCTAD, with suggestions for constructive responses from the United States and other developed nations.

SIMON KUZNETS, *Economic Growth of Nations* (Cambridge, Mass.: Harvard University Press, 1971).

A review of long-term trends in economic growth which makes comparisons between the developed and developing countries. It develops interesting criticisms of conventional national economic accounting.

SIR ARTHUR LEWIS, *Theory of Economic Growth* (London: Allen & Unwin, 1955).

This is an early classic of the literature, taking a broad approach, eclectic in theories and seminal in ideas.

ANGUS MADDISON, *Economic Progress and Policy in Developing Countries* (London: Allen & Unwin, 1970).

The book draws on Dr Maddison's valuable research on the development of Japan, Russia and West European nations. It attempts to quantify the contribution of various factors to economic growth in developing countries. The study is limited to a sample of nations in order to give greater empirical depth.

ROBERT S. MCNAMARA, *One Hundred Countries, Two Billion People* (London and New York: Praeger, 1973).

A series of speeches and essays on the dimensions of under-development. Special attention is paid to population, malnutrition and unemployment issues.

GERALD M. MEIER, *Leading Issues in Development Economics* (London: Oxford University Press, 1970).

A course book for the study of development economics, compiled from major articles on the main issues by a wide range of leading writers, with introductions and summaries by Professor Meier.

GUNNAR MYRDAL, *Economic Theory and Underdeveloped Regions* (London: Duckworth, 1957).

Professor Myrdal argues that economic inequalities between nations are increasing and that they are the necessary result of unfettered economic forces operating through persistent disequilibrating tendencies present in the real world. Theories should be based not on equilibrium but on 'cumulative causation'.

GUNNAR MYRDAL, *Asian Drama: an Inquiry into the Poverty of Nations* (Harmondsworth: Penguin, 1972).

A massively detailed study, mainly concentrated on India.

International Trade and Development

MICHAEL B. BROWN, *The Economics of Imperialism* (Harmondsworth: Penguin, 1974).

This work expounds the main theories of imperialism: classical, Keynesian and Marxist. The author adopts the thesis that imperialism is a mechanism for transforming economies into the sphere of competitive capital accumulation. This process creates an artificial world-wide division of labour amounting to a dual economy. In the final chapter he suggests how it might be possible to escape from this.

JAGDISH BHAGWATI (ed.), *Economics and World Order* (Geneva: World Law Fund, 1970).

This is basically a look, by authors of varying origins and qualifications, at the probable future of international economic relations, often with more optimism than analysis. The authors are worth consideration.

W. M. CORDEN, *The Theory of Protection* (Oxford: Clarendon Press, 1971).

This is a comprehensive treatment of the theory of protection, including considerable attention to the concept of 'effective protection', which has become a commonplace technique in the analysis of commercial policy.

KENNETH W. DAM, *The GATT Law and International Economic Organisation* (Chicago: University of Chicago Press, 1970).

An excellent study by an international lawyer with a good second training in economics and an understanding of how and why the principles of the two frequently conflict.

GERALD K. HELLEINER, *International Trade and Economic Development* (Harmondsworth: Penguin, 1972).

A clear, concise and brief introduction to foreign trade aspects of economic growth.

HELEN HUGHES (ed.), *Prospects for Partnership* (Baltimore: Johns Hopkins Press, for the International Bank for Reconstruction and Development, 1973).

This is a study of industrialisation and trade policies in developing countries based on papers given to a World Bank-sponsored seminar. It is optimistic about the developing countries' capacity to produce manufactured exports efficiently, less optimistic about rich nations' willingness to reduce barriers to these exports.

HARRY G. JOHNSON, *Comparative Cost and Commercial Policy Theory for a Developing World Economy*, Wiksell Lectures (Stockholm: Almqvist & Wiksell, 1968).

This brief survey puts together contemporary ideas on human capital, public goods, education and so on, into a capital-theoretic approach to dynamic comparative advantage and the theory of commercial policy.

HARRY G. JOHNSON (ed.), *Trade Strategy for Rich and Poor Nations* (London: Allen & Unwin, for the Trade Policy Research Centre, 1971; and Toronto: University of Toronto Press, 1972).

A collection of papers on the implications of a free trade treaty among developed countries as the next phase in the movement towards an open world economy. It contains a level-headed examination by M. D. Steuer on the bogey of American capital 'inevitably' dominating any economy which entered into a free trade arrangement with the United States.

HAL B. LARY, *Imports of Manufactures from Less Developed Countries* (London and New York: Columbia University Press, 1968).

Here is a fine piece of research on factor proportions and exports of manufactures from the less developed countries. His work differs from earlier studies in treating human capital as a separate input from labour. On the basis of his empirical work he finds support for neo-classical trade theory.

ALASDAIR I. MACBEAN, *Export Instability and Economic Development* (London: Allen & Unwin, 1966).

The conventional wisdom on the causes and effects of short-term export instability is confronted with statistical analyses which cast doubt on most of the widely accepted conclusions. The second half of the book is devoted to critical evaluation of national and international schemes to reduce export instability.

GERALD M. MEIER, *The International Economics of Development: Theory and Policy* (London: Harper & Row, 1968).

Beginning with a very clear exposition of theory the author moves on in later chapters to policy issues in trade, aid, foreign private investment and commercial policy. The last chapter discusses international economic reform, covering issues raised in UNCTAD.

GUNNAR MYRDAL, *An International Economy* (London: Routledge, 1956).

This is an early treatment of the causes of international inequality.

PETER ROBSON (ed.), *International Economic Integration* (Harmondsworth: Penguin, 1972).

This volume contains several articles on common markets and developing countries, including empirical studies of the East African trading unions.

MONTAGUE YUDELMAN and FREDERICK HOWARD, *Agricultural Development and Economic Integration in Latin America* (London: Allen & Unwin, 1970).

Stressed in this work is the need for conciliation of the different national agricultural policies as a prior need to arrangements for freeing trade in agricultural products. The study highlights the range of problems which a developing region is likely to meet in moving towards a common market.

Planning for Development

A. K. DASGUPTA, *Economic Theory and the Developing Countries* (London: Macmillan, 1974).

The volume provides a concise discussion of the problems of developing countries. Also provides a non-mathematical discussion of the techniques of input-output analysis, linear programming and cost-benefit analysis.

K. B. GRIFFIN and J. L. ENOS, *Planning Development* (London: Addison-Wesley, 1970).

This discusses the need for planning and outlines the main techniques of planning such as input-output analysis and mathematical programming. A good simple exposition of the problems involved in planning.

SIR ARTHUR LEWIS, *Development Planning: the Essentials of Economic Policy* (London: Allen & Unwin, 1966).

Sir Arthur discusses the main snags involved in planning and explains the statistical framework of a plan with the aid of an arithmetic example. This is intended to provide a simple exposition of planning problems to the layman.

MICHAEL LIPTON and PAUL STREETEN (eds), *The Crisis of Indian Planning, Economic Planning in the 1960s* (London: Oxford University Press, 1968).

Two specialists on India have compiled here a collection of papers on India's efforts at planning and especially interesting is Mr Lipton's article on 'Strategy for Agriculture: Urban Bias and Rural Planning'.

I. M. D. LITTLE and J. A. MIRRLEES, *Project Appraisal and Planning for Developing Countries* (London: Heinemann, 1974).

This brilliant exposition of the Little-Mirrlees method of project evaluation is much easier to understand and more precise than their earlier exposition in the OECD *Manual*.

ALBERT O. HIRSCHMAN, *Development Projects Observed* (Washington: Brookings Institution, 1967).

In this book is provocatively continued a Hirschman theme of the success of human ingenuity in the face of adversity produced by human lack of foresight.

WILLY SELLEKAERTS (ed.), *Economic Development and Planning: Essays in Honour of Jan Tinbergen* (London: Macmillan, 1974).

This volume contains a series of essays on topics in the development and planning field by distinguished development economists. The level of technical competence required of the reader varies from very little to honours degree.

W. F. STOLPER, *Planning Without Facts* (Cambridge, Mass.: Harvard University Press, 1966).

Professor Stolper illustrates the operational use of theoretical concepts in making resource allocation decisions in the context of the Nigerian development experience. He presents the provocative thesis that economic profits are the best guide to resource allocation.

Aid

JAGDISH BHAGWATI and RICHARD S. ECKAUS, *Foreign Aid* (Harmondsworth: Penguin, 1970).

The editors present a collection of readings on aid which covers objectives, criteria for allocation, aid burden, multilateral versus bilateral aid, aid-tying and commodity aid.

EDWARD K. HAWKINS, *Principles of Development Aid* (Harmondsworth: Penguin, 1970).

This is straightforward exposition of the main aid issues: measurement of aid, debt burden and so on. It contains a discussion of the Pearson Commission's Report on International Development.

I. M. D. LITTLE and J. M. CLIFFORD, *International Aid* (London: Allen & Unwin, 1965).

Here is presented a comprehensive study of aid with special attention to the British aid programme.

EDWARD S. MASON and R. E. ASHER, *The World Bank Since Bretton Woods* (Washington: Brookings Institution, 1973).

This volume provides a massive and authoritative history of the World Bank family. It ends with a number of questions about the future of Bank policies. Although not uncritical, the study is generally favourable in its comments on the Bank.

GERALD M. MEIER, *Problems of Cooperation for Development* (London: Oxford University Press, 1974).

Another study of aid, private overseas investment and tariff preferences for development. It provides a lot of factual material with sets of questions for students to ponder (and useful to the teacher).

RAYMOND F. MIKESELL, *The Economics of Foreign Aid* (London: Weidenfeld & Nicolson, 1968).

It is an excellent textbook on aid with critical evaluation of formal theories of development and aid. It also surveys comprehensively a broad spectrum of writings in this field.

RONALD C. NAIRN, *International Aid to Thailand: the New Colonialism?* (New Haven: Yale University Press, 1966).

Basically this is a study of the effectiveness of the United Nations' and bilateral donors' attempts to raise the level of education and skills in Thailand through two major projects; one in modernising teaching methods and the other in a community development programme. The failures to mesh with Thai culture are also documented.

LESTER B. PEARSON, *et al.*, *Partners in Development: Report of the Commission on International Development* (Pearson Report) (London: Pall Mall, for the International Bank for Reconstruction and Development, 1969).

This is the work of an impressive group of international figures, with a large research staff, who were given the task of evaluating aid to date and making recommendations for future aid policies. While the report has received many plaudits, it has also been heavily criticised, mainly for not addressing realities vigorously enough.

JOHN PINCUS, *Economic Aid and International Cost Sharing* (Baltimore: Johns Hopkins Press, 1965).

This pioneering study of aid burdens, with the development of a present-value method of reducing loans of different maturity and interest cost to a common grant-equivalent value, also includes the first attempt to estimate the possibilities for resource transfers to developing countries through commodity agreements.

JOHN PINCUS, *Trade, Aid and Development* (New York: McGraw-Hill, for the Council on Foreign Relations, 1967).

Another good book covering the same general ground as Harry G. Johnson's *Economic Policies Toward Less Developed Countries*, but with a different and illuminating personal approach.

Industrialisation and Employment

JAGDISH BHAGWATI and P. DESAI, *India: Planning for Industrialisation* (London: Oxford University Press, 1970).

In this book is a lucid and well documented critique of India's industrialisation and trade policies in the two decades since 1947. The main thesis of the book is that Indian planning was excessively detailed and was characterised by an extravagant display of bureaucratic controls and restrictions which had no economic rationale. The book provides valuable lessons on how neglect of basic economis cost considerations can bring the best laid plans to grief.

HOLLIS B. CHENERY (ed.), *Redistribution with Growth* (London: Oxford University Press, 1974).

The study is a collection of essays on inequalities in income distribution in developing countries. There are general essays on the extent of inequalities and the causes for it. It also provides case studies including one on Cuba. The main theme of the paper is that redistribution and growth are not incompatible.

I. M. D. LITTLE, TIBOR SCITOVSKY and M. F'G. SCOTT, *Industry and Trade in Some Developing Countries: a Comparative Study* (London: Oxford University Press, 1970).

This book is based on earlier individual country studies commissioned by the OECD. It discusses the costs of the strategy of import substitution pursued by these countries and suggests that more emphasis should be placed on agricultural development and that industrialisation should be promoted by direct incentives rather than by indiscriminate tariff protection.

A. K. SEN, *Employment, Technology and Development* (London: Oxford University Press, 1971).

This book provides a menu of topics on employment and technology. The main theme of the book is employment implications of technological choice in development strategy. The major emphasis is on the need to take into consideration the institutional and political framework in formulating employment policies. There is also a methodological discussion of the concepts of employment and capital intensity, an analysis of the problems associated with the measurement of unemployment and a discussion on the use of shadow prices and benefit-cost analysis. The relationships between institutional features and technological choice are illustrated in the context of Indian agriculture.

H. W. SINGER, *The Strategy of International Development* (London: Macmillan, 1975).

A collection of essays on a variety of topics in development economics by H. W. Singer, it includes three papers on employment problems in developing countries. The essay on international policy and its effects on employment lucidly presents the case for promoting exports of labour-intensive manufactures and fashioning the structure of aid and foreign private investment to promote employment. The essay on unemployment in an African setting discusses the report of the International Labour Organization mission to Kenya and its recommendation of redistribution with growth. The essay on employment problems in developing countries discusses the main factors responsible for unemployment in developing countries. From the vantage point of the year 1975 neither Singer's diagnosis nor his prescriptions may appear too novel, although novelty is not entirely lacking (for example, in the suggestion that part of the aid monies should be devoted to perfecting labour-intensive technologies in the donor countries), Professor Singer, however, has been an early exponent of many of the currently popular prescriptions. These essays are well worth reading for the lucidity of exposition alone.

R. B. SUTCLIFFE, *Industry and Underdevelopment* (London: Addison-Wesley, 1971).

This book provides a critical survey of the existing literature on industrialisation in developing countries. A major conclusion of the book is that countries will not become rich unless at some stage they industrialise. Industrialisation is desirable in the long run in the interests of higher productivity and living standards. It may also be imperative in the short run to solve problems posed by urbanisation and social change and also in the interests of political stability. Although the conclusions are open to dispute the book deserves to be read for its comprehensive discussion of the various issues related to industrialisation.

Foreign Private Investment and the Transfer of Technology

PETER ADY (ed.), *Foreign Investment and the Developing World* (New York: Praeger, 1971).

Miss Ady's collection of papers was presented to a conference of Academics and businessmen in London. The papers by A. Mazoomdar and F. Rampresad discuss tax policies of India and the West Indies towards foreign private investment. The editor's introductory article is a good survey of the debate on foreign private investment.

V. N. BALASUBRAMANYAM, *International Transfer of Technology to India* (New York: Praeger, 1973).

Dr Balasubramanyam discusses the role of Indo-foreign Technical Collaboration agreements in international transfers of technology to India. It suggests that such arrangements may be a second-best alternative to foreign private investment in transmitting technology.

CHARLES COOPER (ed.), *Science, Technology and Development: the Political Economy of Technical change in Underdeveloped Countries* (London: Frank Cass, 1973).

This is a collection of articles on science policy and choice of techniques originally published in the *Journal of Development Studies*. Cooper's introductory article surveys the recent issues in the area of science policy for developing countries and transfers of technology. Especially interesting is Frances Stewart's discussion of the scope for labour-intensive technologies in developing countries and Genevieve Dean's discussion of China's policies towards science and technology.

PETER DRYSDALE (ed.), *Direct Foreign Investment in Asia and the Pacific* (Canberra: Australian National University Press, 1972; and Toronto: University of Toronto Press, 1972).

This is a very useful conference volume. The authors are experts on South-east Asian experience and attitudes and provide a useful comparison with the more flamboyant and alarmed discussions of the alleged dangers of foreign enterprise elsewhere.

JOHN H. DUNNING (ed.), *The Multi-national Enterprise* (London: Allen & Unwin, 1971).

A collection of papers presented at a conference on multinational enterprises at Reading University in 1970, it is especially interesting where Paul Streeten, Edith Penrose and Jack Behrman discuss the relationship between multinational enterprises and the host countries. Edith Penrose's article is a sharp attack on the cosmopolitan view of the multinational enterprises propounded by Charles Kindleberger.

JOHN H. DUNNING (ed.), *International Investment* (Harmondsworth: Penguin, 1972).

This is a collection of articles on foreign private investment. Especially interesting are the articles by Paul Streeten and G. M. Meier. The former emphasises the need to assess the effects of foreign private investment with due consideration to alternative arrangements such as licensing agreements. The latter discusses the role of foreign private investment in generating externalities and technology transfers.

HARRY G. JOHNSON, *Technology and Economic Interdependence* (London: Macmillan, for the Trade Policy Research Centre, 1975).

Professor Johnson sets out in this volume to clarify issues in the complex of topics covered by international trade and investment, in respect of both developed and developing countries, focusing on transfers of technology, managerial expertise and human skills.

MICHAEL KIDRON, *Foreign Investments in India* (London: Oxford University Press, 1965).

This provides a detailed account of India's policy towards foreign private enterprise and discusses the magnitude, nature and pattern of foreign private enterprise participation in India. In general it concludes that the costs of foreign private investment have out-weighed its benefits. Interesting from the standpoint of case material discussed and lucidity of style and presentation.

CHARLES P. KINDLEBERGER, *American Business Abroad: Six Lectures on Direct Investment* (New Haven: Yale University Press, 1969).

Professor Kindleberger presents the controversial view that the multinational corporations are going to dominate the world economic scene and 'the Nation State is just about through as an economic unit'.

HLA MYINT, *South East Asia's Economy: Development Policies in the 1970s* (Harmondsworth: Penguin, 1973).

Chapter 5 discusses the opposition to foreign private investment on the grounds of economic nationalism. The book argues that it is irrational to oppose it in primary export industries. It suggests that the correct policy is to make such investment more attractive and charge an economic rent to the foreigners investing in these industries. In general it makes out a strong case for foreign private investment.

Agriculture, Food and Population

PETER DORMER, *Land Reform and Economic Development* (Harmondsworth: Penguin, 1972).

This book analyses the relationship between land reform and economic development and presents a concise account of the diverse types of tenure system prevailing in different parts of the world. It concludes that land reform alone cannot result in development and argues that it should be accompanied by investment in infrastructure, technical assistance, credit facilities and marketing assistance.

RENÉ DUMONT and ROSIER BERNARD, *The Hungry Future* (London: Methuen, 1969).

The authors discuss the population explosion and the food problem in different regions of the third world, including the socialist bloc, and argues that only a change in attitudes and institutional arrangements at the regional, national and international levels can solve the problem.

SCARLETT T. EPSTEIN, *South India: Yesterday, Today and Tomorrow* (London: Macmillan, 1973).

This is a sequel to *Economic Development and Social Change in South India* by the same author. The earlier book described the response of two villages in South India to the coming of irrigation to the region. The book gives a highly readable account of socioeconomic changes that had taken place in the two villages in the ten intervening years since the first book was published. That rural development has been accompanied by increasing inequalities is one of the main findings of the study.

KEITH GRIFFIN, *The Political Economy of Agrarian Change* (London: Macmillan, 1974).

Dr Griffin provides here a study of the effects of the Green Revolution which concludes that the new technology embodied in the Green Revolution has potential for economic development, but if used unwisely can cause further inequality and poverty.

D. GALE JOHNSON, *World Agriculture in Disarray* (London: Macmillan (hardcover) and Fontana (paperback), for the Trade Policy Research Centre, 1973; and New York: St. Martin's Press (hardcover) and New Viewpoints (paperback), 1973).

This is a sensible and sober account of the mess into which shortsighted policies of raising farm prices through tariffs and export controls have got the world's trade in agricultural products, and the basis on which the mess might gradually be cleaned up.

A. M. KHUSRO, *Economics of Land Reform and Farm Size in India* (Madras: Macmillan, 1973).

The study examines the problems associated with land tenure and size of farms in India. It also presents a critical account of land reforms in India. It is shown that the minimum economic size of holdings in Indian agriculture is 5 acres and above the 5-acre size there is nothing to choose between one size and another from the viewpoint of productivity. The study also outlines an integrated strategy for a new agrarian change.

JOHN W. MELLOR, *The Economics of Agricultural Development* (Ithaca: Cornell University Press, 1966).

This is a basic text on agricultural development and presents a comprehensive survey of traditional agriculture and discusses the problems involved in modernising it.

KUSUM NAIR, *Blossoms in the Dust* (New York: Praeger, 1962).

Reporting on the extraordinary variety of responses by farmers to economic stimuli this book also criticises government policy for failing to take account of the variety of social attitudes among farmers.

GORAN OHLIN, *Population Control and Economic Development* (Paris: OECD, 1967).

Presenting detailed discussion of the consequences of population explosion, the book analyses the benefits and costs of population control programmes.

THEODORE W. SCHULTZ, *Transforming Traditional Agriculture* (New Haven: Yale University Press, 1964).

Professor Schultz argues that transforming traditional agriculture requires the production and supply of new inputs and makes out a case for investment in both human and material capital. Also known for controverting the much-debated thesis that the marginal product of labour in traditional agriculture is zero.

GRANT L. REUBER *et al.*, *Private Foreign Investment in Development* (London: Oxford University Press, for the Development Centre, OECD, 1973).

Attempting to quantify the effects of foreign private investment on income, employment and balance of payments of developing countries this book concludes that in general the effects are positive. Although the statistical evidence is weak the study furnishes a fund of data and information on foreign private investment in the developing countries.

ROBERT SOLO and E. M. ROGERS (eds), *Inducing Technological Change for Economic Growth and Development* (East Lansing: Michigan State University Press, 1972).

This was a collection of papers presented to an inter-disciplinary American Seminar of Economists, Sociologists and Anthropologists of the Michigan State University. The focus of the papers is on agents of technological dissemination and technology transfers to developing countries.

P. Strassman, *Technological Change and Economic Development: the Manufacturing Experience of Mexico and Puerto Rico* (Ithaca: Cornell University Press, 1968).

This is a fairly detailed study of the role of technology in the development process. Presents a lucid discussion of the networks available for technological diffusion. Especially interesting is the discussion on the scope for labour capital substitution provided by the use of second-hand equipment and intensive staffing and multiple shifts. Profusely illustrated by case studies from Mexico and Puerto Rico the information for which was gathered by extensive interviews.

Index

Page numbers with the following letters added refer to:
b – selected bibliography,
n – note
t – table.